The Summer of '45

The Summer of '45

Stories and Voices from VE Day to VJ Day

By Kevin Telfer

Aurum
Press

First published in Great Britain
2015 by Aurum Press Ltd
74—77 White Lion Street
Islington
London N1 9PF
www.aurumpress.co.uk

A catalogue record for this book is available from the British Library.

ISBN 978 1 78131 435 7
eBook ISBN 978 1 78131 474 6

1 3 5 7 9 10 8 6 4 2

2015 2017 2019 2018 2016

Typeset in ITC New Baskerville by Saxon Graphics Ltd, Derby
Printed and bound by CPI Group (UK) Ltd, Croydon, CR0 4YY

Contents

Introduction

Stories that Shaped the Twentieth Century

'It was the best of times, it was the worst of times, it was
the age of wisdom, it was the age of foolishness, it was
the epoch of belief, it was the epoch of incredulity, it
was the season of Light, it was the season of Darkness,
it was the spring of hope, it was the winter of despair,
we had everything before us, we had nothing before
us, we were all going direct to heaven, we were all
going direct the other way.'[1]

Charles Dickens, A Tale of Two Cities

Charles Dickens's opening to *a Tale of Two Cities* seems the
most apposite description of May 1945 – in Europe at least.
The war in Europe was over: it was the best of times, and
people danced on the streets in celebration, lit bonfires,
played pianos and sang, kissed strangers, dusted off special
tins of meat and – sometimes – quality bottles of booze that
they had been saving for just such an occasion and drank
freely. Yet the war in the Far East continued, and in Europe
every possible terrible thing that could be done to a human
being was being done to human beings on a staggering scale,
especially in Germany, but also in Czechoslovakia, Poland,
Austria, Hungary and even France and Holland.

1

Victory was not enough to stop torture, rape, robbery, starvation, humiliation, murder and homelessness; and in many cases, victory was actually the catalyst for these things to take place – because of revenge, retribution and victors claiming their spoils. The crimes and heartaches of the war were still being unearthed, concentration camps still being uncovered; people were still being killed, were still living in fear and trying to get home – or find a new home; the agonising hunt to find family members – dead or alive – gripped millions of people across the world; the horror of what had unfolded in the past six years was still fresh in people's minds and for many was ongoing. It was the worst of times.

People felt passionate about the future and how it must be different from the past; it was the epoch of belief. People distrusted politicians more than ever and those in authority who had sent millions to their deaths; it was the epoch of incredulity. The end of the war in Europe coincided with late spring and early summer and the sun warmed those who had endured a hard winter. There was hope in that summer that things would improve, that new buildings, newly enlightened government, new social contracts, new opportunities would spring from the wreckage: it was the season of light. There was despair that people were doomed to do barbaric things to one another for the rest of time; despair from mourning; despair even from long-awaited reunions gone wrong: it was the season of darkness.

These contrasts of darkness and light in themselves make the period from May to September 1945 a particularly fascinating one, full of every shade of human experience. In some senses, there are two different stories – the story of the occupied countries and those that had not been occupied – like Britain and the United States. In what had been fighting zones until very recently, the terror and the suffering were often horrendous. In the non-occupied countries, there were varying degrees of difficulty, but nothing on the scale of what was being faced in Germany, for instance. But the picture is also rather more complex than that. The different stories and experiences of people in this time vary widely – from the joys of a young woman dancing uninhibitedly in the West End of London at the end of the war in Europe to a Japanese schoolboy who, in a heartbeat in August 1945, lost everything and everyone he had ever known. From a female German journalist in Berlin, facing the daily terror of rape by Soviet soldiers, to a British soldier in Germany hoping desperately to be demobbed soon so that he could go back to his family. And, of course, misery and joy, hope and despair, poverty and plenty were juxtaposed more sharply and immediately than that, within each and every country. This is the principal focus of this book – the real lives and experiences of these different people as around them events on the most monumental scale took place.

This mosaic of stories – from those people who witnessed and participated in these historical events – forms its own historical narrative, a social history that offers a uniquely personal perspective of what can otherwise easily become dry historical discourse with little understanding of the impact on people's everyday lives. The events that they were witness to were not just significant at the time, but so markedly defined the post-war, global, geopolitical landscape that the way in which people reacted to those events then seems especially interesting now. Indeed, these are the stories that helped shape the twentieth century – and beyond.

As well as the end of the war in Europe – and eventually in the Far East, too – the summer of 1945 also witnessed the birth of the United Nations and the beginning of the modern welfare state. The United States cemented its position as the pre-eminent global power with military bases and influence all over the world. The first – and only – two nuclear weapons to have been used in warfare were detonated and the world entered the atomic age. The Potsdam conference in July 1945, following on from Yalta, in February, with leaders from the Soviet Union, the United States and Great Britain attending, worked out the post-war settlement – and the future of a continent – on the back of napkins.

Europe was divided in two between the east and the west, with an iron curtain drawn between them and distrust between the Soviets and the West was fast approaching Cold War levels levels by September 1945. This indeed was the beginning of the Cold War: a nuclear face-off between the two new global powers in the heart of Europe and through proxy wars around the world. Nationalist movements – such as in India, Syria, Malaya and Vietnam – developed increasing hope that they would soon be able to cast off their colonial yoke. The concept of a Jewish homeland in Palestine became a tangible hope for many survivors of the European camps. When taken together, these events and developments that all took place within a few months in the summer of 1945, mark the year as one of the most significant of the twentieth century.

The Summer of '45 tells a parallel story of headline events and the human stories that lie beneath them, such as the voices of the pilots who dropped bombs on Nagasaki and Hiroshima, killing tens of thousands of Japanese civilians, and some of the eyewitnesses who were on the ground when it happened.

Some terrible things happened between VE Day and VJ Day, and whether by the end of the war people were optimistic about the future depended a great deal on where they lived. In cities such as Berlin and Nagasaki, Leningrad and Dresden, the outlook was, in the short term at least, rather bleak. For those in American cities, by contrast, there seemed little standing in the way of greater prosperity and opportunity. In France and Britain, by contrast, the period of rebuilding from the rubble could begin with a new social contract and a more benevolent state to look after the people who had worked so hard during the war to ensure the victory that had been celebrated with such fervour.

V did not always stand for victory. Winston Churchill only adopted the two-fingered mannerism that came to define him in the public imagination (as much as his speeches and cigars) in the summer of 1941 after the Battle of Britain, and after his most famous speeches. He even had to be reminded by his advisors to show his fingers the correct way around, because in reverse it was – and is – a lewd and insulting gesture in Britain. The man largely credited with coming up with the common use of 'V for victory' was, appropriately enough, called Victor. On 14 January 1941, Victor de Laveleye, an exiled former Belgian Minister of Justice working as the Director of Belgian French-speaking broadcasts and an announcer for the BBC, urged Belgians to use V (for *victoire* – *victory* in French and *vriheid* – freedom – in Flemish) as a rallying call as they struggled against occupation by German forces.[2] Soon afterwards, Churchill followed suit and from July that year regularly began making his famous salute, often with a cigar between the two fingers as he made the sign. And on VE Day itself, on 8 May 1945, as he stood on the balcony in Whitehall of what was at that time the Department of Health, with some of his Cabinet colleagues alongside him, he made the same gesture again to the boisterous crowds below, puffing merrily on his cigar.

Credit for coming up with the V sign was also claimed by the occultist and writer Aleister Crowley. In 1941, he felt that the British needed a symbol to counter the powerful ancient sign of the swastika, which had become such an essential and potent part of Nazism. 'How can I put it over pictorially or graphically?' he wondered. 'I want positive ritual affirmation.' Crowley felt that the letter V had all kinds of potency attached to it from many ancient cultures, including the well-known Latin phrase '*Veni, vidi, vici*' ('I came, I saw, I conquered'). Using his personal connections with Naval Intelligence and the Air Ministry, he claims that he campaigned for the V sign to be used as a powerful public riposte to the swastika – successfully, if he is to be believed.[3] Regardless, it became the defining motif of the end of the war, a theme that was emblazoned across the sky in fireworks and flares, in shop windows and on posters drawn by schoolboys and girls.

Whoever coined the association and the gesture, there was no doubt that when VE Day came around, for the Allied forces, this was very much a *victory* in Europe rather than merely peace or an end to war. When Churchill stood on German soil in March 1945, he urinated on it with enormous relish, telling nearby photographers that 'this is one of the operations connected with this great war which must not be reproduced graphically'.[4]

The location in which the German unconditional surrender was signed, though coincidental, also seemed to

Introduction

emphasise the notion of a proper victory – a comprehensive defeat of the enemy in every way: militarily, morally, politically. General Alfred Jodl signed the documents at 2.41 am on 7 May in Reims, France, the capital of the Champagne region, where the Supreme Headquarters of the Allied Expeditionary Force (SHAEF) was based. 'Remember, gentlemen, it's not just France we are fighting for, it's champagne!'[5] Churchill had previously said with characteristic ebullience. Hitler once called the British Prime Minister a 'superannuated drunkard', while he, on the other hand, cultivated a reputation at least as an ascetic man – a vegetarian, non-smoking teetotaller.[6]

Churchill made two speeches to the crowds on 8 May in Whitehall – both prefaced by plenty of V gestures. In the second of these two speeches, he celebrated the spirit of the British people in their moment of victory:

'My dear friends, this is your hour. This is not victory of a party or of any class. It's a victory of the great British nation as a whole. We were the first, in this ancient island, to draw the sword against tyranny. After a while we were left all alone against the most tremendous military power that has been seen. We were all alone for a whole year. 'There we stood, alone. Did anyone want to give in? [The crowd shouted "No."] Were we down-hearted? ["No!"] The lights went out and the bombs came down. But every man, woman and child in the country had no thought of quitting the struggle. London can take it. So we came back after long months from the jaws of death, out of the mouth of hell, while all the world wondered.

7

'When shall the reputation and faith of this generation of English men and women fail? I say that in the long years to come not only will the people of this island but of the world, wherever the bird of freedom chirps in human hearts, look back to what we've done and they will say "Do not despair, do not yield to violence and tyranny, march straightforward and die if need be – unconquered." Now we have emerged from one deadly struggle – a terrible foe has been cast on the ground and awaits our judgment and our mercy.'[7]

According to the *Manchester Guardian*, 'Four things saved us. The English Channel; the combined prowess of the navy and the RAF; Mr Churchill's leadership; the fourth was something in the national character which refused to take in the staring prospect of defeat.'[8]

It was a victory after six hard years of fighting and the death of millions; a hard-won victory. The crowds of cheering people in London and Paris confirmed this. And, of course, not just in London and Paris, but in every other town and city in free Europe where there were fancy-dress parades and street parties, and where people got together to ensure that there were treats for the children and to produce between them, in their individual communities, the most extravagant meal that anyone could remember for years.

One woman working at the Women's Voluntary Service (WVS) remembered being part of the crowd in central London that day:

'We all walked to Buckingham Palace. As we got in front of it the flood-lighting flickered on. It was wonderful ... magnificent and inspiring and it seemed we had never seen so beautiful a building. The crowd was everywhere and yet one could walk through it. We edged our way to the balcony, which was draped with crimson, with a yellow and gold fringe. The crowd was such as I have never seen – I was never so proud of England and our people.'[9]

Yet any sense of triumphalism was also tempered by both the losses and privation that had been endured by people across the Continent and in Britain, and by the economic austerity and other restrictions that the vast majority of the population still faced. One television commentator noted that people in London were celebrating in high spirits because they were the only spirits that they could afford. In *The Times* on 9 May 1945, the day after VE Day in Britain (commonly called VE Day plus one), there was an advert for 'New ways of using dried eggs'. According to the same newspaper, the Admiralty announced that the coastal blackout would continue until it was confirmed that all U-Boats 'have received instructions to surrender, and are complying with them'. At the House of Commons service held at St Margaret's Church, Westminster, Canon Don said in his service that 'the fruits of victory have yet to be gathered in'.[10] Many street parties, such as this one in Cardiff, were taking place surrounded by bombed-out buildings:

'What a day. We gathered together on our bombed site and planned the finest party the children ever remembered. Neighbours pooled their sweet rations, and collected money, a few shillings from each family ... and our grocer gave his entire stock of sweets, fruit, jellies, etc. All the men in the neighbourhood spent the day clearing the site. The church lent the tables, the milkman lent a cart for a platform, and we lent our radiogram and records for the music. We all took our garden chairs for the elderly to sit on. Someone collected all our spare jam jars. Blackout curtains came down to make fancy dresses for the children. Everyone rummaged in ragbags and offered bits to anyone who wanted them. That evening, ninety-four children paraded around the streets, carrying lighted candles in jam jars, wearing all manner of weird and fancy dress, singing lustily, *We'll be coming round the mountain when we come,* and led by my small son wearing white cricket flannels, a scarlet cummerbund and a Scout's hat, beating a drum. In the dusk, it was a brave sight never to be forgotten.'[11]

Not just Britain, but all of Europe to varying degrees, was living through a period of extreme privation in May 1945, and many people spent VE Day doing exactly the same things that they had spent every other day doing for the past months and years – women queued for hours to get bread from the bakers; teenage boys headed to the fields to try to catch a rabbit for dinner; workers finished their shift and caught buses home through streets in which many buildings had been reduced to rubble. That was the kind of austerity that existed on a household level – rationing, queues, a lack of any luxury – but on a larger scale, entire nations were also in severe economic difficulties. Germany's economy was destroyed and Italy was in ruins. The Soviet Union had been disastrously affected in terms of its economic infrastructure and 14 per cent of its pre-war population had been killed in the fighting. Britain and France both owed enormous sums of money to the United States, without whose help they could not have continued to wage war against Germany.

In the major Australian cities, there were also celebrations, but overall the mood across the country remained sober as the continuing Pacific conflict was much closer to home. The Japanese bombing raids of 1942–43 were still fresh in the memory and many Australian soldiers were still prisoners in Japanese Prisoner-of-War camps with no hope of release. Churches everywhere held thanksgiving services, and on 9 May, 100,000 people attended the service at the Shrine of Remembrance in Melbourne.

In America, there were huge celebrations in many of the major cities, such as Los Angeles, San Francisco and Chicago, and in Times Square in New York. 'The War in Europe is Ended!' shouted the front cover of the *New York Times* on 8 May.

For President Harry Truman, there was more than one reason to be pleased that day – as well as victory in Europe, it was also his 61st birthday. He had been President for just twenty-six days and had moved into the White House only the day before on 7 May, so it was an auspicious start to his incumbency, though he was also painfully aware that the Pacific War was still going on and would result in many more American casualties.

When Truman met with reporters on the morning of 8 May to discuss the surrender, he soberly dedicated the victory to his predecessor Franklin D. Roosevelt, who had died less than a month earlier, then spent the rest of the day with friends and aides: there was certainly not the same official public display of jubilation as there was in Britain.

Roosevelt had insisted to the other Allies that the German surrender be completely unconditional and this was criticised in some quarters at the time, and since, for extending the war in Europe and allowing the Soviets to advance further than was necessary. It had also raised that same spectre of Germany on its knees that Hitler had used so effectively at the start of his rise to power. And with this partly in mind, General Dwight Eisenhower, the Supreme Allied Commander, issued a non-triumphant communiqué on the German surrender. It read: 'The mission of this Allied Force was fulfilled at 0241, local time, May 7th, 1945.'[12]

But even in Britain, where there were great scenes of official celebration – including appearances by the royal family at Buckingham Palace and Churchill in Whitehall – there was also a sense of disquiet amongst some that the war as a whole was not really over. There were still many British troops in the Far East. *The Daily Telegraph* editorial on 9 May 1945 stated: 'At the moment when the guns have fallen silent in Europe, hundreds of thousands of British fighting men are in the full blaze of battle in the Far East; and Japanese spokesmen continue loud in petulant defiance.' One veteran of the First World War, whose son was one of those troops, did not feel like celebrating:

'I thought of the sufferings and miseries of tens of thousands in Europe yet to come; I thought of the grim outlook for the future; I thought of my son in Burma. I compared my feelings with my feelings on Armistice Day of the last war (when I was on active service on the Western Front), and remembered how wild with joy and excitement I was then, how eagerly I looked forward to the New World that was to be built, how glad I was to be alive. My feelings on VE Day were something wholly different. Relief was there, enormous relief; but no triumphant excitement, no zeal about the future, no gladness to be alive. There was a sense of anti-climax in me, a curious deadness, a disappointment that I felt so different from what I was expected that I should feel. This is due, I expect, largely to old age, because there is no useful work left for me to do; but partly because the future for Europe seems to me so gloomy. Everyone seems to be thinking in terms of force, violence, revenge and national interest. There is no idealism anywhere.'[13]

The fact that the war was over – but not over – was a strange and important part of this period from VE Day to VJ Day. For some historians, though, the war continued long after the Japanese had surrendered and ended only in 1989 after the fall of the Berlin Wall – the Cold War was in effect a direct and indistinguishable extension of the 'hot' Second World War. And for some individuals, the war remained a more tangible everyday reality for an extraordinary length of time: two Japanese soldiers held out separately until 1974 before surrendering – one, Teruo Nakamura, in Indonesia, the other, Hiroo Onoda, in the Philippines – both believing that the war had continued the entire time. Onoda even insisted that his commanding officer from the war – Major Yoshimi Taniguchi – give him the order before he gave up his arms. The ex-major was working as a bookseller and was flown out to the Philippines in order to relieve Onoda of his duty. Onoda died in January 2014.[14]

War in Europe may have been over in the summer of 1945, but occupations were just beginning – with all their attendant problems and challenges for occupiers and occupied. In Germany, the great wrath and terror that the Nazis had waged against their enemies had now been turned back on the civilian German population. The chickens came home to roost. Whether or not that was deserved was a matter of debate then as much as it is now. Only slightly more than 30 per cent of the German population had voted for Hitler in the last free elections in the country. But as the occupation began, many Americans, British, French and Soviets occupying the country lumped the Germans all together as an evil race. And there was sometimes more than a tinge of the Nazi's own racialism in doing this, which made the Germans also seem sub-human (*untermensch*) themselves.

This book has been written to coincide with the seventieth anniversary of the end of the Second World War and, as such, it marks a lifetime in Shakespeare's terms between then and now. That in turn means that eyewitness testimony from 1945 is now largely restricted to those people who were – at most – in their teens or early twenties by the time peace arrived. Martin Gilbert's book *The Day the War Ended*, published in 1995 to commemorate the fiftieth anniversary of VE Day, used extensive accounts from those who were alive at the time. However, there is now sadly a dwindling number of people that fall into this category and the material in this book has necessarily been mainly built from narratives gleaned from letters, diaries, memoirs, Mass Observation reports, autobiographies and other books.

In many ways that is no bad thing: after all, memories from seventy years ago tend to fade and so to get the immediacy and also the authenticity of what it was like to be alive in 1945, material that was written at the time – or soon after – generally provides a far better guide than shakily remembered recollections. But at the same time, it would be criminal not to take the opportunity to get first-hand testimony from those who were there and who are still alive, and I have tried to do this as far as has been possible. So the stories of Bernd Koschland, who arrived in London on the *kindertransport* in 1939, and Fred Aiken, who was an explosives scientist during the war, for example, are among those included in this book.

There have been many great and serious books written about many of the subjects that this book covers in brief. This book is an overview of the period between VE Day and VJ Day and in single chapters records narratives of events of such enormous scale that they cannot in any sense be considered comprehensive. They are snapshots, composed of a series of smaller snapshots and cameos, attempting to tell a story using the voices of the people that witnessed these events in some form or another: from politicians and field marshals to actors and writers, as well as ordinary people – soldiers, civilians, workers, housewives and children. This mixture of different voices means that it cannot claim to be the 'voice of the ordinary people' alone, whatever that may mean – there are plenty of contributions from people at the top of the political and military decision-making processes and well-known cultural figures. Excerpts from newspapers and broadcast media also form an important part of this picture. What is important is to hear those voices together which offer multiple viewpoints, ideas and insights. This is what this book aims to achieve. Together, these voices constitute a layered chorus that rejects a tendentious and reified view of history. The witnesses are not always well-informed and credible witnesses. But they were there and they have a story to tell, and that is all the credibility that they need in this book – their very experience has value in itself.

Where possible, I have tried to include contradictory narratives – to tell of someone who was having a miserable time on VE Day as well as someone who was celebrating the best night of their lives, for instance. This has not always been possible. But that is not to suggest that those voices do not exist. This account is selective and eclectic and the object is not to try overly to interpret the source material or, in general, to use it as the basis for empirical claims – I leave that to far more serious historians – but to present it as part of the wider historical fabric.

There is an enormous ongoing fascination with the Second World War, especially with what happened in Europe, as can be seen in the prolific number of books printed on the subject and widespread continuous media coverage. In part, that is because of the sheer horror and scale of the events – the Holocaust, the immense displacement of people, the destruction of entire cities. In the relative post-war calm, it seems unimaginable that those things happened on this continent. It is also because of the enormous political ramifications of what happened during the war not just for Europe but for the world as a whole, which remain relevant now. Yet during the writing of this book, I have realised that many of the most terrible things that happened between May and September 1945 are also happening today on a massive scale – in places such as Syria, the Congo and Somalia. Lots of the stories I have read about the summer of 1945 – and especially those set in places like Germany, Poland, Austria and Czechoslovakia – have been horrendous and emotionally exhausting. Yet writing this book has also made me think that now, with a lifetime's distance, a little less time could probably be spent agonising over the suffering of people in 1945 and a little more time spent trying to prevent the suffering of people in conflicts now that do not receive the same attention as the Second World War still does.

Kevin Telfer
February, 2015

Chapter 1

Uneasy Excesses

VE Day in Britain

'A day disorganized by victory!'

Field Marshal Alan Brooke[1]

'They played us a dirty trick – a proper dirty trick,' said a woman in her forties to a bunch of similarly disgruntled Londoners in a newspaper shop in Chelsea on the morning of 8 May 1945 at about 11 o'clock. The mood was rather sour despite the fact that outside the weather was warm and humid, the street was vivid with red, white and blue from bunting and flags, and shop windows were decorated with letter Vs and Union Jacks.

'A muddle it was. Just a muddle,' agreed a twenty-five-year-old man in the same shop.

'People waiting and waiting and nothing happening. No church bells or nothing,' chimed in a thirty-year-old woman.

An older man, in his fifties, perhaps slightly crossly, said, 'Yes – what 'appened to them church bells, I'd like to know?'

Another man, in his early thirties, jokingly – or perhaps not – asked whether anyone else had 'heard that thunderstorm in the night? God's wrath, that was!'.

One more party – a man – chimed in: 'Telling us over and over the church bells would be the signal. And then there was <u>no</u> signal. Just hanging around.'

The elder man, rather angrily added, 'Well, I'm sick and tired – browned off of them I am. The way they've behaved – why, it was an insult to the British people. Stood up to all wot we've stood up to, and then afraid to tell us it was peace, just as if we were a lot of kids. Just as if we couldn't be trusted to be'ave ourselves.'

The thirty-something man chided, 'Do 'em no good in the general election – the way they've gone on over this. People won't forget it. Insult's just what it was. No more and no less.'

Another woman: 'Oh, well, I expect people will get excited enough later in the day.'

But the elder man was insistent: 'It's not the same. It should have been yesterday. When you think of it – peace signed at two forty in the morning, and then people wait and wait all day, and then nothing, but it would be VE Day tomorrow. No bells, no All Clear, nothing to start the people off.'

The woman who began the discussion said, 'That's just what they were afraid of, I reckon.'[2]

Rumours had been rife that the war would officially be declared over for the past few days and there was such a thirst for confirmation of this rumour that on 7 May a paper seller on Kensington High Street, who had been continually pestered all morning, told one passer-by, 'They'd buy a paper every hour if there was one printed.'[3]

In fact, earlier that same day, General Alfred Jodl had travelled to Reims to sign the instrument of surrender on behalf of Karl Dönitz, who had assumed the role of head of state after Hitler's death on 30 April. The surrender document stated: 'The German High Command will at once issue orders to all German military, naval and air authorities and to all forces under German control to cease active operations at 2301 hours Central European Time on 8 May and to remain in the positions occupied at that time. No ship, vessel, or aircraft is to be scuttled, or any damage done to their hull, machinery or equipment.'[4]

Jodl was granted permission to speak after he had signed the document: 'With this signature, the German people are, for better or worse, delivered into the victors' hands,' he said.[5] The mood of the German delegation was understandably sombre and Admiral von Friedeburg, Commander-in-Chief of the *Kriegsmarine*, said that he had not slept properly for a month. Just fifteen days later he committed suicide.

The reason that the surrender did not become widely known more quickly was that behind the scenes the Soviets were unhappy with the way that the surrender ceremony had been conducted – orchestrated by the Americans and with a Soviet general only a witness to the ceremony – and insistent that the Germans must also surrender their troops on the eastern front in the seat of German power – Berlin. Therefore, Stalin suggested that an additional ceremony be held in Berlin on 8 May, and this in turn meant that Churchill eventually conceded that he would not formally announce victory in Europe until 3.00 pm on 8 May and the formal start of peace in Europe was timed for one minute past midnight on 9 May. But the fact that 8 May would be a holiday in Britain was nonetheless announced on 7 May because, according to the American Admiral William Leahy at least, Churchill had said to him in a telephone conversation that 'the crowds celebrating in the street of London were beyond control'.[6]

But the *Manchester Guardian* reported on the 8th:

'Manchester throughout yesterday afternoon preserved
a restrained expectancy, which gave way to a little flag-
waving and a few street cheers only when the news of
the unconditional surrender of Germany reached the
waiting public in printed form. A little later flags began
to unfold from the tops of high buildings. All afternoon
Manchester though working as usual had more or less
of a holiday aspect, thanks to the combination of genial
weather and high anticipations.'[7]

Lancasters from RAF Bomber Command landed in Germany
for the first time on 7 May to bring back freed prisoners of
war. Four and a half thousand men were flown back to
England on VE Day. Another important shipment also
arrived: 1,700,000 Irish eggs came from Fishguard for the
London market.[8]

Victory over the Germans in one form or another had been
more or less assured since the summer of 1943, when the
reversal of the Wehrmacht's military fortunes had reached a
critical point. The BBC had begun planning in the autumn
of that year for their victory coverage once the day arrived.
In an internal memo the Controller of Programmes wrote to
senior BBC staff telling them:

'It is assumed that the Armistice will see an immediate
official and unofficial holiday of several days, during
which the public will no doubt be celebrating much of
the time but nevertheless will be in the mood to listen
(even at day-time non-peak hours for the first two or

three days) if the BBC broadcasts the right programmes; but whether they are expected to listen or not, the BBC should make the gesture.

'It is assumed also that the public mood will change fairly rapidly from the deliriousness of the first two or three days to a mood of more sober thankfulness and retrospect, and ultimately of thoughts about the future, and in particular remembrance of the necessities of the war against Japan. It is important that these necessities should be put consistently and constructively before the public directly after the first raptures of celebration have worn off. The past and present situation of Australia must be sympathetically emphasised.'[9]

The first drafts for a programme schedule that were drawn up in 1943 were not very different from the actual programming that took place on VE Day and in the days that followed it, though among the changes of note was the replacement of Beethoven's 'Fifth Symphony' (after the Second World War often called the 'Victory Symphony') with Elgar's 'Pomp and Circumstance Military Marches'.[10]

In April 1945, the Mass Observation Project gave its volunteer investigators a directive – or questionnaire – to ask people. It contained two questions: 'What do you expect to do the day peace is declared?' and 'What's going to be your personal worry after the war?'.

A 45-year-old male chemist and journalist in London replied to the first question that he would 'go around in buses (if they are running) tearing the sticky net off the windows'. The windows had been covered because of the blackout, and everywhere there was a rush to bring light

23

back into life. In answer to the second question, he stated: 'I am afraid we shall lose some good things which the war has brought us e.g. full employment, greater comradeship between all kinds of people, state care of children, increased birth rate, and general willingness to overcome strong personal resistances to change.' A 35-year-old architect replied to the second question that his worries after the war would be no different to those during it.

A 30-year-old female secretary predicted that she would 'have a bit of a fling in town and then take the midnight train to Bournemouth' on VE Day and that she had no worries for after the war because she was in 'the prefabricated housing business'.[11]

It was a warm and muggy day across most of Britain on 8 May, with sunny intervals, rain threatening in some places in the morning and thunderstorms expected in the evening. Yet, as the *Manchester Guardian* reported, 'For the first time since the war began it is possible to tell the world what weather Britain is having while it is having it – and what it is likely to have.'[12] During wartime this had been regarded as sensitive information but now the war was over, a great British obsession could be renewed in public.

The first weather forecast since the start of the war, issued by the Air Ministry, recorded that 'A large depression between Ireland and the Azores is almost stationary and small disturbances are moving northward over the British Isles. Weather will continue warm and thundery, with bright intervals in most districts'.

The following day, the *Manchester Guardian* reported that on VE Day 'Rain fell almost everywhere. Winds off the sea kept day temperatures down to around 50 degrees along the east coasts of England and Scotland, but inland and in western districts the day was warm. 70 degrees being exceeded in most places in south-east and South England, South Midlands, and East Anglia. London was the warmest place with 78 degrees.'[13]

In this fecund time, as bluebells were carpeting the floors of woodland all over Britain, the *Western Daily Press* recommended that now was the ideal time to

'dig the trenches for celery seedlings, remembering that this crop will appreciate all the manure that can be spared. It is now safe to sow seeds of the popular ridge cucumber on specially prepared outdoor stations. Make a successional sowing of lettuce. A variety slow in running up to seed heads is Continuity. If more radishes are to be grown choose a moist, semi-shady spot for the reception of seeds. Keep the hoe moving between rows of spring-sown onions.'[14]

It was an early start for Dr J. J. Beeston on the morning of 8 May. He was to be awarded the George Medal by the King at Buckingham Palace that day in recognition of an act of bravery he had performed at the end of 1944, administering a blood transfusion to a woman in a bombed-out building at great personal risk, and saving her life.

'May 8th 1945 was a beautiful day,' he remembered. 'Spring was in the air and also, it was a bright sunny morning.' A chauffeur-driven car arrived at his father's house in Catford, South London to take him and his family to Buckingham Palace.

'Because everyone was in a holiday mood and going to celebrate that day, there was quite a bit of traffic.

Nevertheless we arrived at the palace just after 8am. Already there were a lot of people outside the gates. Some had been there all night and many more would arrive, later in the day, to join the traditional gatherings at the Palace when the royal family greets the crowds from the balcony.

'As our car approached the palace, I wondered if we would have to get out and walk the rest of the way. When we stopped at the gate, the policeman came forward and I showed him the card with the command to attend. After looking at it, he told the driver to go ahead and saluted me and wished me luck.'[15]

On his journey to the Palace – much of which would have been through severely bomb-damaged parts of the capital – he would have seen most of the occupied houses decorated with Union Jacks, bunting and even fairy lights strung out on trees, over porches and bay windows. Flags were in enormous demand and enterprising sellers of VE merchandise – including rosettes, blowers and hats – were doing a brisk trade. One West End hawker selling Churchill button badges cried out, 'Churchill for sixpence. Worth more!'[16] In the *Daily Telegraph* the following day, the London Day by Day column told the story of 'A retired Guardsman friend who lives in Mayfair.' He tried to buy Allied flags for the windows of his flat. 'He encountered a flag vendor in Davies Street. The price asked for a Union Jack, the size of a handkerchief and of the commonest material, was 6s. A larger one was £5 and a Russian flag cost £2 10s. He forbore to ask the price of the Stars and Stripes, and went home unbeflagged.'[17]

E. van Someren, a 41-year-old research scientist living in Broxbourne, Hertfordshire, had a more prosaic start to his day than the doctor on his way to the Palace, spending a little longer than usual in bed. He then took the opportunity of a day off to do the washing-up, 'aided by both children, the first time we had done this together', while his wife Kay went to the shops.[18]

Not all children were enthusiastic about spending the day with their parents. Ronald McGill from Vauxhall, South London was looking forward to going fishing in Richmond Park with his friends. But his parents had other ideas: '"No you're not, you're going to Buckingham Palace." And I said: "I don't want to go to Buckingham Palace, I want to go fishing." We had a terrible row and my friends went off. And I had to go up on the railway to Vauxhall, walk up to Buckingham Palace and stand there with the rest of them cheering the king and queen and my heart was in Richmond Park fishing!'[19]

Bernd Koschland had come over from Germany on the *kindertransport* in 1939 in order to escape the Nazi wave of hatred and persecution against Jewish people. When he arrived in London as an eight-year-old, he knew only one phrase in English that his parents had taught him before he left: 'I'm hungry, please give me a piece of bread.' By 1945, he was living in a hostel for Jewish refugees in Tylers Green in Buckinghamshire run by a Jewish organisation called the Refugee Children's Movement. 'We probably all cheered and were happy when the war ended in Europe,' he said.

'I can't remember exactly – but I'm certain we took it in our stride. The next thing we were concerned about was the whereabouts of our parents. But even when people were reunited with their parents this had its own problems. Life in concentration camps had changed them. Their children had grown up and had

27

also changed from living in a different country. They were like strangers meeting one another. And there was a lot of resentment from many of the children. Why had they been sent away? Can you imagine what it must have been like?'[20]

Tony Bray was a teenage boy who had been evacuated from his home in Gosport on the south coast early in the war and moved to Rottingdean, just east of Brighton. 'Although there was great jubilation in the large towns and cities throughout the land,' he wrote, 'nothing much seemed to happen in Rottingdean. We wandered about in a group, somebody had got a few fireworks from somewhere, and we let these off, but the village was strangely quiet. I guess the grown-ups were relieved that the killing – in Europe, at least – was over.'[21]

For many, though, the celebrations that were just beginning would be epic in nature.

Joan Styan, who was fifteen at the time, travelled in to central London from Clapham with her mother to see the royal family and Winston Churchill at Buckingham Palace. 'No more suffering,' she later wrote,

'peace at last; survival and freedom were all that mattered. London was submerged in jubilation and screams of relief from humanity. People climbed on anything they could, statues, buildings, cars, and every lamp-post was scaled. Noisy dustbin lids were banged and the hysterical crowds were totally beyond any order. Nothing mattered, only freedom. The ultimate heights of pent up human emotion were as they had never been and will probably never be again.'[22]

Churchill in his memoirs wrote:

> 'The unconditional surrender of our enemies was the signal for the greatest outburst of joy in the history of mankind. The Second World War had indeed been fought to the bitter end in Europe. The vanquished as well as the victors felt inexpressible relief. But for us in Britain and the British Empire, who had been alone in the struggle from the first day to the last and staked our existence on the result, there was a meaning beyond what even our most powerful and most valiant allies could feel. Weary and worn, impoverished but undaunted and now triumphant, we had a moment that was sublime. We gave thanks to God to the noblest of all his blessings, the sense that we had done our duty.'[23]

There was a great demand for church services. E. Van Someren and his wife took their two children a thanksgiving ceremony at the local parish church, 'which was well attended (about 300)'.[24] John Snow, a pacifist civil defence clerk from Edmonton in North London went to a local service with friends.

> 'The church was quite full, although not packed. The greater number were strangers. The hymns were "Praise my soul the king of heaven", "All people that on earth" and "Now thank we all our God". The prayers were restrained but somewhat bloodthirsty – prayers to a tribal deity who had been "on our side" – at the end, rather incongruously a prayer for peace (a prayer for peace has been said regularly in our church for at least the past eighteen years).'[25]

At St Martin-in-the-Fields on Trafalgar Square there were services every hour between 11.00 in the morning and 9.00 in the evening on both VE Day and the following day. At the first service, the church was full. One of the Mass Observation investigators noted, 'People are standing in the doorway.' And at the next service that there wasn't 'a vacant seat and people are standing. It's a very mixed congregation. Men and women in service uniform and of many different nationalities. Old people dressed very drably and looking very solemn; young people hatless and sporting victory colours and looking very jaunty in gaily coloured frocks; children in victory dresses and wearing victory hair bows and holding Union Jacks.'[26]

People went to these services for a number of reasons – for hope, for remembrance and for thanks. One woman had lost her husband: 'He got killed in Italy two years ago and that was a big blow to me. Today I feel all pent-up, not exactly bitter but sad to think that my husband won't be coming back with the others. I've got to remake my life and carry on for the sake of my little girl. I feel much better for coming and sharing in this thanksgiving service.' Another woman's son was taken prisoner by the Japanese in Singapore: 'I've had one postcard from him from the Red Cross and since then nothing. I'm hoping that he's alive – you have to keep on hoping. I couldn't stay at home today, it'd choke me if I did. I had to get out and be with the crowds.' But two young women from South London had just 'come to see the sights': 'Vi and I thought we'd like to start off with a service of thanksgiving and join in. We're glad we did.'[27]

Outside, crowds of people were beginning to congregate in the West End. One female investigator writing reports for the Mass Observation Project set off from her home in

Chelsea at 2.30 pm with 'three young Marxist neighbours' –
one female and two male (twins), heading in to the centre of
town: 'Their first discovery is that all the buses are packed to
overflowing and just sail past the stopping places. They walk
down towards Lower Sloane Street. Outside the Rose and
Crown a large ring of people, several in uniform and mostly
quite young, are dancing "Knees Up Mother Brown" and
singing loudly. Cars dart across the road ignoring the traffic
lights.'

Whitehall was packed with people, with thousands lining
the pavements. The Chelsea investigator recorded that
everything was 'good-humoured but somehow shapeless.
People just drift about rather uncertainly'.[28]

For Dr Beeston, who had received his George Medal from
the King, getting to the restaurant he had booked was a bit
of a battle:

'After I knew that May 8th was to be my day at the
palace,' he wrote, 'I had invited a number of family
and friends to be my guests for lunch to celebrate the
occasion. Several weeks before, I made reservations at
the Regent Hotel at Marble Arch for sixteen guests for
1pm that day and ordered the food and wine for the
meal. The guests were to assemble in their own at the
hotel while my parents and I planned to take a taxi
there after the ceremony, and in time for a toast at the
bar before lunch.

'We had not counted on the presence of hundreds
and thousands of people in festive mood outside the
palace gates shouting "We want the King! We Want
the King! We Want the King!" Not only were there no
taxis anywhere since all the surrounding roads had

31

been closed, but we had to fight our way out of the crowds who wanted to go in the opposite direction to get to the Palace gates. Everyone was in good humour which was a blessing, but it did not make it any easier for us to try to get through the crowds. Eventually we were able to cross Green park and reach Piccadilly where we though we might get a taxi. What a hope! Only people, people, people!'[29]

Mary Tisdall was one of those people outside Buckingham Palace. She was responsible for army pay slips and worked in an office next to Harrods in Knightsbridge. She described her work as a 'horrible accounting job' but enjoyed breaking the monotony with dancing and jazz. On VE Day, she was photographed by a *Daily Express* photographer on the Mall. 'When we were photographed we were singing "Knees Up Mother Brown" – you can see that I'm lifting my knees up. And Monika on the same row as me eventually became my bridesmaid.' Her boyfriend at the time was on active service with the RAF, and for Mary this was the main reason for her joy at the end of the war. 'I was excited because I thought there might be a chance I would finally see the man I would eventually marry.'[30]

Churchill gave his speech on the radio at 3.00 pm. In it, he clarified the slightly confusing nature of the surrender arrangements, saying that the existing agreement signed on 7 May 'will be ratified and confirmed at Berlin' that same day. He also told his audience that the one part of the British Isles that had been occupied by enemy forces during the war, 'our dear Channel Islands', 'are also to be freed today'. In fact, it wasn't until the following day that HMS *Bulldog* and HMS *Beagle* arrived in the Channel Islands to accept the unconditional surrender of the German forces still on the islands. Churchill said:

> 'We may allow ourselves a brief period of rejoicing; but let us not forget for a moment the toil and efforts that lie ahead. Japan, with all her treachery and greed, remains unsubdued. The injury she has inflicted on Great Britain, the United States, and other countries, and her detestable cruelties, call for justice and retribution. We must now devote all our strength and resources to the completion of our task, both at home and abroad. Advance, Britannia! Long live the cause of freedom! God save the King!'[31]

The vast crowds assembled on Whitehall listened intently over the loudspeakers that had been specially erected for the occasion. A female Mass Observation reporter wrote:

> 'People hang on to every word he has to say. When he tells them that as from midnight tonight hostilities will cease, there's loud cheers and again when the people hear that the Channel Islands will likewise be freed as from midnight tonight. But there's whoops of joy and waving of hats and flags when he comes to that point in his speech when he declares that "The German war is, therefore, at an end". Mention of Eisenhower's name and "our Russian comrades" starts the crowd clapping once more. He ends his broadcast with "Advance Britannia" and Buglers of the Scots Guard sound the ceremonial cease-fire.'[32]

One of Churchill's most important advisors during the war was his Chief of the Imperial General Staff, Field Marshal Alan Brooke, later 1st Viscount Alanbrooke. He combined his day job of military strategy with a keen private interest in ornithology and was an avid photographer of birds in his spare time. On the afternoon of VE Day he was hunting for a rare bird book on Museum Street, opposite the British Museum. But due to the crowds swarming all over the West End, he

> 'had a difficult journey and found the place closed when I got there. At 4.10 pm left [the War Office] for Buckingham Palace where I was due at 4.30 pm. A meeting of War Cabinet and Chiefs of Staff with the King. I crossed Whitehall with difficulty, through Horse Guards, battled my way down the Mall and came into an impenetrable crowd outside the Palace. However, with much honking and patience we gradually got through and arrived in good time. PM was very late as he insisted on coming in an open car!'[33]

Brooke called it '"A day disorganized by victory!" A form of disorganization that I can put up with.' Like many others, Brooke also saw the end of the war as a day of reckoning. For him, it was vindication of all of his behind-the-scenes work, planning and strategy that never got the recognition he felt it deserved. Instead, he saw his political master, Churchill, taking credit on one side, and commanders in the field, like Montgomery, receiving it on the other. Yet his contribution was barely even known to the public at the time. There is perhaps a hint of this in his statement about Churchill being late because of his insistence of travelling in an open car – of wanting to accept all the adulation. In his memoirs, he sought to set the record straight.

'There is no doubt that the public has never understood what the Chiefs of Staff have been doing in the running of this war. On the whole the PM has never enlightened them much, and has never once in all his speeches referred to the Chiefs of Staff or what they have been doing in the direction of the war on the highest plane. It may be inevitable, but I do feel that it is time that this country was educated as to how wars are run and how strategy is controlled. The whole world has now become one large theatre of war, and the Chiefs of Staff represent the Supreme Commanders, running the war in all its many theatres, regulating the allocation of forces, shipping, munitions, relating plans to resources available. Approving or rejecting plans, issuing directives to the various theatres. And most difficult of all handling the political aspect of this military action, and coordinating with our American allies.

'It is all far less spectacular than the winning of battles by commanders in the field, and yet if the COS make any errors the commanders in the field will never be in a position to win battles. Their actions are not in the limelight, indeed most of the time they are covered by secrecy. We therefore find the COS working and working incessantly, shouldering vast responsibilities, incurring great risks without the country ever realising we were at work. It has been a wonderful experience, of never ending interest. At times the work and the difficulties to be faced have been almost beyond powers of endurance. The difficulties with Winston have been of almost unimaginable proportions, at times I have felt that I could not possibly face a single other day. And yet I would not have missed the last 3½ years of struggle and endeavour for anything on earth.'[34]

For Brooke it was also an opportunity to look back over the past six years and to think beyond questions of battlefields and supply lines, diplomacy and endless meetings.

'Many more wars,' he wrote, 'and much suffering is required before we finally learn our lesson. However humanity in this world is still young, there are still many millions of years to run during which high perfection will be attained. For the present we can do no more than go on striving to improve more friendly relations to those that surround us.'[35]

Churchill was at the centre of everything in Britain on VE Day. Immediately after his radio broadcast at 3.00 pm, he went and addressed the House of Commons. He was driven to Parliament in an open-top car that was pushed as much as driven through the vast crowds.

Churchill later wrote, 'Apprehension for the future and many perplexities filled my mind as I moved about among the cheering Londoners in their hour of well-won rejoicing after all they had gone through.'[36]

According to the *Manchester Guardian*:

'It would be a sweeping statement to say that no British Prime Minister was ever received with such tumultuous acclaim as Mr Churchill today. Let us be restrained, and say that there has been no comparable scene in the House of Commons for at least a generation. Today, at the first glimpse of Mr Churchill, coming in from behind the Speaker's chair, a House packed in all parts rose as one man and broke into a prolonged burst of ecstatic cheering – yes, "ecstatic" is not too extravagant a word. And, of course, it all went to a wild waving of order papers.'[37]

After his speech, Members of Parliament filed out of the House and went to a service at St Margaret's Church in Parliament Square. 'St Margaret's, I thought, had never looked more beautiful,' wrote the London Day by Day columnist for the *Daily Telegraph*. 'A splash of colour was given by the two new Union Jacks which hung at the side of the altar.'[38] Then it was back in the open-top car for Churchill, making a dash for Buckingham Palace through the crowds. On Whitehall, more than 50,000 people stood in the afternoon warmth waiting for Churchill's return. For many of them it was too much, as detailed in one of the Mass Observation reports from that day:

'Occasionally an ambulance drives through and the crowd makes way. Now and then two or three or half . a dozen people feel ill, and file out through the people, with green faces. Here and there someone falls, and someone else produces smelling salts and supports him or her. It is usually a woman, but one or two of the men are seen to collapse momentarily too.

'Time passes. Sporadic bursts of shouting from crowd. "We want Winnie! We want Winnie!" There are occasional shouts of "Here he comes!" but the balcony is still empty. There is a lot of restless activity around the parapet near the balcony; men keep walking along it to further windows and back again. Now and then people look up enviously to those sitting at windows opposite or sitting down on the roofs above. A few people pipe up weakly, "He's a jolly good fellow," and there are more shouts, "We want Winnnie." The minutes seem to pass very slowly in the intense heat. More people keep feeling ill, and the crowd makes way for them, sympathetically. A stout man collapses and is helped out. Shouts of "Hurry up, Winnie, old man!"[39]

The crowd was getting a little impatient. They did not want to be disappointed again after the shenanigans of the previous day. A voice from the back asked why he wasn't coming out. A woman answered loudly, 'Ee's 'avin' a drink, dear!'

It was 5.40 pm before the man they had all been waiting for stepped out onto the balcony of the Ministry of Health making the V sign and with the trademark cigar in his mouth, along with some other members of the government, including Ernest Bevin. The crowd roared and waved anything they had to hand – hats, flags, umbrellas, fans and gloves. Churchill spoke, very briefly: 'God bless you all,' he said. 'This is your victory.'[40]

After his short speech, Ernest Bevin urged the crowd to give 'Three cheers for victory', which they duly did, and also sang 'For He's a Jolly Good Fellow'.

As Churchill, Bevin and the others headed back inside the Ministry of Health and the cheers died away, people formed orderly queues to head away from Whitehall. Some went towards the river, trying to find a pub or a café that was open for a cup of tea or a pint of beer. Most were closed, though, and amongst the cafes that were open, many were serving rather dubious fare: 'weak tea and nasty cake' in the case of one establishment at Milbank.[41]

A more festive atmosphere was to be found for those who headed north to Trafalgar Square where, at 7.00 pm,

> 'a very pretty girl about eighteen dressed in a red frock with white polka dots, a blue neck square, and shoeless and stockingless, stands on the edge of the fountain. She's been fooling around with three pompous looking officers of the Norfolk regiment. Lifting up her skirts she paddles into the water. Two of the officers roll up their trousers and follow suit. They climb to the very top of the fountain carrying the girl. When they reach the top they get a cheer from the crowd, and the pretty girl kisses them. British movietone cameramen take photographs. After a while they paddle back. Lifting up her skirts she calls: "Oh my, I've never shown so much leg in my life". Male cries of "Don't Mind us".'[42]

It was still light at 7.45 pm, but in the West End fireworks were already being thrown among the crowd and people screamed and leapt back as they went off with big bangs. Various vehicles with people hanging off them – such as a jeep filled with girls and American soldiers – passed through the crowds, honking their horns. On one of them a girl sat waving a Union Jack and a Stars and Stripes. One American soldier's face was covered with lipstick. He asked a girl:

'Won't you join in my collection?' A young woman complained of her 'poor feet'. A man in the crowd shouted out: 'Come on grin and bear it. You only get a celebration of this sort once every twenty-five years.'[43]

Out in the suburbs and across the country, children who had been collecting firewood for much of the day were now assembling great pyres to light and dance around. The more enterprising were also crafting effigies of Hitler to burn on them – though for some it took until the following night to organise this. A group of children in south London managed to inveigle the whole road into helping them, as described by a Mass Observation investigator: 'Everyone participated in the making of Hitler. One lady gave the jacket, another the trousers, and so on until Hitler's rig-out was assured. A dressmaker in the road gave the dressing up the professional touch.'[44]

In Manchester, the celebrations, according to the *Manchester Guardian*, had begun 'a little diffidently' in the morning with overcast weather and

'soft, warm rain that fell generously for several hours. But it did not spoil the decorations and it did not unduly damp the spirits of the young, who were the chief merrymakers and who poured from the outskirts into the city centre in their jubilant though somewhat aimless thousands well in time for the one local ceremony that served as a common focus and cue – the broadcasting of the Premier's message from before the Town Hall, with the Lord Mayor and other dignitaries outside, flanked by the newly floated flags of all the friendly nations lined across the building's face.

'Official sanction having been given, the rejoicing that the Prime Minister said we might allow ourselves for a brief period became warmer and more general. The sun came to show the gay decoration in improved colours and the jollity that was released in the centre spread to the outer parts of the city: all the suburbs had their own brave, glad shows.'[45]

In Trafalgar Square, as the sun sunk low in the sky, the celebrations were getting a little rowdier. Two sailors with their girlfriends sat on top of one of the fountains. An American soldier fell in, stripped off to his waist, then dived back into the water. 'My goodness, he'll catch his death of cold,' one lady called out. Men and girls climbed up lamp-posts and waved flags.[46]

According to the *Daily Telegraph,* 'Piccadilly Circus was reminiscent of a Venetian carnival, as the sober Britons threw off restraint for the biggest night of their lives.' People were dancing, women were fainting 'on this sultry night' and a bonfire was lit in the middle of the street.[47]

But there was one rather more serious thing still to do before the night was out. At 9.00 pm, the King spoke on the radio. Crowds swarmed into hotels around Piccadilly to hear the broadcast. In Trafalgar Square there were loudspeakers and most people stood attentively to listen to it.

'Today we give thanks to Almighty God for a great deliverance. Speaking from our Empire's oldest capital city, war-battered but never for one moment daunted or dismayed – speaking from London, I ask you to join with me in that act of thanksgiving.

'Germany, the enemy who drove all Europe into war, has been finally overcome. In the Far East we have yet to deal with the Japanese, a determined and cruel foe. To this we shall turn with the utmost resolve and with all our resources. But at this hour, when the dreadful shadow of war has passed far from our hearths and homes in these islands, we may at last make one pause for thanksgiving and then turn our thoughts to the tasks all over the world which peace in Europe brings with it.'[48]

In London pubs people stood as the national anthem was played at the end of the King's broadcast. The lady from Chelsea who had come in to the centre of London earlier in the day had returned to her home borough and sat in a local pub with her three young neighbours drinking gin. But when the King began talking, far from listening intently, one of her neighbours put his feet on the table, sat back and groaned. And when the pub rose for the national anthem at the end of the speech, the Marxist twins refused to stand. Half a dozen naval officers came to investigate and then rounded on another table that had congratulated the brothers on having the courage to remain seated. There was a scuffle, glasses were broken and the Marxist brothers spent the following day in bed.[49]

Charlie Matthews, who was part of a merchant navy escort that night, was still on edge – as the King was speaking, the escort he was serving on spotted a U-boat:

'The greatest day in English history, everyone ashore wild with joy but just another contact for us, another evening, another convoy.

'We make several attacks when oil and air bubbles come to the surface from the wreckage. We pull this inboard and find that we have got German rubber dinghies and interior woodwork of a German U-boat. We have had the honour of killing the last U-boat of the war. He was probably trying to have the honour of sinking the last British ship. Hostilities cease at midnight but we still hammer at our U-boat as I turn into my hammock at 0030.'[50]

For Fred Couling, an injured sailor recovering in hospital, it was the most raucous night of his life, though he clearly felt a little ashamed about it in a letter he wrote to his relatives. 'It was an outlet because [I] have been in here getting on eight months and really was feeling very depressed,' he explained.

Writing the day after VE Day he noted that 'it scarcely seems possible that we can go about freely without fear of being bombed and blasted to pieces'. And he goes into some detail about his exploits – and those of the other injured sailors in the hospital – on VE night: 'Last night is a night I shall never forget; I got well and truly plastered. It all began like this; the Admiral of this joint said there wasn't to be any rejoicing, no leave, or anyone found in drink or with it would be severely punished.'

Clearly, orders were ignored. The men who were mobile enough went to the pub and it was only when they returned, stocked with booze, that the party in the hospital really got going.

'One chap has a broken neck and is completely encased in plaster from his head to his thighs with just holes for his ears and a round part cut out for his face.

43

Where these holes were they had stuck daffodils in, and completely encased the top with beer bottle labels. Another fellow had a stirrup pump wrapped around him complete with hose. Yet another had gone off on crutches and came back without them. Of course loaded up with a big box full of beer and then the party began. The antics these chaps cut made us cry with laughter, one of them was wandering around with just a small cricket shirt, shoes and socks and his sailor's hat on. The nurses couldn't drum into him how immodestly dressed he was. Anyway, the party continued unabated until after midnight and we were all plastered.'[51]

The author Iris Murdoch, who at the time was working for the United Nations Relief and Rehabilitation Administration (UNRRA) also indulged in boozy celebration on VE night. In a letter a few days afterwards, she wrote that

'It is extremely hot & I am sobering down after the uneasy excesses of VE. We did all the right things in London, such as dancing in Piccadilly at 2am. Now I suppose one will cool down, think about poor old Europe, & wonder if our rulers have learnt a great deal from all this. Yet to hell with such gloomy reasonings! Thank God part of the damned war is over. I did thank God very earnestly in the RC Cathedral on Tuesday where the emotion was as thick as incense & the Cardinal (or is he a Cardinal) made a dreadful speech which was happily soon drowned in the Hallelujah Chorus. After that I went & got drunk, which was good too.'[52]

A female London bus conductor, who had worked all day, got home at 2.00 am and found a half-bottle of rum belonging to her sailor husband and sat on the step of her house drinking it with a friend of hers.[53] A young woman working in an Army Records Office in Bournemouth remembered, 'My sailor husband took my mother and I for a tour of Hampshire villages, joining in their bonfires, singsongs, dancing in the streets, drinking our way through dozens of country pubs, swapping our personal stories of how we won the war. We even hugged and kissed complete strangers in the streets, to have those dreadful years behind us was so incredibly wonderful.'[54]

But according to many reports, mass drunkenness was not in general a feature of the VE Day celebrations. For instance, the author Norman Longmate, at the time a serving soldier on leave in London, said that he 'walked all through the West End that night and saw no drunkenness or rowdyism, only cheerful high spirits'.[55] A teenage boy in Glasgow wrote afterwards, 'I didn't see too many drunks, now that I think on it. There was no need. The spirits were lifted high enough as it was.'[56] However, there were a number of fatal traffic accidents reported in the press the following day, and it seems probable that alcohol may have played a role in at least some of these.

For some, there were reservations about the nature of the celebrations. One young woman said that

'There were three things wrong, I think. There should have been guns sounded, salvos of guns as they have in Moscow and the planes shouldn't have been past in ones and twos skimming over the rooftops, they should have organised formations of bombers to fly over London. And another thing they should have sounded the sirens. Actually as a government organised VE Day I don't think it was particularly good. But I suppose they don't think that they ought to organise things on a big scale with the war with Japan still to be fought. They could have had bands in the park and people marching about I think.'[57]

For John Snow, in North London, the reality did not live up to his expectations. 'Perhaps I expected something on Spanish Armada proportions?' he mused ruefully. As darkness fell over the city 'the searchlights came out, swirling around the sky, and then centering as a cone over the centre of the city. I was disappointed and would have liked something a little more spectacular.' For him, 'there was no atmosphere at all … . The man next door had some fireworks – three! Three fireworks don't make a victory!' Although there were bonfires burning everywhere, the party atmosphere was distinctly low key. 'We moved into other roads. The same bonfires and the same lethargy.' The usual songs were being sung – 'Knees Up Mother Brown', 'Roll Me Over' etc. and people had brought a piano out onto the street – but 'even "Roll Out the Barrel" lasts for only a bar or so and peters out. Thus ended my VE Day.'[58]

The celebrations were clearly at their peak in central London and many thousands of people travelled into the city from outside in order to take part. They included Yvonne Milne, who recalled, 'I felt that I had to go to London, the London that I had been with and had suffered with through the blitzes and from whose limits I had been taken as an evacuee and had later escorted evacuees. It was sentiment that made me take my decision as London forms such a big part of my mind.'[59]

But across the country, all the major cities had mass celebrations. The *Daily Telegraph* reported that in Liverpool, the sirens of beflagged liners formed the background to 20,000 people signing 'Land of Hope and Glory' outside the Town Hall. In Birmingham, crowds in Victoria Square sang songs for hours on end. Buildings across the city were floodlit and huge bonfires burned in every suburb. In Cardiff, 30,000 people congregated to hear Churchill speak. In Glasgow, the sound of the ships on the Clyde could be heard reverberating around the city and people tore off their blackout curtains to light up the streets for the first time in six years. In Nottingham, effigies of Hitler and Mussolini were burned and the church bells across the cities had been hung back in their bell towers in time for them to ring loudly on both sides of the River Trent. In Beeston, then just outside Nottingham, Ella Glen had spent much of the war doing secretarial work and being a firewatcher in her spare time. She said,

'On VE Day we all got together and danced in the street. One of the ladies was a very good pianist and she sat and played some popular tunes that we could all dance along too. It sounds silly when I describe it now, but everyone was very happy and excited that the war was over.

'My husband at that time was still in Italy. He had been wounded outside Perugia and got taken down to Naples to be treated in the army hospital there. But I was happy – the war was over and at least he was safe even if he wasn't at home with me.'[60]

The BBC coverage included all the regions and met with acclaim in the *Manchester Guardian*:

'It began at the centre of events, with Buckingham Palace again and the Royal Family on the balcony, then moved to Piccadilly with its immobile cordon of amiable London bobbies watching the revels without interfering. This was a crowd, as the commentator said, "Milling about – but wonderfully behaved." From there to Lambeth, where they were singing the "Lambeth Walk". And gradually the scene widened, to cover Dover seen from the cliffs above, then Caernarvon with song rising from the town square by the Castle, and farther again to Belfast and Edinburgh. The field marshals spoke; the soldiers, sailors and airmen spoke, and we returned at the last to a little village in Dorset with a Dorset farmer to describe the village pub and the quiet but heartfelt thankfulness of the people. For late listeners there was still the promise of further broadcasts from the London night scene, to end a day in which the BBC had acted as a wholly admirable agent for bringing the news and rejoicing of the people to the people everywhere.'[61]

In London, the partying went on late into the night. Another great cheer went up at a minute past midnight when the war was officially over. Champagne was quaffed in large quantities at the outrageous price of £6 a bottle. Sailors drank from bottles in the streets. Men and women stole away to London's parks to kiss and, according to some, much more as well. It was a very warm night, certainly for May in London. Kathleen Tipper had been at a party at the parade ground in Woolwich, South London where 'the soldiers from the garrison put on a fireworks display which was reminiscent of the blitz, with hand grenades and Verey lights going off and rockets and various other noisy fireworks adding to the din.' Some of the children were scared, not quite understanding the distinction between these celebratory bangs and the ones from bombs that they had learned to fear. As Kathleen Tipper and her friends walked home they watched 'the wonderful searchlight display, at one point there seemed hundreds of these lights all concentrated on one spot. On our way home wirelesses were playing through open doors and windows and people were sitting in gardens, in fact it was a grand night.' But for her, at least, the celebrations were over for the night: 'I went to bed about 1.30 with searchlights still popping and bonfires going, and was exhausted!'[62]

Chapter 2

VE Day Across the World

'Europe has never known such a calamity to her civilization and nobody can say when she will begin to recover from its effects.'

Manchester Guardian, 2 May 1945[1]

What was happening in Britain on VE Day was a tea party compared to what was happening in mainland Europe at the same time. Yes, in the liberated countries like France, Belgium and Holland there were great celebrations. In the Soviet Union and countries under Soviet control, these celebrations would take place on 9 May rather than 8 May. But the backlash against collaborators, traitors and fascists was also well under way, which meant a great deal of summary justice being handed out, often extremely violently. In places like Germany, Austria, Czechoslovakia and Poland, there was widespread terror, and atrocities were still being committed. In areas that had been liberated across Europe, populations of German civilians were now subject to brutal mass attacks aimed at revenge, enrichment and sexual gratification. The Prague Uprising ended on 8 May when the Czechs were put down for the final time by the occupying Germans, just before the Red Army took control of the city

51

the following day and Czech civilians took their revenge on those who had ruled their city since 1939. And just because the war was over, it did not mean that life was suddenly more enjoyable for Allied soldiers either. There were new duties that they had to undertake and new concerns that they had. In the first hours and days after surrender, Allied soldiers were still on high alert for potential reprisals and secret 'Werwolf' German resistance units. German soldiers were being disarmed and placed in camps. German concentration camps had been uncovered by the Allied forces for months, leading to widespread outrage, anger and disgust. The Soviets liberated Auschwitz on 27 January 1945; the Americans went into Buchenwald on 11 April; the British liberated Bergen–Belsen on 15 April and American forces freed the prisoners in Dachau on 29 April. When British troops liberated Bergen–Belsen in April, footage was widely shown soon after and became known as the 'atrocity films'. On 8 May, the Soviets liberated Theresienstadt, a concentration camp around 40 miles north of Prague, where 155,000 Jews had been sent during the war, including Sigmund Freud's sister, Esther Adolfine.[2] Tens of thousands of people died in the camp and many more were sent from there to be killed at Auschwitz.

The *Manchester Guardian* reported that 8 May saw the final demise of the Nazi salute in Europe. A supplement to the last German High Command communiqué said:

'The British have in several places prohibited the use of the German (Nazi) salute by the Wehrmacht. Military discipline makes it advisable to have a unified form of salute and, therefore, the army salute is being made compulsory for all parts of the Wehrmacht.'[3]

Allied servicemen on German soil had very little opportunity to celebrate that the war was over on VE Day. For most it was business as usual. And that included the British actor David Niven, who was a major in the army. He recalled his memories of VE Day:

'On a country road near Brunswick, I drove through an attractive red-roofed village on the outskirts of which was a large manor house. Two tow-headed little boys were playing in the garden. A mile or so away, I passed a farm wagon headed for the village. I glanced casually at the two men sitting up behind the horse. Both wore typical farmer gear and sacks thrown over their shoulders protecting them from a light drizzle. We were just past them when something made me slam on the brakes and back up. I was right, the man who was not driving was wearing field boots. I slipped out from behind the wheel, pulled my revolver from its holster and told the corporal to cover me with his Tommy gun.

'I gestured to the men to put their hands over their heads and told them in fumbling German to produce their papers.

'"I speak English," said the one with the field boots, "this man has papers – I have none."

'"Who are you?" I asked.

'He told me his name and rank – "General".

'"We are not armed," he added, as I hesitated.

'Sandhurst did it – I saluted, then motioned to them to lower their hands.

'"Where are you coming from, sir?"

'He looked down at me. I had never seen such utter weariness, such blank despair on a human face before. He passed a hand over the stubble of his chin.

'"Berlin," he said quietly.

'"Where are you going, sir?"

'He looked ahead down the road towards the village and closed his eyes.

'"Home," he said almost to himself, "it's not far now … only one more kilometre."

"I didn't say anything. He opened his eyes again and we stared at each other. We were quite still for a long time. Then I said, "Go ahead, sir," and added ridiculously … "please cover up your bloody boots."

'Almost as though in pain, he closed his eyes and raised his head, then with sobbing intake of breath, covered his face with both hands and they drove on.'[4]

Private Sid Verrier from Stoke Newington, North London, was also having a sober time. In a letter to his family – 'Mum, Dad, Violet and Len' – he wrote: 'Believe me folks, I've never felt so fed up since I joined the army. No beer here, no decent grub worthy of such an occasion, no mail, no fraternisation with civvies, absolutely nothing.'

However, the consolation for Sid was that he knew his family back home were safe, that he had survived and in all likelihood he would see them all again. 'There is one thing I am very grateful for,' he wrote, 'that is the war is over in Europe and there will be no more suffering for you all in England – no blackouts, no V bombs. You are all safe at home, and I am okay. That means a lot to us all.'

Clearly he wished that he could be at home in London to celebrate rather than stuck in Germany:

'Well today is the day of victory and I hope you have been enjoying yourselves at home. I keep wondering if you are getting together now like the good old days. I expect Aunt Lil and Aunt Ede and Julie have been to see you.

'I heard Churchill's speech on the wireless and the broadcasting of the celebrations on the programme after the speech had been read in all Allied languages. Gosh, I would like to have been there very much. If I am lucky enough perhaps I will be on the marches that might take place. At the moment, I would march anywhere in England.'

He also made his feelings known about Germans, though he was very keen to make a distinction between those that supported the government and those that did not:

'Five and a half years is a long time, but at last it is finished, and may the SS and Nazis and all the Germans who supported the regime die of frost bite and starvation whilst road building in Siberia. Shooting is too quick for them, too relieving, slow torture and nothing less to teach them a lesson.' As a reminder of the fate that still faced any Germans still prepared to put up resistance he mentioned that 'Two days ago the boys caught the last German sniper – an SS trooper. If the German civvies like to see him he's hanging in the market square, riddled with his own ammunition. Poor sod!!'

By contrast, an ex-German soldier was working with Verrier's unit as an interpreter who 'did not agree with the Nazi Party, told them what would happen, was disgraced because he remained reserved from the Nazi Party' was 'terrifically interesting' and 'the type of chap that any average Englishman could talk with for hours.' So much so that

Private Verrier decided that is how he would spend the rest of his time on VE Day, 'chatting with a sensible German'.[5]

Staff Sergeant John Armas Lethi from Brooklyn, New York was serving with the 104th Infantry in Germany in 1945. In a letter to his mother, typed on a 'liberated' typewriter just over a week after VE Day, he apologised because 'it doesn't work the way a real democracy typewriter should'.

'Well, I see from your letter and from the newspapers that there was quite a bit of celebrating on VE Day. Over here we didn't do any kind of celebrating where we were, on account we were mostly too darn tired and the end of the festivities were more or less an anti-climax, because we all knew by the fourth that the whole thing was over and all they had to do was sign the paper and have their pictures taken. I guess that when you heard the war was over, you pictured us all over here as laying aside our weapons and resting up. I suppose in some cases that would be correct but in my own case, my last bit of combat activity didn't end until today.'[6]

Lethi described how on the 17th, he had to persuade some well-armed SS troopers who 'had the idea that the war wasn't over' that it was. It turned out to be a routine operation without a shot being fired. Mopping up was going on across Germany and Austria on VE Day too as Wehrmacht and SS units surrendered to the Allies.

One of those who surrendered that day was Rudolf von Ribbentrop, the son of the Nazi Foreign Minister who was later sentenced to death at the Nuremburg Trials. Von Ribbentrop, a highly decorated captain in the Waffen-SS, was captured by the Americans in Austria.

The last city in Germany to fall – Breslau (now Wrocław in Poland) – was taken by the Russians on 6 May after a three-month siege. On 8 May, the Russian soldiers moved into the city, taking any remaining German soldiers prisoner and raping the women. 'The Russian soldiers reached our cellar the next morning, May 8,' recalled one woman, who was then a young schoolgirl. 'Women of all ages were raped openly, in sight of everyone, including their own small children. A drunken soldier pushed me to the floor and raped me, but he was only the first.'[7]

In April and May 1945, a nineteen-year-old Jewish man called Michael Etkind had been on a death march through western Sudetenland. On the night of 7 May, he and the others he was with slept in a barn. The next morning

> 'We had to get up at dawn. At least ten men were dead, and half that number just could not get up and were shot. We were lined up on the road and counted a number of times. I felt exceedingly weak. I knew that I could not possibly survive another day's march. I had to have some food, but how? I positioned myself near the head of the column. We were about to start marching when suddenly a group of German soldiers appeared. They had no arms and no military insignia. We at once understood what had happened. They must have been captured, or they had surrendered, and were disarmed and told to go somewhere.
>
> 'Our guards talked to them for a few minutes. In the meantime the village women and children gathered round to look at us. A boy of about ten was holding a large beetroot in his hands. I had to think fast: "Even if he manages to throw it, which seems doubtful, the

chances that I will get it are very small". I stepped out of the line and grabbed the beetroot. As I was stepping back into line, I felt a swingeing blow to my left ear. The SS man nicknamed "The Dwarf" hit me with the end of the knobbly stick he always carried. I heard ringing in my left ear, the upper part of which seemed stuck. There was sticky blood on my fingers after touching the ear.

'"Achtung, attention, forward march!" We started to march at a fast pace, and going back in the direction from which we had come three days earlier. My head began to spin, and the ringing was still there. I began to fall back, and before long I was near the end of the column. The road was going downhill so the pace quickened. Suddenly we heard a shot behind us, and a command, "Halt". Two American tanks had appeared higher up the road down which we had just come.

'I ran towards them as fast as I could, and climbed on to the first tank. I thought that the shooting was about to start, but the Americans were laughing and saying, "Germany kaput". We looked down and observed the strange scene. The "boys" – the strongest of our men who were carrying the Germans' rucksacks – threw themselves on the guards and began to wrestle with them. The Germans would not dare to shoot now, but they all managed to extricate themselves after throwing away their weapons. Some of them ran into the fields without their boots, which remained in the arms of their "boys". Turning to the Americans, I pointed my finger in the direction of the escaping SS men and said "Boom, boom". The Americans kept on laughing, shaking their heads, and repeating, "Germany kaput" and "Hitler kaput".'[8]

For an anonymous German woman living in Berlin, the two weeks before VE Day had been nothing less than a descent into hell as the Soviets burst into Berlin, killing, raping and looting as they went. She recorded the often harrowing daily events between the end of April and the middle of June in her remarkable diary, which was published in 1955 as *A Woman in Berlin.* On VE Day, she completed her half-written diary entry from the day before when she and one of her neighbours had found a dead man lying outside their apartment block on their way back from collecting water from a nearby pond. 'We wonder whether we should search him for papers, notify possible relatives. But we don't feel up to it.'

In the spring and early summer of 1945, women in Berlin and many other cities in Germany and Austria did not ask one another whether they had been raped or not, only how many times it had happened. The Soviets were the worst, but French, American and British soldiers were also guilty of the same crime. For the anonymous woman in Berlin, 'This collective phenomenon of rape will also be overcome. Each woman helps the other by speaking about it, by airing her experience and giving her fellow woman a chance to air hers, thus ridding themselves of their sufferings.'

At 9.00 in the morning of 8 May, she heard the secret signal on the front door they had established to let the people inside know that it wasn't Soviet soldiers about to charge in. Instead,

'It was Frau Wendt, the eczema woman, who brought news of peace. It is rumoured that the last organised German resistance in the north and south has been broken and that we have surrendered.

'The widow and I breathe a huge sigh of relief. Thank God it happened so quickly. Herr Pauli is still very bitter about the *Volksturm*, about the senseless killing during the last hours of the old, the exhausted; helpless men bleeding to death for the lack of a rag with which to bandage their wounds; splintered bones sticking out of civilian trousers, human bundles on stretchers from which blood kept dripping ... Herr Pauli has seen some frightful things. And I'm sure that the cause of the sciatica which has kept him in bed for more than a week is at least partly psychological – a refuge, an escape into sickness. There are several men in this house taking refuge in inertia for various reasons: the bookseller has his party membership, the deserter his desertion, and several others their Nazi pasts for which they fear punishment by deportation and behind which they shelter when it comes to water fetching or other activities. The women themselves do their best to hide their husbands and protect them from the enemy. For what, after all, can the Russians do to us women now? They've already done their worst.'[9]

The anonymous woman reflects that 'I often think that from now on I shall be able to endure anything on earth, so long as it takes place from without and not from the ambush of my own heart. I feel so burned out I can't imagine what could move or excite me much in the future. If life must go on I suppose it could be lived on a desert of ice.'[10]

The sun was shining in Berlin on VE Day and the woman took the opportunity to clean her linen 'which was badly needed after all the booted guests'. She could hear the queue of people standing outside the baker's in the street outside her window. There was no bread for the people in the queue, but the baker was giving out tickets for the following day and the day after, depending on a delivery of flour and coal. However, the woman already had her bread that the baker had given to her out of gratitude after she 'defended his wife when the Ivans were trying to drag her away'.[11]

In general, life was infinitely better for women in Paris, and certainly for writer Simone de Beauvoir. Returning from a trip to Portugal in early spring she had managed to carry with her 'fifty kilos of food', including 'hams, rust-coloured chorizos, Algarve cookies sticky with sugar and eggs, tea, coffee, chocolate.'[12] On VE night 'when all Paris was out in the streets signing and dancing', she went with a group of friends to the Place de la Concorde on the Metro. During the day, there had been jeeps full of American soldiers and young women driving around town; American aircraft flew low overhead and church bells sounded across the city. Everywhere was decorated with tricolour flags and the crowds – mainly of young people – were thick. There were so many people on the streets that de Beauvoir's group was soon broken up 'as the surging crowd carried us toward the Place de l'Opera: the opera house was streaming with red, white and blue lights, flags were snapping and snatches of the *Marseillaise* floated everywhere: we felt suffocated; one false step and we could have been trampled where we stood. We made our way up to Montmartre and stopped at the Cabana Cubaine; what a crush!' The major monuments in Paris were lit up for the first time since the war began. The *Garde républicaine* (Republican Guard) made a ceremonial appearance on their horses, though many of them also had a girl behind them, clinging onto their Napoleonic uniforms.

The liberation of Paris in August 1944 and the subsequent celebrations perhaps meant that the end of the war in Europe did not quite have the same meaning in France as it did in Britain. Certainly, for Simone de Beauvoir, the celebration did not have the same intensity.

'My recollection of this night is much more confused than my memories of other, earlier festivities, perhaps because my feelings were so confused. The victory had been won a long way off; we had not awaited it, as we had the liberation, in a fever of anxiety; it had been foreseen for a long time, and offered no new hopes. In a way, this end was like a sort of death … The war was over; it remained on our hands like a great unwanted corpse, and there was no place on earth to bury it.'[13]

General de Gaulle broadcast to the nation at the exact same time as Churchill did in London. He told his audience that France was one of the victors in the war, though many were unconvinced by the claim. France had been humiliated and almost destroyed. But members of the Resistance and the Communist Party felt like victors – they felt that the future of France belonged to them.

Elsewhere in France, Staff Sergeant John Rhys, a fluent German speaker who would be recruited soon after VE Day to work in the British Zone in Germany, celebrated the end of the war in Bayeux in Normandy. The celebrations began early with a major military parade of all the British units still stationed in the area. Bayeux had been captured in the early days of the Normandy invasion and was virtually unscathed by the war. According to Rhys, 'The church bells were pealing all day long and the many sidewalk cafés and bars were lit up for the first time since the beginning of the war in September 1939. There was much singing, cheering and alcohol-fuelled toasting which lasted until the next morning.'[14]

Mary Pettit was in the Women's Auxiliary Air Force (WAAF) in 1945 and based just outside of Brussels.

'I was back in the barracks by 4.30 pm with time to get ready to go out to meet an airman friend of mine. The trams into the city were running, although few and far between. We had been waiting interminably, when an American pulled his jeep up and asked if we wanted a lift to the city centre. We climbed in and had to hang on very tight indeed as he went like a bat out of hell. It was a relief to get out in one piece. In the city we wandered through the main streets or, more correctly, went along in the direction the crowd was going. Everywhere was crammed. By chance the crowd took us along to the Malcolm Club where we stopped for a visit. Leaving there, we were pushed along to the Porte de Namur. After a visit to a nearby hostelry, we got back to the barracks at 2.00 am and finally retired to bed at 3.00 am. That hostelry was the *En Passant* bar that would, one day, hold very dear memories. VE Day had been a very long, but a very happy day; one never to be forgotten.'[15]

The American writer Edmund Wilson toured through Europe in the spring of 1945, later writing up his experiences as the book *Europe Without Baedeker: Sketches among the ruins of Italy, Greece and England.* In a 'stunned and stopped' Milan at the start of May he reported that it looked 'like a slice of hell'. The people there, he noted, were 'bloodless undernourished people, wrapped in any old cloth that could protect their skins'. However, he also found that the teenage boys in the city were 'exhilarated at getting a chance to let themselves go against somebody', and saw them 'cruising around in cars with machine guns, looking for Fascist collaborators to shoot'.[16] In Rome, there were wild celebrations. British soldier Noel Mander was stationed on the outskirts of the city and later recalled that 'the city was throbbing with excitement and jubilation, drinks were pressed on everyone, bands playing. Towards the evening celebrations became rowdy, Americans became particularly aggressive. Many girls were on the streets offering their favours.'[17]

Edmund Wilson also noticed the prodigious trade in prostitution that was going on in Rome, particularly with the American soldiers. It was a trade, he noticed, that was not always popular with the local people.

> 'The hotels in the Via Veneto that have been commandeered by the AC [Air Corps] are picketed by tarts and pimps. The Air Corps are great spenders on furlough and they are allowed to have women in their rooms, so that the aviators' hotel in this section is the center of activity and gaiety. Women stream through the lobby, perch in the bar and flutter about the entrance like starlings. I saw one little girl coming out, wild-looking, red-haired and slim, who gave me the impression that she was having an intoxicatingly good

time as well as making a great deal of money. In another of these hotels, one night, some soldiers threw a girl out of the window and broke her back so that she died. Such incidents have antagonized the Italians, and the "better class" of people are disgusted by the spectacle of the Roman women – and many who come into Rome for the purpose.'[18]

In Preveza, on the west coast of Greece, Major T. C. Howes of the 2nd Battalion Royal Fusiliers was without a chaplain, but nonetheless decided to organise his own thanksgiving service for his troops. He needed a church, so he decided to ask the local archbishop if he could borrow his. The archbishop agreed.

'Doug Lambert and some of the others had been choir boys in their youth. We had a few choir practices. I invited the mayor, the nomarch, the archbishop and everyone else to the service. We marched to the cathedral. The NAAFI and UNRRA and everyone for miles was there. I took the service, said a few words, and in typical British fashion took a collection – half for the cathedral, half for the Royal Fusiliers Benevolent Fund. The nomarch insisted on calling me "pappas" for ever afterwards.

'After the service there was a triumphal tour. I provided the jeep. In it was the archbishop, the nomarch, the major and me. We went to the town hall where the four of us appeared on the balcony to the cheers of the crowd. As soon as it was dark we arranged a firework display on the quay. This consisted of shooting off all our spectacular weapons. Verey lights, parachute flares, mortar bombs (in the sea), smoke bombs and a big "V" sign with machine gun tracer bullets.'[19]

For Edmund Wilson, Greece was in a far worse state than even Italy at the end of the war:

'Greece now is really the country where nobody has anything at all. In Italy there are still many commodities that are being produced and sold – striped neckties, pink silk slips and lace brassieres, new books in crisp, bright covers, perfume and candy and cakes – and that revive some of the brilliance of the shops in places like Milan and Rome. But in Greece there is not much beyond remnants of old stocks that must predate the war, and, in clothing, a scanty supply that only meets rudimentary needs. No woman in the street wears make-up, and they have only rather dreary cheap dresses, mostly of the national blue; none of the men has a necktie on, even when his shirt collar is buttoned. If you got a better-class restaurant, you can get little but a slice of fish, a dish of cut-up tomatoes, a bottle of resinated wine and a slice of watermelon.'[20]

Charles Pennethorne Hughes had just been appointed as the director of the New Delhi office for the BBC in the spring of 1945 and on his way to his new post he stopped off in Cairo. He warned in a letter to the senior controller in London that the BBC should not expect triumphalism in the Middle East and India when the war was declared over.

'When peace was imminent last year, we were asked to provide programmes illustrating the extravagant elation which it was imagined would greet the event amongst British Forces and indigenous peoples of the Middle East. So, I gather, was India. Both I and my predecessor here had to reply that demonstrations were, if permitted at all, highly unlikely to be desirable ones – either the soldiery breaking up the local institutions it most disliked, or the local populace demonstrating against the Raj. With peace again looking as though it is likely to happen at any moment, I do think that another warning note may be necessary, although I know there have been warnings to individual producers, both from Stephenson and myself.

'Whilst naturally, there will be tremendous relief at the end of fighting in Europe, it will mean to the serving man out here merely that at last he will get a bit more help from the West, and to the peoples of the Middle-East countries and, I am afraid, of India, that the military cork is now at least half way out of the bottle of their political aspirations.'[21]

The British War Office had similar feelings and felt that the end of the war was encouraging nationalism in India. The day before VE Day, the official report by the British Government had been published into the Bengal famine of 1943 and 1944 that had killed more than 1,500,000 people. The political atmosphere was certainly not poised to celebrate British success.

Like Charles Pennethorne Hughes, Tony Benn had also been in Egypt in April 1945, serving with the RAF. But he was on leave in Palestine when peace was declared. In a letter to his family, Tony Benn wrote that:

'We hired a rowing boat and rowed out into the sea of Galilee, trying to pick out Capernaum on the side of the lake further up. Coming in, we entered a little Arab restaurant for refreshment and as we walked towards the place, a Jew hurried up with a smile and said "The war – finished!"

'We didn't know whether to believe it or not so we smiled back. It seemed to be confirmed by a special edition of the paper. So we solemnly celebrated with an orange squash and an ice cream each – hardly believing it could be true, hardly thinking of it, it seemed so remote. Returning later to Shaar Hagolan, via another settlement, we found them preparing for a festival to celebrate peace.

'It was nearly ten o'clock and we understood that the King was to speak so we asked to listen to the wireless. As you know, he didn't, but in consequence we missed the gathering on the lawn when the leader of the settlement gave an address in Hebrew to the "three English officers". Think of the wonderful opportunity for replying with a speech – what we missed! I was disappointed.

'Outside on the grass an effigy of the swastika was burned and the settlement crowded into the eating hall, where a little wine and lots of biscuits and nuts were laid along tables.

'I asked for an orange squash and was given one, however one old boy emptied half a cupful of wine into it, and I drank it up – it was practically communion wine – rather an appropriate beverage to celebrate peace.

'Then the national dances began – Germans, Czechs, Poles, Turks, Yugoslavs, all did their national dances. Then there was a pause and an announcement in Hebrew. Everyone looked at us and it was explained that the RAF officers would do an English national dance. Hurriedly deciding to do the boomps-a-daisy, two of us took to the floor – it was an instantaneous success and everybody joined in.

'That is how I celebrated the peace.'[22]

In Burma, peace was a distant dream for Captain I. A. Wallace, who spent VE Day engaging the Japanese in the tangled, remorseless jungle. He was an Observation Post (OP) officer in 115th Army Field Regiment, Royal Artillery, which meant that it was his job to direct artillery and mortar fire to targets over the radio. He recalls in his memoirs, *The Diary of a Junior Officer*, that on the morning of VE Day 'I was ordered to wait with battalion HQ and I was able to get a cup of tea and some breakfast. We also picked up the news that the war in Burma was virtually over with the fall of Rangoon and that VE Day was being celebrated with dancing in the streets at home. We knew that no one at home could appreciate what was really happening in those Burma jungles while they celebrated victory at home.'

The objective that day was for two companies to occupy a cross-tracks 'which was regarded as important to control'. It was hot and sunny and Wallace was ordered to join the leading company. He and the rest of his OP party walked through dense teak forest with a visibility of just ten yards – 'the ensuing uncertainty proved a terrible strain on the nerves'. Once they had reached the leading company, they started to dig holes because the company commander expected the Japanese to be firing mortars at them at some point. At that moment, they got the order to attack the Japanese position and it was Wallace's job to train the guns on the right spot. He had an hour to get it right: 'It was a most anxious hour as the lives of so many men depended upon the accuracy of the artillery.'

Just before the attack was about to happen – at 1.00 pm, and in sweltering heat – Wallace encountered a problem when he could not find his water bottle: 'This was very serious, as water was precious and one did not feel justified in borrowing it.' He eventually found it buried under some loose earth that had been thrown up when he and the other men were digging their foxholes. Now he had just to sit and wait for the assault to begin. Every man fixed their bayonets and waited: 'Lining up in the jungle for an assault was always a heavy strain on the nerves. I was particularly anxious in this instance as the whole artillery support was my responsibility.'

The guns opened up at the right time, but in reply machine gun bullets came hissing through the teak leaves at Wallace and the rest of the company, who dived for cover.

When the bullets had stopped, they stood up and advanced through the barely penetrable foliage with less than ten yards of visibility. Within just thirty yards, a Japanese soldier unwittingly ran towards them: 'Almost every man had fired his rifle at him and he fell riddled with bullets.' They stepped over his body and carried on, expecting to be fired upon at any moment. They eventually reached the cross-tracks that had been the objective at the start of the day, but in breaking cover, two men in the company were cut down by enemy fire: 'On we went past the dead bodies on the ground and secured our objective.' They were joined by another company which came through and assaulted a nearby hill, which was taken 'for a few more English lives'.

They now had to dig more foxholes, as it seemed that they would spend the night there. It was oppressively hot, and they had had very little to eat. But for Wallace, the day was not over yet. Their zealous colonel sent a third company forward to try to exploit the new position and Wallace was sent to accompany them. He was 'getting pretty near the end of my tether', but nonetheless got his party together, 'loaded up our wireless sets and other paraphernalia and we trudged on'.

But the next push forward was to be a far more perilous one. The leading scout was killed. Another man was sent forward through the thick jungle and he too was fired upon. They stopped and waited for orders. The order came through: 'Push on'. Two more men were ordered forwards.

> 'I suppose such an order was an everyday occurrence but to me it seemed altogether wonderful that two men could bring themselves under whatever compulsion to walk forward again into that dense jungle, knowing what was in store for them there.
>
> 'We waited… half an hour or so later one man came running back. Haggard and lathered with sweat he stammered out his story – the same old story. Then the other man came crawling in desperately wounded. The Japanese had shot him, searched him, taken away his gun and left him for dead. But he lived.'

They decided to try once more to push forwards and two more men – a corporal and a private – went on. The corporal did not make it, but the private came back alive.

'It was when this corporal died that men's nerves began to go. The platoon commander, a hard-bitten sergeant with an MM, suddenly turned his face away and broke down. The tears poured down his cheeks and he sobbed bitterly. He had to be led back to battalion HQ. As may be imagined everyone was felling pretty near breaking point, but the sight of this tough sergeant sobbing like a child was completely unnerving.'

They decided to dig in for the night, and as they did so, some of the men fell down unconscious from exhaustion and dehydration. Eventually, water came from behind on mules and they were able to drink. 'That was how we spent VE Day – the war in Europe over, the war in Burma virtually over except for a little "mopping up!"'[23]

The Soviet Union sustained far more casualties in the war than any other country; estimates vary as to exactly how many, but between twenty-six and twenty-seven million seems credible. This includes millions of civilian deaths as they were caught up in the ebb and flow of armies between 1941 and 1945. Victory was celebrated on 9 May across the country and by Red Army soldiers everywhere – in Poland, Germany, Austria, Yugoslavia, Hungary and Czechoslovakia. In Moscow, there were spectacular fireworks that even, at one point, attempted to draw a representation of Stalin's face in the sky. On the streets of the city, there were scenes of enormous jubilation similar to those already described in London and Paris – dancing, singing, drinking, hugging and kissing. A thousand-gun salvo was fired into the air. The *Daily Telegraph* in London paid tribute to Russia's role in the defeat of Germany: 'Her contribution in blood to the common victory has been immeasurably the greatest. Mr Churchill has asked us to pay tribute to her prowess and it will be paid without stint.'[24]

While celebrations were going on in Moscow and elsewhere, the Soviet counter-intelligence agency, known as SMERSH, was guarding a significant body part found right in the centre of Berlin. Elena Rzhevskaya was the female operative charged with looking after what was suspected to be Adolf Hitler's jawbone, and two dental bridges, which had been removed from a body discovered in the wreckage outside Hitler's bunker on 5 May. According to the historian Anthony Beevor, Rzhevskaya was given the job because she would be less likely to get drunk and lose the items during the VE Day celebrations than a male operative would.[25] The evidence was entrusted to her in a red satin covered cigar or jewellery box.

In an interview in 2005 with the *Observer*, she said: 'Can you imagine how it felt? A young woman like me who had travelled the long military road from the edge of Moscow to Berlin; to stand there and hear that announcement of surrender, knowing that I held in my hands the decisive proof that we had Hitler's remains. For me it was a moment of immense solemnity and emotion; it was victory.'

According to the *Observer* report, 'On 8 May, as Soviet soldiers in Berlin's streets shouted with joy at the news of German surrender, Rzhevskaya poured wine for her colleagues with one hand – while clamping the little box to her side with the other.'

A few days later, her unit managed to track down the dental technician Fritz Echtmann, who had been an assistant to Hitler's dentist, and he provided a positive identification of both bridges – one belonging to Hitler and the other to Eva Braun.[26]

Looting might have been expected in Berlin in May 1945, but in Halifax, Nova Scotia it would have seemed, to outsiders at least, a rather unlikely eventuality. But to those who had been in the town for some time, the possibility of a riot was not a great surprise as there had been considerable and long-standing tension between the town and the large number of service personnel based there. When preparations for the victory celebrations began in September 1944, the mayor asked 'as to what protection the armed services could give against damage'. And in March 1945, at a meeting of the naval police in Ottawa, 'It was generally anticipated by the meeting that V-Day celebrations are apt to be of a boisterous nature and that insofar as possible, civil and Service authorities should make preparations against breakage of windows, overturning of vehicles and the customary forms of property damage occasioned by mass celebration.'[27]

Despite the fear that there would be trouble, poor decisions in the run-up and on VE Day itself meant that the likelihood of rioting was increased rather than decreased. Liquor stores, restaurants and cinemas were shut on the afternoon of 7 May and the trams were not running. But the most conspicuous reason for the riots was the fact that the Navy decided on an open-gangway policy, flooding the town that afternoon with around 12,000 sailors who could not travel, eat, drink or find any form of entertainment. So they decided to make their own. They smashed windows and stole enormous amounts of alcohol, set fire to trams, looted shops and fought in the street. The following day, another 9,500 sailors were allowed on shore and the carnage continued unabated for much of 8 May, before a curfew was finally imposed. Three men were dead – two from alcohol poisoning.

More than 350 sailors were arrested and more than $5 million of damage had been done.

Further down the east coast of North America, in New York, the celebrations were enthusiastic but mainly lawful. They had started spontaneously on 7 May, but as VE Day was proclaimed in the papers (though not by the government) on the morning of 8 May, lots more people turned out on the streets. 'The War in Europe is Ended!' screamed the cover of the *New York Times*. According to Louis Sobol in his column for the *New York Journal-American*, 'The people were hysterical. There were wild scenes, especially in Times Square, all through the day. There were shouts, and tears, and people kissing each other and banging each other on the back. And, of course, there were thousands who went to church or stayed indoors, remembering that VE Day had come too late for a husband, a brother, a sweetheart, a son who wasn't coming back – who'd never come back.'

In the *New York Times*,

'The terms made ready for Germany by the European Advisory Commission are believed first of all to call for the disarmament of all forces, the surrender of war criminals and complete obedience to the orders of Allied Military Government authorities for restoring order in Germany.

'At a time to be jointly decided by the Allies, the Allied Control Commission, composed of the Commanders in Chief of the British, American, Soviet and French forces in Germany, will take charge of the Reich.

'One question that may be settled "promptly" is that of drafting labor from Germany to rebuild the devastated European countries. More than 10,000,000 men may soon be in Allied captivity and until peace has been signed they will remain prisoners of war and can be sent to work wherever they are needed.

'The British and American forces will soon have captured more Germans than the total number of men in their own forces and consideration must be given to the reallocating of these prisoners.'[28]

To reflect this fact and the fact that the war against Japan was still going on, President Truman, who broadcast to the American people at 9.00 am on 8 May, described it as a 'victory only half won'. In fact, Truman had another reason to celebrate the day – it was also his birthday – but he was keen to strike a statesman-like tone and dedicated the victory to Franklin D. Roosevelt who had died less than a month before. 'My only wish is that Franklin D. Roosevelt had lived to witness this day,' he said. Truman had been president for only 26 days and had just moved into the White House the day before VE Day.

Truman continued: 'If I could give you a single watchword for the coming months that word is – work, work, work. We must work to finish the war. Our victory is but half won. The West is free but the East is still in bondage to the treacherous tyranny of the Japanese.

'When the last Japanese division has surrendered unconditionally, then only will our fighting job be done.'

He also paid tribute to the British contribution to the war effort: 'The Government of the United States is deeply appreciative of the splendid contribution of all the British Empire Forces and of the British people to this magnificent victory. With warm affection we hail comrades in arms across the Atlantic.'[29]

Rather than a public holiday, a day of thanksgiving was declared for the following Sunday. But according to the *Daily Telegraph*, the American people did not resent the fact that Britons had two days off: 'After five and a half years of blackout and bombs they have earned it,' was the common refrain.

The driver of a taxi in New York told a *Daily Telegraph* journalist when President Truman made his broadcast, 'I could not celebrate today. I have a boy at Okinawa.' And he added to his passenger: 'Do you mind if we keep the radio on? I do not want to miss Churchill. He is the best speaker we have now.' Speeches by both Churchill and King George VI were relayed to American audiences. 'Reception was excellent, and his Majesty's firm and resonant voice was heard as clearly as if he had been in the same room.'[30]

After the surrender ceremony on the morning of 7 May in Reims, General Eisenhower, the Supreme Commander of the Allied Expeditionary Force in Europe, held the two pens that had been used to sign the document in the shape of a V. Addressing the troops under his command on VE Day, he said:

'Though these words are feeble, they come from the bottom of a heart overflowing with pride in your local service and admiration for you as warriors.

'Full victory in Europe has been attained. Working and fighting together in a single and indestructible partnership you have achieved a perfection in unification of air, ground and naval power that will stand as a model in our time.

'Blood of many nations – American, British, Canadian, French, Polish and others – has helped to gain the victory. Each of the fallen died as a member of the team to which you belong, bound together by a common love of liberty and a refusal to submit to enslavement.

'No monument of stone, no memorial of whatever magnitude, could so well express our respect and veneration for their sacrifice, as would perpetuation of the spirit of comradeship in which they died.'[31]

In Australia, the scenes of celebration seen in New York, Moscow, Paris and London were not repeated. The mood was sombre. The Japanese bombing raids of 1942–43 were still fresh in the memory and many Australian soldiers were still fighting in the southwest Pacific in Borneo or were being held in Japanese prisoner of war camps with no hope of release. 'Thank goodness we had the wireless to cheer us on Wednesday recording the joyousness in England,' wrote one reader of the *Melbourne Argus* in a letter to the newspaper. 'Here it was more like a solemn funeral than a great victory achieved.'[32] But others, like John Laffin, an Australian Platoon Commander, were jealous of the situation in Europe:

'I have to admit a certain amount of envy of the British that they were no longer at war in Europe, especially when I paraded my men in the training camp the next day. Some of them were broken almost beyond repair and I (with others) had to restore their morale and motivation. We realized that it was going to be even more difficult now that one part of the war was over. Sooner or later the Japs would be beaten and none of my men wanted to be the last Australian killed in action.'[33]

Churches everywhere held thanksgiving services, and on
9 May, 100,000 people attended the service at the Shrine of
Remembrance in Melbourne. An editorial in the *Canberra
Times* wrote that the floodlights over the Australian War
Memorial stood 'in bright relief against the darkness which
is now passing from Europe, and soon from the entire
world'.[34] But the darkness, of course, had not even left
Europe; the continent was still thick with it. On 8 May, Private
Lawrence Saywell became the last Australian to die in the
war in Europe. He had originally been captured in Crete in
1941, then escaped from a prisoner of war camp in Bohemia
in January 1945 and joined a Czech Resistance group. Saywell
fought with the partisans against the Germans for four
months but, on the day the war ended, he was shot and badly
wounded by a German soldier near the village of Miretin
(now in the Czech republic). He died of his wounds. Saywell
was awarded the Czech Military Cross, which is now in the
Australian War Memorial collection.[35]

Chapter 3

The Future of a Ruined Germany

'Germany today is a State in dissolution, a State without leadership, without civil organisation, almost without hope.'

Manchester Guardian[1]

A month before the end of the war the *Observer* correspondent George Orwell followed the Allied forces as they made headway into the heart of Germany. The sheer scale of the destruction that Orwell saw amazed him and he wrote that 'almost every observer' of it made three comments about the state of Germany: 'The first is: "The people at home have no conception of this." The second is: "It's a miracle that they've gone on fighting." And the third is: "Just think of the work of building this all up again..."'

Such was the extent of the damage that Orwell suggested that 'to walk through the ruined cities of Germany is to feel an actual doubt about the continuity of civilisation as a whole'.[2]

It is a picture that almost every account of Germany at the end of the war hammers home again and again. Britain had been bombed, but Germany had been flattened. Richard Dimbleby, the first Allied correspondent to enter Berlin in July 1945, was also astounded by the scale of devastation:

'It's not a very pleasant experience to drive around Berlin,' he said in a broadcast on 3 July. 'This is not the capital of before the war. That impression of solidity and a certain grandeur that atoned for the ugliness of mien of the place has gone. Blown away by thousands of tons of bombs and bitter street fighting. I have never seen widespread ruin to equal that of the centre of Berlin; whole buildings – complete German Ministries – have dissolved into dust. The famous dome of the Reichstag rises like a rickety rose pergola above the trees of the Tiergarten, the Hyde Park of Berlin. And the trees themselves are battered and uprooted, and many of them are stripped of their bark. The wreckage of German aircraft lies smouldering by the side of the great Charlottenburger Chaussee, the broad avenue that runs from the west right into the centre of Berlin. The green horses that surmount the pock-marked Brandenburg Gate gallop madly – drunkenly – straight up into the air; and behind them, in the Soviet zone, the heart of Nazi Germany – the Wilhelmstrasse and the Government buildings – lie in shapeless ruin. Through all this chaos, the pulse of life runs slowly, and haltingly.'[3]

On 10 May, the eponymous – and anonymous – woman in Berlin set out with a friend for a walk to the centre of the city. It was the first time that she had left the confines of her district for some time, and over the past weeks, she and every other woman in her building had been raped by Russian soldiers. Yet her curiosity remained undimmed, and she was keen to find out what had happened to the city in which she lived. She walked through a Berlin that was now almost completely unrecognisable to her, later writing:

> 'I really don't know how to describe what I saw.
>
> 'Everywhere remnants of the army, disembowelled cars, burned-out tanks, twisted gun carriages. Here and there a sign, a poster in Russian celebrating the first of May, Stalin, victory. Here too very few people. Once in a while a miserable figure staggers past us – a man in shirt sleeves, an unkempt woman. No one pays much attention to us. "Yes the bridge is still standing," says a ragged woman in bare feet in answer to our question. A woman in bare feet? I've never seen that in Berlin before. In front of the bridge there's still a barricade of rubble. We slip through an opening. My heart is beating wildly.
>
> 'The sun blazes down. Not a soul on the bridge. We stop for a minute and gaze down the tracks. A maze of yellow rails, deep craters between them. Strips of rail, some straight, others twisted, point toward the sky. Pieces of upholstery and stuffing hang out of bombed sleeping cars and diners. The heat broods over it all; a smell of burning rises from the tracks. Everywhere waste and desolation, not a breath of life. This is the carcass of Berlin.'[4]

Beyond the obvious physical damage, Germany and its citizens faced many other problems in those first weeks and months after the end of the war. The threats of starvation, disease and homelessness hung over the population. The country had no government. Hitler, by refusing to surrender, had invited the complete annihilation of organised society in Germany. Indeed, as historian Ian Kershaw commented, 'Hitler had invariably posed total destruction as the alternative to the total victory for which he had striven.' If Germany lost the war, Hitler said, its people had 'no right to live'.[5] As German troops retreated, they had also been under orders from Hitler to destroy infrastructure and industry that could otherwise be used by the invading nations. Many of these orders were disobeyed and undermined – most notably by Albert Speer – but extensive self-inflicted damage was caused which made the country's difficulties all the greater when the final reckoning came. And for the Soviets in particular, reparations were an essential part of their incursion into foreign territory. Russian soldiers on their way into Germany read road signs saying 'Soldier, you are in Germany, take revenge on the Hitlerites'.[6] This took the form of the dismantling of factories, train tracks and buildings, which would then be sent east to be reconstructed, as well as mass looting, rape and other violence. In the streets of Berlin in the summer of 1945, it was a common sight for Russian soldiers to requisition bicycles with people on them, then try to cycle off, often falling off in the process as they were unfamiliar with how to ride a bike.

Staff Sergeant John Rhys was transferred to Germany to join the newly formed Planning and Intelligence Section of the Control Commission immediately after the end of the war. He was stationed in Hanover. He writes in his memoirs that 'my ability to speak fluent German and my familiarity with Berlin and Germany as a whole (as well as Austria etc.) led to my becoming the general factotum.'

He described the sight of Russian soldiers stealing bicycles from the local people in a way that almost feels like pantomime, if it were not also done with such menace:

'The Mongolian (Russian) troops stationed in Berlin all apparently considered the possession of a bicycle the ultimate luxury in personal transportation. Obviously many of them had no prior experience in riding bikes, so their inability to use one resulted in wobbly, pathetically comical rides. Consequently this led them to believe that the bike they had was faulty and when they saw a German riding a bike properly, the Mongolians would immediately want to acquire that bike. I saw one Russian soldier forcefully, with the aid of his Kalusha (Tommy Gun) demand the "exchange" of the bike he was on with the one the German had. However, after the trade he quickly fell off this one as well.'[7]

Rhys also witnessed general looting by the Russian troops and noted that there were often fights between soldiers 'vying amongst themselves for the best acquisitions'; things such as alarm clocks, light bulbs and water taps that had been ripped out of walls and sockets. The main target of the soldiers was the poor Berliners who carried everything they owned with them.

'When Berliners had to move from one bombed out place to somewhere else,' wrote Rhys, 'their hand drawn carts full of belongings were of special interest to these scavengers, and as most desirable goods and chattels were visible it did not take them long to fill their sandbag size sacks and throw them over the handlebars of their bikes. One such looting incident occurred during one of our many duty trips trying to trace Germany Ministry offices and their records. We came upon a looting going on in the middle of the street where an elderly couple's belongings had been searched and most of their stuff was thrown around the cart. As usual watches and clocks were of special interest to the Russian, but suddenly an alarm clock started ringing in one of the loot sacks. Startled, he immediately fired his Tommy gun at the bag emptying a whole magazine of ammunition into it and ran off as quickly as he could, leaving everything he had packed behind. There was not much we could do except leave the distressed couple to sort things out by themselves.'[8]

For George Orwell, it was important that Germany be rehabilitated rather than being further humiliated and bankrupted. 'The impoverishment of any one country reflects unfavourably on the world as a whole,' he wrote. 'It would be no advantage to turn Germany into a kind of rural slum.'[9]

This was the line from the *Manchester Guardian* on 9 May as well. The newspaper wrote in its editorial that it was surprised.

'But we have seen what hardly any of us thought possible, the visible overthrow of the whole system we set out to destroy. When Dönitz said yesterday "The foundation on which the German Reich was built is a thing of the past. The unity of State and Party no longer exists. The Party has disappeared from the scene of its former activity," he was recording a tremendous fact. Germany today is a State in dissolution, a State without leadership, without civil organisation, almost without hope. It shares the relief the victors feel that the peace satisfies the deepest of human instincts, but it looks forward in bewildered fear to the future.'[10]

The newspaper suggested that the next stage in dealing with Germany was as important as the military victory in itself: 'The moment of defeat and internal crisis is the time for this surgical operation that must be the complement of military victory.' The Allies needed to 'be severe but we must also be just', or else they ran the risk of alienating the German population. It was vital, the editorial urged, to stamp out any remnants of militarism and Nazism in order that the Germans can 'start the rebuilding of the community under our supervision'.[11]

Germany was divided into four zones in line with agreements made in 1944 and later ratified at the Potsdam Conference in July 1945. Field Marshal Bernard Montgomery was in charge of the British Zone. In his memoirs he described some of the problems that were apparent to him when he took up his post.

'In the area occupied by 21 Army Group there were appalling civilian problems to be solved. Over one million civilian refugees had fled into the area before the advancing Russians. About one million German wounded were in hospital in the area, with no medical supplies. Over one and a half million unwounded German fighting men had surrendered to 21 Army Group on May 5 and were now prisoners of war, with all that entailed. Food would shortly be exhausted. The transport and communication services had ceased to function, and industry and agriculture were largely at a standstill. The population had to be fed, housed, and kept free of disease. It was going to be a race for time whether this could be achieved before the winter began; if by that time the population was not fed, and housed, famine and disease would run riot through Germany and that would prove a most serious embarrassment to the western Allies.'[12]

For Julian Bach Jr, a roving reporter for *Army Talks*, the official US Army magazine devoted to military and political subjects that was distributed each week to troops in the European Theatre of Operations, 'the ends for which the defeated enemy is being occupied are several'. He listed them as being:

'One is to make certain … that the Germans can never again be a threat to peace. Another is to reduce German industry to the extent that Germany will increasingly resemble a pastoral state, concentrating on the production of food and consumer's goods, without most of the heavy industries that have three times running made it possible for the Germans to wage war. A third goal – and the most difficult to achieve – is to "reconvert" the German heart and mind so that eventually, instead of Nazis, the Germans will be democrats, and Germany, instead of being a law-breaker among nations, will become a law-abiding member of the family of nations.'[13]

Bach also writes about the 'denazification' of Germany. In his eyes 'the word does not mean *reconversion*. It is not part of the educational program, but part of the punishment

Germans must undergo. Denazification means *getting rid of Nazis, just as delousing means getting rid of lice.*[14] In theory, that meant bringing war criminals to justice and purging party members from their roles in public life. In practice, it became one of the messier aspects of the Allied administration.

One of the difficulties was that people were pragmatic and saw no sense in owning up to having a Nazi past. As a member of the resistance in Berlin, Ruth Andreas Friedrich, put it: 'The *Führer* is dead. If you want to live you must eat, and to eat well, you'd better not be a Nazi. So they aren't Nazis. Therefore they weren't Nazis and they swear by all that's holy that they've never been.'[15]

For others, not knowing the nature of the retribution that they might face, suicide was the only option. As well as famous senior Nazis like Hitler himself, Goebbels and Himmler (who killed himself in British custody on 23 May 1945), many ordinary rank-and-file soldiers and local party leaders gave up hope in the final days of the Reich and beyond. The anonymous woman in Berlin records in her diary that just near her apartment block 'in the midst of the debris and craters are three double graves, three double suicides. An old woman cowering on a stone tells me, with bitter satisfaction and many nods of the head, further details about the dead: on the right there lies the local Nazi leader with his wife – revolver. In the grave in the middle, on which several branches of lilac are wilting, a first lieutenant and his wife – poison.'[16]

For important visitors to Berlin that summer, one visit was obligatory – the trip to the ruined Reich Chancellery building and Hitler's office within it to see the root of the poison of Nazism which had spread across the world. Richard Dimbleby broadcast from there on 4 July 1945.

'In this room, were hatched many of the major plots of National Socialism. It was, in its time, a grand – almost overbearingly grand – apartment; a huge, high chamber with brown marble walls on which great tapestries were hung. Those tapestries now have disappeared into rubble and the chaos that lie along the marble floor, making it with the dust that lies powdered on it so slippery that you have to pick your way across. Here by the window where Hitler sat and Hitler worked, I found his chair and I am sitting in that chair now, what's left of it is just the back, which has been ripped up; it looks as though it was done by bayonets. The tapestried seat and one broken arm. And by its side, turned upside down and crashed to the floor, is his grey marble desk, fifteen feet long and five feet wide. That is where Hitler worked. Today it lies in the filth and the rubble that are found in every corner of this huge building in Berlin.'[17]

Dimbleby took a prize with him from the building – a set of cutlery – which I am reliably informed is still owned by the Dimbleby family. Just under two weeks later Dimbleby was back, this time watching the British Prime Minister Winston Churchill make his inspection of the seat of Nazi power.

'Mr Churchill made no comment as he entered the Reich Chancellery,' said Dimbleby on 16 July, 'but by the way he stopped for a moment and looked around, you could sense that this was an historic moment for him. He followed the Russian staff officers through and round the piles of rubble, until his once shining shoes were white with dust. He stopped here and there, generally in silence, and once when I was standing next to him in Hitler's study, I saw on his face, what I can only describe as a stern and hard look. He clenched his unlighted cigar very firmly between his teeth, and went down into the garden where there was so much bitter fighting in the last stage of the Berlin battle. There he turned to the Russians, and then went towards Hitler's air raid shelter. Together, with one or two of the party following, they vanished down the stairs into the ground.'[18]

Writing about the visit later in his memoirs, Churchill wrote that his 'hate had died with [the German people's] surrender and I was much moved by their demonstrations, and also by their haggard looks and threadbare clothes'. As he went down into the bunker, Churchill was shown where Hitler had committed suicide with his wife and when they were back upstairs the Russian guides showed him where Hitler's body had been burned. 'The course Hitler had taken was much more convenient for us than the one I had feared,' wrote Churchill.[19] Alanbrooke, visiting with Churchill, wrote that 'it was possible to imagine the tragedies which had occurred there only some 2½ months ago. Hitler's study in ruins, with his marble top writing table upside down!'[20]

Even Staff Sergeant John Rhys managed to get a tour of the Chancellery and he too walked away with some mementoes.

'When I was rummaging through the document repository shelves, I was thrilled to find several dry file boxes from the secretarial office that contained a

91

small quantity of unused notepaper with gilt adorned letterhead embossed *Adolf Hitler* and others with *Der Fuhrer*, also gilded dinner guest invitations and table seating cards for state banquets and gala functions at the Chancellery. [...] I tucked all this memorabilia into my uniform tunic, which made me look quite portly, as it seemed the best way to carry this material past the Russian guards.'

Rhys had lived in Germany with his parents before the war and he was curious to see their old apartment in Berlin.

'After visiting the Chancellery there was just enough time to drive to the prewar Berlin residential area where my parents and I had been living before the war. Our erstwhile family flat was gutted and the entire district was an awesome sight as almost half of the city dwellings were severely damaged or had been shored up to stabilize them, the result of the frequent heavy bombing raids and the later street fighting with the Russian troops.'[21]

In fact, according to Julian Bach, in 1945, 'Germany today is a country without cities. The countryside is practically untouched and in many spots as picturesque as ever. But in a physical and to a large degree psychological sense, the cities no longer exist.'

He suggested that there were only three cities that had remained intact in the whole country: 'Heidleberg, with 130,000 people, in the US Zone, and Celle, with 60,000, and Flensburg, with 62,000 in the British zone. A few other cities like Luebeck [Lübeck] and Bamburg are in good shape. Otherwise German cities are the world's vastest ruin. Today high canyons of maroon rubble and rusted iron, twisted into snake-like shapes, stand sentinel to Germany's defeat.'[22]

For many back in Britain and America, the Germans deserved what was now coming to them. In Heswall in Cheshire, one female diarist, Ms K. M. Carruthers, recorded how in her office a middle-aged typist that she names only as 'Mrs V', remarked, 'slowly', 'There's only one thing to do with the German people. Our men should use flamethrowers on every town and village they come to, and wipe them all out. Show no mercy.'[23]

And Bach quoted one US officer as saying: 'To look at these Germans ... and at the same time read scare stories about "German starvation" is embittering. After all a good many thousands of persons pulled through years in concentration camps on a diet of thin soup.' Bach suggested that although this was certainly true, the Americans should not 'reduce ourselves to the moral level of the Germans and their concentration camps'. But then he also rather more controversially suggested that 'we hold each German individually guilty for having allowed concentration camps to exist and having thrived while Europe suffered'.[24]

Even British Private Sid Verrier, based in Germany, who said of the hard-core Nazis that 'shooting is too quick for them, too relieving', conceded that there were sensible Germans who did not agree with the Nazi Party.[25] In response to the atrocity films that were shown in Britain in April, depicting the conditions inside the Bergen–Belsen concentration camp, one of the other women in K. M. Carruthers' office commented that 'our fellows fraternise with the Germans and feel sorry for them because they're women and kids without homes. They won't *see* that it's these people who are responsible for such awful things.'[26]

Strictly speaking, this wasn't true, as there was a strict non-fraternisation policy on the part of the western Allies. Major P. M. Barrington of the Royal Horse Artillery, based in Germany, complained in a letter to his parents on 25 May that 'life is dull at the moment. No fraternisation and no fighting'. On 12 July, he says that he organised a dance for 130 Polish girls and 200 men in a local dance hall (the non-fraternisation rule only applied to Germans). He wrote that 'everyone got very hot and rather noisy, but it is the first party the men have had since peace and it went down very well. This non-fraternisation is very difficult, but people are playing very well, and we have no trouble.'[27]

Private Sid Verrier wrote to his family in London,

'In our billet was a lovely girl, yes a lovely girl, really marvellous, although a German. The second day we were there, her mother said to us, "The British are gentlemen, so will you not interfere with my daughter." She spoke very good English. The answer she received was: "Don't worry we are very particular". Upset the poor old cow, but we don't fraternize. The civvies sweep the streets around our billets, clear up the mess they make after looting and those that come to our lines getting away from the Russians, live in the woods. It is a sight worth seeing.'[28]

The British were probably the most conscientious of all the occupying forces at not fraternising with Germans. But for the Americans and French, the reality was somewhat different, and keeping the conquering troops away from

German women was patchily enforced. According to Julian Bach, 'by banning Yankee-Kraut dalliances, the "furlines" became forbidden fruit, thus making them in the minds of many men all the tastier.'[29]

German men were almost uniformly emasculated by being on the losing side of the war. Many of them simply weren't at home – around 11 million German soldiers had been captured. Accounts vary as to the number of those who died in captivity. Montgomery wrote about the challenges he faced in trying to administer so many prisoners – for one thing, they could not fit into any facility or camp. Instead,

> 'all German troops were to be moved into peninsulas along the coastline, and then sealed off in those peninsulas with their backs against the sea. There was no other way of dealing with a million and a half prisoners; we could not put such a number into camps or POW cages. The selected peninsulas were on the east and west coastlines of Schleswig–Holstein, in the Cuxhaven area, and about Wilhelmshaven and Emden.
>
> 'Once in these areas, prisoners were to be documented and checked over. They were then to be demobilized and directed back to their civil vocations, as and when they were needed and work became available – the farmers, the miners, the post office workers, the civil servants, etc. etc. When they left the POW areas to go back to civil work, they were to be dressed in plain clothes.'[30]

Those German men that were not in captivity were generally subdued and servile. The anonymous woman in Berlin wrote in her diary in May 1945, 'It's difficult to imagine an armed

German lying in wait for a Russian. In any case, I've not so far run into this type of man. We Germans are not a nation of partisans; we wait for leadership, for orders – which reminds me of an ironic remark made by a Russian in whose company I travelled for days on one of those endless trips by train across that country: "German comrades would storm a railway station only if they could first of all buy platform tickets!" In other words, Germans have a horror of the unlawful, spontaneous act. Besides, just now they are afraid; reason tells them that they have been conquered and that any kicking against the pricks would only lead to more suffering and do no good.'[31]

According to Giles MacDonogh in his book *After the Reich*,

'German men, such as there were, received a cold shoulder from their women. Poorly nourished, dressed in rags, penniless and morally suspect, they did not have the heroic smell of the conqueror. Carl Zuckmayer spoke to two pretty waitresses who worked in an American mess in Berlin. Neither would have anything to do with German boys. As one put it: "They are too soft, they are not men any more. In the past they showed off too much." The other described German men as "worthless".'[32]

There were millions of displaced persons (DPs) in Germany – not just Germans but also immigrant labourers, prisoners of war captured by the Germans and the liberated inmates of concentration camps. For many of the Jewish people who were placed in DP Camps, the experience to begin with was not always sufficiently different from their previous experiences to reassure them that their future would be brighter than their past. In Bavaria, for instance, General Patton insisted that all camps should be surrounded by barbed wire and armed guards and DPs were allowed out of the camps only if they had an acceptable reason. Jewish DPs were also often placed in camps with the very people who had manned the concentration camps during the war years: Ukrainians, Latvians, Hungarians and Poles who were now homeless and stateless. In some of the camps where malnutrition had been a significant problem – such as Bergen–Belsen, the first interventions by the Allies were disastrous, giving the emaciated inmates rich food that they could not possibly digest. Very quickly, better and more sophisticated techniques were used to nurse these people back to health, but many thousands died. In Bergen–Belsen around a quarter of the 60,000 inmates perished after liberation.[33] Many Jewish people wanted to get to Palestine, but their emigration there was discouraged by the British.[34] Many others wanted to emigrate to the United States and so they tried to move into the American Zone in order to make this more easily possible.

Ordinary Germans became widely aware of the concentration camps in those first few months of occupation. It was a deliberate policy of the Allies to make them aware and in some cases local people were forcibly brought into camps in order to see what had been going on. However, many who saw films or read reports in newspapers did not believe it. And those that did believe it were mainly too concerned with finding food and shelter to think too much about it.[35] In most cases, survival itself was the key priority in those first few months in which Germany had no real institutions or government and almost nothing in the way of schools or hospitals or a legal system. Hunger was the greatest enemy for many. According to Julian Bach, writing in 1945, 'Some Germans are starving, millions are suffering from malnutrition, while other millions are neither starving nor suffering.' He reported that in the French Zone, Germans received an allowance of just 800 calories a day, though he mentions that this is '200 more than the diet fed prisoners in the main compound at Dachau'. However, he suggested that a simple story was the most eloquent of all: 'Near Hamburg one evening, in a marshy plot of land, an elderly German in a business suit takes his cane and clubs a duck to death. More will be said about the food situation, but that in essence is it.'[36]

For Montgomery, 'the greatest problem was food and much would depend on the coming harvest. I ordered that the armed forces were not to purchase or requisition any foodstuffs from the civil population; the latter would need it all themselves.'

It was an unique historical situation to have four conquering countries co-operating with one another to administer their collective foe. 'Germany,' said Lieut. General Lucious Clay, 'will be the great test tube of international co-operation.' Things started off well and there were various friendly get-togethers between the nations in the early days in May 1945. For Field Marshal Montgomery, these types of social events were sometimes rendered slightly tricky because of his abstemious personal habits. According to him,

'The Russians were clearly anxious to make a good impression and they sent a special envoy to the HQ of the 6th Airborne Division in Wismar to find out what sort of entertainment I liked, and what were my tastes and habits; he was told that I disliked wine, never drank any alcohol and preferred water. He then said they proposed to produce some very fine cigars at lunch. Did I like cigars? He was told I did not smoke. By this time he was somewhat shaken; but he had one more suggestion to make. They had some very fine women and dancing girls and they would produce these for the Field Marshal. He was told that the Field Marshal did not like women. That finished him and he exclaimed: "He doesn't like drink, doesn't smoke, and doesn't like women. What the devil does he do all day?"'[37]

On another occasion, Montgomery was in the impressive US headquarters in Frankfurt (in what had previously been the IG Farben building) as Eisenhower hosted the Russians:

'Before lunch some 1700 American and British aircraft flew past in formation giving an impressive display of Western air power – which was not lost on the Russians. During lunch the Americans produced a colourful cabaret show, with swing music and elaborate dancing by negro women who were naked above the waistline. The Russians had never seen or heard anything like this before and their eyes almost popped out of their heads! Nonetheless they enjoyed it thoroughly and encored every time. The whole organisation of the day was on a most elaborate scale, so was the lavishness of the welcome extended by the Americans. It was a day which revealed undeniably the wealth and power of the United States.'[38]

But Montgomery and the Americans also had a significant distrust of the Soviets. Monty noted this not in terms of a comment on countries, but as a comment on race:

> 'From their behaviour, it soon became clear that the Russians, though a fine fighting race were in fact barbarous Asiatics who had never enjoyed a civilisation comparable to that of the rest of Europe. Their approach to every problem was utterly different to ours and their behaviour, especially in the treatment of women, was abhorrent to us. In certain sectors of the Russian zone there were practically no Germans left; they had all fled before the onward march of the barbarians, with the result that the problems of food and housing seemed almost insoluble. I wrote the following in my diary at that time: "Out of the impact of the Asiatics on the European culture, a new Europe has been born. It is too early yet to say what shape it will take. One can only say it will be wholly unlike the old Europe. Its early infancy and growth will be of supreme importance to our civilization."'[39]

General Patton, too, was another who expressed his problems with the Soviets in racial terms. He was disparaging about the Russians, spoke sympathetically about the Germans and expressed disgust at the condition of Jewish displaced persons (DPs). He described one set of Jewish prisoners in September 1945 as 'the greatest stinking bunch of humanity I have ever seen'.[40] On another occasion, talking about the Germans, he said that 'we have destroyed what could have been a good race of people and we are about to replace them with Mongolian savages and all of Europe with communism'.[41] This type of language brings to mind the Nazi concept of the *untermensch,* or subhuman, such as that expressed by Heinrich Himmler: 'We shall take care that never again in Germany, the heart of Europe, will the Jewish-Bolshevistic revolution of subhumans be able to be kindled either from within or through emissaries from without.'[42]

Though he was outspoken, Patton also reflected a wider distrust of the Russians which grew in May and June 1945 amongst the Western Allies. Truman noted in his diary in May that relations with Russia were 'deteriorating' as well, and for many in Britain and America, the threat from Russia was becoming almost as great in the summer of 1945 as the threat from Germany had been six years previously.[43]

Yet, outward co-operation was maintained even at the same time as secret agents were being recruited and primed to infiltrate both sides. In August, John Rhys was allowed into the Russian zone as part of an observation party. 'They treated us as objects of curiosity wherever we went,' he wrote. 'Fully armed we explored the various areas around Berlin, including the Russian zone, by jeep with a gunner at a mounted Bren Gun as protection and authority.'[44]

Major P. M. Barrington had moved with the Royal Horse Artillery into the Olympic Stadium in Berlin by early July. This clearly had some advantages, such as 'swimming pools and every sort of games facility'. However, the downsides were that 'there was no glass in the windows and the barracks were not good'. It did not bother Barrington himself much as he had his mess in a 'big, and rather luxurious house in Charlottenburg'. It sounds like one of the better residences in the city at the time, with 'electric lights, refrigerator, radiogram, and fountain playing in the garden, which is a pleasant spot of grass and trees'. His regiment was there mainly for ceremonial duties; there was a big parade in Berlin on 13 July and again on 21 July with Churchill, Stalin and Truman all present.

Barrington described the parade on the 21st to his parents:

'Today has been a historic occasion – a great parade for Churchill, and others. The audience was impressive and rather staggering. Montgomery, Alexander, Wilson, and Brook heading the army, Andrew Cunningham the Navy, and Portal the Air Force, General Marshall from US and hundreds of red blue and other coloured hats. The saluting base was like a herbaceous border. We fired a salute of 19 salvoes, the first and the last from all 24 guns. The Charlottenburg Chausee was filled with smoke, and the salute thundered down the avenues and echoed among the trees. There were press men everywhere and as you have probably heard Richard Dimbleby whom we primed first, and made certain he got his facts right! Everyone in the regiments is very proud and pleased, and we marched past with great feelings of achievement. It may be better to trot or gallop in service order, but to go past, making a thundering noise of tanks 6 abreast, followed by the rattle and jingle of guns is very impressive. You will see it in the papers and the Gaumont British News, and when you next go to London, perhaps you might try and get some photos out of them – I believe it is possible, and it should be well worth it. I had my tank wireless on as we went past, and heard Dimbleby describing us as we went past – it was most amusing. Churchill looked very well, but Monty very liverish. We had the Chiefs of

Staff, Alexander and Georgie Patton pay impromptu calls on us already and Anthony Eden is visiting us tomorrow. By virtue of the fact that our guns are in the arches of the Olympic stadium we get lots of visitors.'[45]

The Potsdam Conference in July formalised the arrangements within Germany and began to put life in the country on a more institutionalised footing. However, this varied widely between the four different zones. In the British zone, the rule of law was reintroduced in the form of military courts that presided over civil matters like theft. Richard Dimbleby visited one of the courts, which sat in the directors' room of a big Berlin sugar factory. The room had a small Union Jack on the wall, though Dimbleby said that it would later be joined by the flags of the other occupying countries. The court was presided over by a British colonel, who was the military commandant for the area. The court was packed with German civilians, curious to see how the court would conduct itself.

According to Dimbleby,

'The cases heard today were fairly normal ones; stealing a ton of marmalade from the British Army; unlawful possession of firearms – an offence that can be punished by life-imprisonment or death (but was met on this occasion by a year in prison) and (a case more unusual) unlawful arrest and imprisonment. As the cases were heard, quietly and as thoroughly as in a Magistrates Court in England, I watched the faces of the public and the German lawyers. Many of these barristers and solicitors, have been coming up to our military government officials and telling them with what joy they welcome the return of free and real justice to Berlin – something they have not known for thirteen years.'[46]

However, even the rule of law was a long way down the list of priorities for broken Germany – food, housing and the prevention of disease were key at the beginning. And after a poor harvest in August, the need for food became even more acute. It was going to be a long struggle for Germans and all the other displaced people found within her borders. For Montgomery, the pressure was acute: 'I had suddenly become responsible for the government and well-being of about twenty million Germans. Tremendous problems would be required to be handled and if they were not solved before winter began, many Germans would die of starvation, exposure and disease.'[47]

But for some, the basis of a new Germany was already evident, and Hitler's insistence on total destruction also meant a total rebirth. The German writer Alfred Döblin had emigrated from Germany at the outbreak of the war. When he returned in the summer of 1945 to Baden-Baden, he saw industry and determination to create a new future:

'The main impression I got in Germany, was of people who were like ants running back and forth through a destroyed nest, in a state of excitement and desperate to get to work in the midst of their ruination. Their only worry is that they can't get to work at once without the requisite tools and directives. They are less depressed by the destruction than inspired to want to work even harder. If they had the means, which they lack today, they would rejoice tomorrow, rejoice that their antiquated, badly laid out places have been demolished, offering them the chance to build something first class and modern.'[48]

Chapter 4

The Pendulum Swings

Elections in Britain

'This is the beginning of the new world.'[1]

Iris Murdoch

While for many people in Britain the end of the war in Europe concentrated their minds on their own personal future and what life might bring next for them, others were already thinking on VE Day about the political future of the country as a whole. H. W. Kemshall from Scarborough wrote a letter to the *Manchester Guardian* that was published on 9 May urging that the government not call a snap election, that he complained would be 'fought on the unreasonable and emotional atmosphere of victory celebrations'. According to Kemshall, there was 'no need for a general election at the present time and it should be delayed until at least the autumn, when emotions have settled and the electorate can think and judge more clearly and dispassionately'.[2]

A Conservative-led coalition government was in power, as it had been since 1940, with four Labour MPs also in the Cabinet alongside their Conservative colleagues. These four were the leader of the Labour Party Clement Attlee as well as Ernest Bevin, Herbert Morrison and Arthur Greenwood. In this sense, with representation from both main parties in the government, there was no great clamour for a quick election, and the comradeship that had developed within the coalition was such that they were quite happy to continue to work with one another for a while longer – perhaps to the end of the war against Japan, for instance. When Bevin stood alongside Churchill on the balcony of the Ministry of Health in Whitehall waving to the cheering crowds below, Churchill invited him to come and accept the applause with him. But Bevin refused: 'No, Winston: this is your day,' he said.[3] Bevin was proud to have served with Churchill and admired him hugely. Churchill himself had said on 15 March, at the Conservative Party Conference:

> 'We have all worked our hardest in the national cause and we have been too busy for party politics. We have all abstained from doing or saying anything which would be likely to impair the unity of the British people or the smooth working of the coalition government of all parties which delivered us from mortal peril and won for itself a memorable place in our long history. We held in abeyance all party activities and allowed our organisations, both local and national, to be devoted entirely to the prosecution of the war.'[4]

But with the victory in Europe assured, partisanship had been gathering steam on both sides in March and April. Conservative and Labour loyalists did not want this arrangement to begin looking too cosy. The Conservative Party strategists were desperate for a quick election which they saw as offering the likeliest opportunity for a victory – as

Roy Jenkins put it, 'They wanted an early cashing in of the cheque of Churchill's victory popularity.'[5] And Churchill himself warned his party in March that 'we must prepare ourselves for the loss of many loyal and capable fellow workers in the administration and for a full clash of party principles and party interests, inseparable from appeal to the judgment of the people'.

Seldom has a prime minister been more popular than Churchill was in the hour of victory. The *Manchester Guardian* noted in its coverage of VE Day in Parliament that every member of the House rose when Churchill arrived in the chamber. The newspaper compared it with Chamberlain returning from Munich, but remarked that the enthusiasm that day was mainly from the Conservative side. On this occasion, though, not just every member of the House rose from their seat, but virtually everyone else in the chamber as well: 'All the diplomatists ... were seen to be standing, all the peers, too, and the body of the general public, and last the supposedly blasé Press gallery. Even the journalists had forgotten themselves. For, remember, it is rank disorder for anyone to stand up like this in any of the galleries of the House of Commons – even the Royal Gallery.'[6]

On 23 May, just over two weeks after VE Day, Churchill resigned, bringing an end to the wartime coalition, and called elections for 5 July. In the meantime, he asked permission from the King to form a Conservative caretaker government until the result from the election was established. And a few days later, on 28 May, he gave a farewell party at Downing Street for the Labour ministers who were leaving. Labour MP Hugh Dalton, who had served in the coalition as the Minister of Economic Warfare from 1940 to 1942, described how, 'with tears visibly running down his cheeks',

Churchill spoke to them all: 'The light of history will shine on all your helmets,' he said.[7]

The following day, a BBC directive for Overseas News Department Editorial emphasised how careful the Corporation had to be in terms of its impartiality. The overseas audience for the election was unusually large because of the number of troops still posted abroad. Their votes could be decisive and whereas the people at home had easy access to newspapers and could go to political meetings to hear politicians talking, overseas services relied almost exclusively on the wireless and letters from home.

The directive stated, 'We have now entered into a vastly difficult period of news coverage. Most of our treatment of political events until 5 July will have to be dictated by common sense and the strictest adherence to objectivity.'

In order to guide BBC editors, a few rules were laid down:

No MP or candidate may be used in any programme heard on the home air or in General Overseas Service or A.E.F Programmes. It is our responsibility to know whether a speaker is a candidate or not.

The customary broadcasting periods will be allotted later to the spokesmen of the principal parties. These broadcasts can, of course, be used in our service, but if one is used, all must be used.

Speeches and statements by ministers and ex-ministers must be dissected into political utterances and utterances emanating from the head or ex-head of a government department. Thus a statement about the part played by British workers during the war by say Mr Bevin as ex-Minister of Labour is admissible, but a plea that this should be rewarded by the return

110

of a Labour majority clearly brings it within the political sphere.

Official party declarations of policy should be given in the news but here again all must be given with equal prominence.

Treatment of outstanding electioneering speeches must be referred. Other electioneering speeches should be left alone.[8]

Accusations of bias and criticisms of the BBC's coverage were still levelled in letters to the Corporation, as they undoubtedly had been before and have been at every election since. J. T. Sharkey from Haringey, North London wrote on 4 June complaining, 'If the Prime Minister had to speak, why is he allowed twenty minutes and not ten as the minority parties, anyway it's a foregone conclusion that the Tory Party has had its innings, so let's quit the cackling and get down to materializing the conditions that were promised our people in 1918.' The BBC replied that the speaking duration had been agreed independently by a committee (the Ullswater committee) in 1935.[9]

Others had suggestions about the nature of the coverage. E. J. Pankhurst from Crosby, Liverpool proposed that after each politician had spoken, there should be some critical analysis of what they had said from 'an unknown elector'. E. Valentine, from Manchester, made a similar proposal when he suggested to the BBC that 'you should give the common people an opportunity of expressing their views on the varied subjects under discussion. I feel that this would be very useful and give the politicians some idea of what the common people want.' His suggestion was rejected by the BBC, who wrote to him that 'the BBC is confining itself during this period to placing the microphone at the disposal of the political parties'. A letter with a number of signatories from Huddersfield urged that the BBC invite 'Mr Harry Pollitt of the Communist Party of Great Britain' to speak. They wrote,

> 'Before the war this party was small and in many ways insignificant, a fact which is evidenced by them having only one representative in Parliament. During the war they have generally observed the political truce, and have thus prevented their representation from being increased. It is said however, and we believe it is correct, that the armed forces have "gone left" and although we do not suggest that it has turned to communism in its original form, we feel that the Communist Party should be entitled to present its views and suggestions.'[10]

Again, the suggestion was turned down. The internal directive within the BBC predicted that 'in the heat of the election wild accusations of non-cooperation, obstructionism, etc. during the coalition will be made'. It made it clear that if this should happen then these should be referred to a higher authority rather than answered by the editor directly responsible.[11]

For Churchill, perhaps surprisingly given that he had just guided the country to victory in Europe, June was 'hard to live through'. He spent most of the month giving speeches. 'Strenuous motor tours to the greatest cities of England and Scotland, with three or four speeches a day to enormous and, it seemed, enthusiastic crowds, and, above all, four laboriously prepared broadcasts, consumed my time and strength,' he wrote. But his mind was elsewhere: 'All the while I felt that much we had fought for in our long struggle in Europe was slipping away and that the hopes of an early and lasting peace were receding.'[12] Others realised, too, that Churchill's heart was not in it – including many of the electorate. He came under fire in particular for his remarks in a speech on 5 June in which he said that the Labour party would 'have to fall back on some form of Gestapo' in order to enforce its socialist policies.[13] Churchill also targeted the Labour Party Chairman, Harold Laski, whom he suggested would be the power behind the throne of any Labour administration. It was one thing to break with his former colleagues in the coalition government, but quite another to ascribe to them, however implicitly, the potential for the crimes against humanity that had been perpetrated by the Gestapo, and by implicating Laski in this attack, who came from a Jewish family, the offence was all the greater.

G. Bamber, a female civil servant and Mass Observation diarist in Blackpool, wrote in her diary that she thought Churchill 'has let himself down very badly in this electioneering, but many consider they owe him allegiance – and because of this are prepared to let us in for a Tory government, which I'm convinced will be bad for this country as things are in the world at the moment'.[14] Kathleen Tipper in South London worked in an office and was also a volunteer bar worker at her local YMCA, which was a popular place to congregate for servicemen from across the world when they were in London. She was keen to go to as many political meetings as possible in the run-up to the election and on the day before polling day she went to listen to Major Francis Beech, her local Conservative MP, who was seeking re-election. She was not impressed: 'He was pretty offensive about certain of his opponents, and in all it was a rather unpleasant meeting. He called Mr Laski "the descendant of a dirty little Hungarian Jew" which brought forth abuse from the audience.'[15]

The Labour Party leader's response to Churchill's speech was restrained, statesmanlike and quietly impassioned. Attlee said,

'The Prime Minister made much play last night with the rights of the individual and the dangers of people being ordered about by officials. I entirely agree that people should have the greatest freedom compatible with the freedom of others. There was a time when employers were free to work little children for sixteen hours a day. I remember when employers were free to employ sweated women workers on finishing trousers at a penny halfpenny a pair. There was a time when people were free to neglect sanitation so that thousands died of preventable diseases. For years every attempt to remedy these crying evils was blocked by the same plea of freedom for the individual. It was in fact freedom for the rich and slavery for the poor. Make no mistake, it has only been through the power of the State, given to it by Parliament, that the general public has been protected against the greed of ruthless profit-makers and property owners. The Conservative Party remains as always a class Party. In twenty-three years in the House of Commons, I cannot recall more than half a dozen from the ranks of the wage earners. It represents today, as in the past, the forces of property and privilege. The Labour Party is, in fact, the one Party which most nearly reflects in its representation

114

and composition all the main streams which flow into the great river of our national life.'[16]

Twenty-year-old RAF pilot, Tony Benn, returned from Egypt in June on the troop ship *Carthage*, which was also carrying many servicemen who had fought with General Slim in Burma. They decided to organise hustings on board and Benn spoke on 'Why I will vote Labour', even though as a twenty-year-old he was actually ineligible to cast a vote (the voting age was then twenty-one).

On the *Carthage*, on 7 June, Tony Benn talked to the troops in a way that would become familiar to a far wider audience over the following decades.

'One of the most pressing problems of all is housing,' he said. 'Before the war, slums were a running sore – disease and squalor were rampant in many areas. The submerged tenth were a forgotten minority. The position is even more serious now than it was then. Inability to effect ordinary repairs and the damage caused by enemy action is incalculable. Are we going to let Jerry Builder do his worst and breed a new series of slums for the next generation or are we going to plan decent homes for the future?'

Benn recalls that 'The atmosphere on board ship was electric and it was at that moment that I realized that Labour might possibly win.' Labour were promising 'food, work and homes', full employment and a national health service. Out of the ruins of Britain's bombed out cities, they planned to build a New Jerusalem. Their motto was: 'Let us Face the Future'. 'The nation needs a tremendous overhaul,' exclaimed their manifesto, 'a great programme of modernisation and re-equipment of its homes, its factories and machinery, its schools, its social services.' The idea of social security was central: 'Labour led the fight against the mean and shabby treatment that was the lot of millions while Conservative governments were in power over long years. A Labour Government will press on rapidly with legislation extending social insurance over the necessary wide field to all.'[17]

But even the Conservative Party proposed an improved national insurance scheme in their manifesto, as well as a health service for all and the building of enough homes to meet the country's needs. 'The health services of the country will be made available to all citizens,' declared the Conservative manifesto. 'Everyone will contribute to the cost, and no one will be denied the attention, the treatment or the appliances he requires because he cannot afford them.'[18] In fact, there was far less difference in policy terms between the two parties than might be imagined – there was, largely speaking, a consensus around the findings of the 1942 Beveridge Report which had recommended an updated national insurance scheme and the foundation of the NHS – but the tone between the two parties was entirely different.

On Benn's return to Britain, he was stationed with the RAF in Harrogate and went down to London to help in the election campaign, working in the Westminster Abbey constituency. The Labour candidate there was Jeremy Hutchinson, a young lawyer, and Benn's job was to drive the loudspeaker van around carrying Hutchinson and his wife, the famous actress Peggy Ashcroft. Ashcroft herself spoke to people on the Peabody Housing Estates in Westminster about the need for a National Theatre. Tony Benn also drove to Downing Street, where Hutchinson attempted to canvas the Prime Minister. In a time before public opinion polls, Benn wrote that 'we never seriously thought we could win'.[19]

There was clearly an enormous appetite for public involvement in the election. After a Labour Party meeting that Kathleen Tipper's father and friend went to in Eltham, Southeast London on 18 June, she wrote in her diary, 'There were thousands at the meeting, and since this is happening everywhere there must be a revival of interest in politics in this country – I wonder if the politicians are worthy of the people they are to represent.' The meeting itself featured Henry Berry, the Labour candidate who was standing against the incumbent Tory, Major Francis Beech. However, the meeting was a 'fiasco' and Berry was 'uninspired'.[20] On 20 June, Tipper went to the local Conservative Party meeting and watched her MP and fellow South London Conservative MP (Croydon South) Sir Herbert Williams get a grilling from an audience member.

'One fellow got up and asked him what [Williams] felt about the Tory Government supplying arms to Japan, up to the time she attacked us in 1941. Sir H denied this, and said it was quite untrue, and added that he was on a committee which enquired into this very matter. He then asked the young man belligerently to give him date, amount of stuff, and the port from which it left this country, and much to his surprise the fellow rattled date, and further details about a shipment. Sir H trying to catch him out, asked for the name of the ship, which his questioner supplied, adding that he was a member of the crew, and he then named the firm in Japan to which the shipment was delivered. Sir H was a bit taken aback, and said that he would look into the matter, and at one of Major Beech's later meetings they would read out his answer. The audience cheered the young man heartily.'

Kathleen Tipper felt that this was a positive contribution to democratic debate: 'I feel that this sort of questioning, or heckling, is most intelligent, and really is a more dignified way of carrying on politics,' she wrote. She felt, though, that the press owned by Churchill's ally Lord Beaverbrook – principally the *Daily Express* and the London *Evening Standard* – was not contributing to the debate in a positive way. 'The *Standard* is carrying on a most undignified campaign in this election,' she wrote. 'No doubt Beaverbrook ideas are being forced on the editor, because sometimes I can hardly believe I am reading the same paper that I read 3 or 4 months ago – the critical, reasoned editorials, are now nothing but trashy attacks on the Labour party and any folk who dare to oppose Mr Churchill.'[21]

Elsewhere, she noted how the *Express* exaggerated the figures of audiences attending Churchill's speeches compared with newspapers like the *Daily Herald* and the *News Chronicle*.[22] The *Daily Express's* uncritical reporting of Churchill's Gestapo statement was widely seen as a misjudgement by Beaverbrook and his newspaper which failed to engage with how the electorate felt.

On 21 June, Kathleen Tipper's father went to see Sir Stafford Cripps, who until 23 May had been the Minister for Aircraft Production and was previously the British Ambassador to the Soviet Union. According to her father, 'it was a fine meeting, with Sir S in grand form'.[23]

At the YMCA, Kathleen had many of the men at the hostel talking to her about the election, regardless of their nationality. 'It is fairly difficult now to keep off politics with "foreigners",' she complained. 'I don't think some of these men would thank us for interfering in their election if one happened to be in their countries on the occasion of one, but they just talk as if they were taking part in it themselves. I chuckled to myself when I thought how careful I have been when talking with Americans at the time of their elections.'

On 25 June, Kathleen Tipper made a small wager with a friend that her local Labour MP would not be elected, even though she hoped that he would be. 'Mr L & I have a 3d. bet,' she wrote. 'He says Mr Berry the Labour candidate will win, I fear he won't, especially as a Labour canvasser delivering bills, told my aunt that Mr Berry really didn't have a hope. I hope I lose my 3d.'[24]

Another Labour canvasser made a strong impression on Kathleen.

> 'During the evening the Labour Party canvasser called and we asked him in to tell us his candidate's policy. Mrs L was with us and we had quite an interesting talk with the old man. He was rather pathetic – a last war veteran, shell-shocked slightly too I think – he had lost his eldest son in Italy, and his other was in a hospital suffering with fits caused by air-raids. He had a childlike faith in the ability of the Labour party to help the people of this country – I hope he won't be disillusioned. However one looks at politics, I think people like this man do deserve a better deal, and I can't understand why people in high places in all parties don't for their own benefit, raise the standard

of living of the ordinary folk. A contented man is rarely a revolutionary – and our canvasser doesn't want much I know, just security.'[25]

With the election looming ever closer, Kathleen Tipper records how emotions were running high. 'Such an argument in the train going home – a violent sort of Irishman asked a young boy reading a newspaper who he was voting for. The boy answered, "I haven't a vote as a matter of fact, but if I had one I wouldn't vote for Churchill." The Irishman was furious and called the young man traitor etc. but the boy rushed in and said that he hated the crowd Mr C was attached to, and wouldn't vote for them. These violent people usually crumple up if they are attacked in their turn, and Irishman sank back into silence, much to all our relief.' In her own straw poll at the YMCA, she found that 'most of those I talked with were voting Labour'.[26]

As the election approached in Blackpool at the start of July, G. Bamber wrote in her diary, 'Things are certainly hotting up a bit in the election campaign. The Tories and the Socialists have definitely started to get lively, at long last. But it's true to say that Blackpool's mood is predominantly that of holidaying.'[27] She seems quite engaged with politics in general, but when given the choice between going to hear the local Conservative candidate speaking or playing tennis in the warm weather on 3 July, she opted for tennis, 'which was very enjoyable'. It seems unlikely that going to this meeting would have changed her mind anyway. She also wrote, 'Churchill's popularity and the split Tory opposition (Liberal and Labour candidates in practically every constituency) will be the two factors responsible for putting the Tories back, but I hope they are not.'[28]

Bamber had the option of going to another political meeting the following night, but she chose not to again because it was a 'fine evening'. The weather was warm and sultry further south as well on the night before election as the politicians made their final appeals to the electorate.

> 'This is election day,' G. Bamber wrote on 5 July in Blackpool, 'and everyone I asked said they had voted. Certainly the officials at the polling booths had a busy day. There were also crowds of people just standing about round the school I voted at and there was an air of excitement about. I should say a high proportion of the electorate in Blackpool voted and I expect the Liberal to get in the north and the Conservative in the south division. I didn't hear of one person who'd been left off the register here.'[29]

Kathleen Tipper also voted:

> 'Election day, I cast my first vote, and felt very good afterwards, somehow there is something pleasant about the fact that I can help to choose my government. Dorothy's brother, in an RAF Camp near London, home on leave, says that the camp is solidly Labour, and he seems quite reactionary as he is voting Liberal. She is most impressed by her Liberal candidate, he is a young naval officer, and at the Liberal meeting she attended last night, the candidate dealt with questions of world policy, and conditions in every part of the Empire, also how to keep peace in Europe, as well as the eternal housing question, and the various sections of the trade disputes act. I still think the Liberals will astonish the

121

country and even the Tory press is beginning to admit that they may make considerable gains.'[30]

E. Van Someren, the research chemist, placed his vote in Hertfordshire. 'Polling day,' he wrote, 'work much as usual but my chief had to go to Birmingham, he voted first and had the works car to pick him up at the works at 8am to take him to Padd[ington]. I voted on the way home, it was a hot evening and we sat in the garden drinking cider and gin and talking to Dorothy Lea who dropped in unexpectedly to visit us, had a pleasantly lazy time and enjoyed ourselves.'[31]

Chief of the Imperial General Staff Alan Brooke, also cast his vote. 'Polling day, thank heaven we are getting on with the election,' he wrote in his diary, 'and I hope we shall soon have a sane government prepared to govern the country. Went down to Camberley to give one of my usual end of term talks. We then drove on to Ferney Close for lunch.'[32]

The waiting game began once the polls had closed. Major P. M. Barrington, who was still in Germany at the time, had written to his parents on 1 July that 'if a proxy voting form comes to you, will you vote Conservative for me please'.[33] But most men and women in the services who decided to vote got their own voting card and registered their votes in the normal way. The delay in shipping and counting all those votes meant that life returned to relative normality from 6 July until the declaration on 26 July. Churchill took the opportunity to head to the southwest of France for a well-earned holiday on 7 July, and found himself 'agreeably installed at General Brutinel's villa near the Spanish frontier at Hendaye'.[34] G. Bamber wrote in her diary on 6 July, 'Things are back to normal today, no be-ribboned cars dashing about the streets and the election placards have disappeared; it will seem a long while waiting for the results – 3 weeks.'[35] For Churchill, his holiday was short-lived because the Potsdam Conference with his Soviet and American counterparts began on 17 July just outside Berlin. Due to the fact that the election result was uncertain, the Leader of the Opposition, Clement Attlee, also attended so that he would be equipped to take over the negotiations, were Churchill to lose his place as Prime Minister. It was a good job that he did, for when the results came in, Labour had not just edged it – there had been a landslide result.

'Socialists In' screamed the *Evening Standard* headline on 26 July. 'Britain swings to the left – and the Churchill government goes out in landslide.' The turnout had been 73 per cent and Labour had a resounding working majority of 145–393 seats to the Conservative's 197: 47.7 per cent of the vote against the Conservative's 36 per cent. The swing was 11 per cent from the previous election. The other major statistic was that the Liberal Party had won only 12 seats, which led the *Evening Standard* to declare a 'Massacre of the Liberals'.[36] Iris Murdoch captured the excitement for many of the first hours and days after the election result was announced. 'Oh wonderful people of Britain!' she gushed. 'After all the ballyhoo & the eyewash, they've had the guts to vote against Winston! I feel really proud of them, & ashamed not having believed in them. I thought they would be fooled. But they have sense, they can think! I feel proud to be British. This is the beginning of the new world.'[37]

Kathleen Tipper, too, was thrilled.

'One of the most astonishing days of my life,' she recorded in her diary on 26 July. 'I didn't hear any

123

news this morning, then I went to lunch and saw headlines saying "8 cabinet ministers fall" and "socialist gains", but had no idea of what was to come. Joyce telephoned me and told me that Brenden Bracken, Duncan Sandys had been beaten, and that Morrison, our man Berry and Bevin were in. Astonishing, we have never had a Labour member in our constituency, not even in 1929 – and E[ast] Lewisham has always been Tory. By this afternoon we realised that the Labour Party was winning hands down, and Joyce telephoned me several times to give me odd snippets of news – another piece of good news that Randolph Churchill had been beaten – how catty are we?'[38]

As a Liberal, G. Bamber was a little more ambivalent about the result, but she was nonetheless pleased that the Conservatives had been defeated.

'This has certainly been an exciting day,' she wrote on 26 July, 'results began to trickle through in the office from 11am onwards and from the start it was obvious that there was a big swing to the left. We haven't had such an exciting day for some time. Personally I am very confident that as the Labour Party have got in, they have a good majority and power to carry out their programme. The position which I feared would arise – no party having a working majority – would have been disastrous in the present stage of our history, but now we can adopt a definite policy both at home and abroad. As a liberal, I am shocked and sorry at the small number of liberal seats in the new House – a revival of Liberalism now seems unlikely.'[39]

A few days later, she wrote,

> 'Many of the Tories are obviously very much upset by
> the prospect of socialism, but I think the majority of
> people are hopeful that social reforms which would
> have taken years under Tory administration will come
> quickly now. Myself I am very heartened by the way
> this country has behaved – we are grateful to Churchill
> for his help during the war, but do not consider that a
> sufficient reason to saddle ourselves with Tory
> government for another five years. Frankly, the man
> in the street has got more common sense than I dared
> to credit him with.'[40]

E. Van Someren was more relaxed in his assessment in his
diary on 27 July. 'Found everyone talking at work,' he wrote,
'and browsed through the political news in the *Express*,
Telegraph and *Chronicle* before settling down to work myself,
being more unsettled than usual. Most of my colleagues
thought it was a good thing, some more enthusiastically than
others. My chief, who voted Tory, is still in Germany.'[41]

Norman Longmate, who was a soldier in 1945, felt as
though the election success was the equivalent for those in
the forces that VE Day had been for civilians: 'It was by far
the most cheerful day I ever witnessed in the Army: VE Day
had been the civilians' moment, a time of hope and fresh
beginnings; this was ours.'[42] However, less than half of the
services did vote in the end – only 1.7 million out of 4.5
million did.[43]

Tony Benn remembers 26 July in his memoirs:

'On the day the Election results were announced I went to Transport house where they were flashed up on a screen using an epidiascope as they came in. As we sat in that darkened room and saw Tory Ministers falling like ninepins, we knew there was a landslide Labour victory. At one point the door opened and, blinking as he came out of the sunshine into the darkness, we saw the familiar figure of Clem Atlee, who had driven from Northholt Airport, after flying from Potsdam, where he had attended the Potsdam Conference with Truman, Stalin and Churchill. The police car in which he travelled did not have a radio and it was only at that moment, as he came into the room, that he heard what had happened. A BBC man came up to me with a microphone and said "Will you shout 'Three cheers for the Prime Minister'?" but I was too shy to do so. That evening in central Hall, Westminster, packed to the doors with Labour supporters, Clem Atlee walked on to the platform and amid tumultuous cheers announced that the King had asked him to form a government. Among his very first ministerial appointments before his return to Potsdam, this time as Prime Minister, was a new secretary of State for Air: my father, then an air commodore in the RAF, complete with his wings from the First World War, was sent to the Air Ministry.'[44]

The *Daily Telegraph* also reported on events as senior Labour Party members waited for the results to come in. 'Mr and Mrs Attlee played the leading parts in an emotional drama enacted at Transport House yesterday,' wrote the London Day by Day columnist. 'As they walked into the large darkened hall, after the Socialist victory was known, the lights were turned on. Immediately the company, comprising party officials, trade union leaders and members of the staff, stood on their chairs and greeted their leader with prolonged cheers.'[45] Kathleen Tipper wrote two days after the election that 'much of Mr Atlee's private life is being made public, although they are a family difficult to make glamorous I should think, and none the worse for that'.[46] In the evening of 26 July, Clement Attlee's wife Violet drove their family car – a humble Standard 10 – to the Palace with her husband alongside her.[47] They only just missed Churchill leaving the palace in his chauffeur-driven Rolls-Royce. Kynaston tells the story of how, inside Buckingham Palace, as Attlee stood with King George VI to declare his intention to lead the next government, the two men stood not talking to one another for some time. 'I've won the election,' Attlee eventually told the King. 'I know,' replied the King, 'I heard it on the *Six O'Clock News.*'[48]

Churchill recounted listening to the results come in. 'By noon it was clear to me that the Socialists would have a majority,' he wrote. 'At luncheon my wife said to me, "It may well be a blessing in disguise." I replied, "At the moment it seems quite effectively disguised."'[49] He resigned the same day and issued to the nation the following message:

'The decision of the British people has been recorded in the votes counted today. I have therefore laid down the charge which was placed upon me in darker times. I regret that I have not been permitted to finish the work against Japan. For this however all plans and preparations have been made, and the results may come much quicker than we have hitherto been entitled to expect. Immense responsibilities abroad and at home fall upon the new Government, and we must all hope that they will be successful in bearing them. It only remains for me to express to the British people, for whom I have acted in these perilous years, my profound gratitude for the unflinching, unswerving support which they have given me during my task, and for the many expressions of kindness which they have shown towards their servant.'[50]

The demise of Churchill was as much a major theme of the newspaper coverage as the wild success of the Labour Party. For the *Daily Telegraph*, a newspaper that Churchill had written for as a young man, it was a rather sad moment. 'In those calm sentences Mr Churchill accepts the startling decision of the British people,' the editorial recorded in elegiac prose on his statement to the British people. 'At the plenitude of high achievement a potent leader passes from supreme authority. The country has declared against the Conservatives and given the Socialists a victory of almost unprecedented magnitude.' The editorial went on to record the admiration expressed across the political spectrum for Churchill's achievements. 'Mr Attlee spoke during the election of the memory of "comradeship in this tremendous adventure … and the spirit of friendly co-operation in a great cause which prevailed." The election result has denied Mr Churchill the opportunity to prove himself as great in winning the peace as he was in winning the war, but he will ever be great in the hearts of his countrymen.'[51]

For the *Manchester Guardian* it was quite a different story. Underneath the headline, 'Britain's Revulsion Against Tory Rule', the newspaper's political correspondent wrote:

'So Mr Churchill has not been able to save the Tory party from defeat! It has fallen as low as that. One of the half-dozen greatest leaders in war that we have produced, while at the summit of his achievement and prestige, could not induce the British people to give the Tories another lease of power. Such is their disrepute. Where, then, would they have been without him? They would have been annihilated. It would have been the debacle of 1906 over again, only worse. Most things were obscure about the election, but not this.'[52]

But for the *Evening Standard,* 'the decision reveals a perhaps natural desire on the part of the people, not so much for a change of government, as for one of party and personalities'.[53]

Alan Brooke had been in Potsdam with Churchill just before the election result had been announced. He wrote in his diary on 26 July,

'The Potsdam Conference is apparently over as far as we are concerned! The Conservative Government has had a complete landslide and is out for good and all! If only Winston had followed my advice he would have been in at any rate until the end of the year! But what was my advice to him a mere soldier!!! Now he is gone, and PJ [Sir Percy James Grigg, Secretary of State for the Army]. Who shall I be dealing with in the future, Attlee as PM and who as [Secretary of State]? I feel too old and weary to start off any new experiments. It is probably all for the good of England in the long run, any government in power in the next year is not going to last long. But what a ghastly mistake to start elections in this period in the World's History! May God forgive England for it.'[54]

129

The following day, 27 July, was for Alan Brooke 'a day of partings!' He had a final meeting with the Secretary of State for the Army, 'then at 5.30 pm had to go and see Winston at 10 Downing Street, with others chiefs of Staff. It was a very sad and very moving little meeting at which I found myself unable to say much for fear of breaking down. He was standing the blow wonderfully well.'

In his memoirs he recalls how he felt in a little more detail about his political master leaving office after such an intense few years.

'The thought that my days of work with Winston had come to an end was a shattering one. There had been very difficult times, and times when I felt I could not stand a single more day with him, but running through all our difficulties a bond of steel had been formed uniting us together. We had been so closely linked together in this vast struggle that it would have been impossible for us to go on striving together unless a deep bond of friendship had existed; had this not been the case there would have been only one alternative, that of parting. No doubt Winston must frequently have felt that he could stand me no longer, and I marvel even now that as a result of some of our differences he did not replace me. There are few things that can bind two individuals more closely than to be intimately connected in a vast struggle against overwhelming odds and to emerge on top of all.'[55]

There were many popular expressions of support for Churchill and this letter written to the BBC from Ms E. Thornton from Taddington in Derbyshire, was typical of a common sentiment that existed following the election: 'I would like to suggest that some tribute be paid publically to Mr Churchill. I think it is disgraceful the way this country has just cast him aside with no comment. If ever a debt was owed by the whole country to one person, that one is Mr Churchill. To me it is unthinkable that at this time he is not still at the head of this country.'[56]

But for many others, it was Churchill's misjudgement that had played a significant role in his own demise. Kathleen Tipper wrote in her diary:

'Our boss took the fact that his entire typing staff voted Labour in good part, but expressed his opinion that something Mr Churchill did turned the people against him. Personally I think the bitterness of his first radio speech, and the consequent campaign of Government supporting papers turned many waiverers against him – but I think the Russian view, that Mr C forgot the 7 million young people enfranchised since the last election is probably a better summing up. The forces I am sure voted solidly for Labour (at least in this country, those overseas probably voted about 50/50) but a great many people, ordinary civilians voted Labour too, otherwise they wouldn't have this vast majority, so I don't think the Forces vote decided the election, but combined with the young people's vote in this country, it was the dominating factor. Foreign countries, particularly America, seem rather surprised at the result, and seem to think we have turned communist.'[57]

G. Bamber wrote in her diary on 27 July, 'The Labour victory is still all the talk in the country – America is staggered – we shall see how Russia reacts (not much doubt about this, I think) – many of the liberated countries will be glad – for Spain it is bad news indeed.'[58] And the *Daily Telegraph* was concerned by the international reaction to the result. 'Allied and foreign countries are showing some natural bewilderment at the dismissal of Mr Churchill by the electors,' the newspaper wrote in its editorial. 'The decision of the poll certainly does not indicating weakening of resolve to fight the war through and maintain allied unity. Doubts on that point should disappear in time, but we must make our account with the unpleasant, ineluctable fact that confidence in British steadfastness and British influence on world affairs has to be justified afresh.'[59] The Soviet Foreign Minister, Vyacheslav Molotov, later said, 'I still cannot comprehend how this could happen that he lost the election!'[60]

The financial markets were also shocked by the outcome of the election. The *Manchester Guardian* reported, 'The Stock Exchange was taken utterly by surprise at the result of the poll, and considerable sales of lightly held stock embarrassed the unprepared market. Prices were first widened and then dropped sharply.'[61]

But for the political Left in Britain – and the many millions who had voted for the Labour Party – it was the start of an exciting new era – the birth of the modern welfare state in Britain and a programme of nationalisation; a dream of full employment and improved productivity, better housing, healthcare and education. For Fred Aiken, who as a recent graduate had worked as an explosives chemist during the war, the investment in education and improved pay for teachers was a significant boost at the start of his career as a teacher that began in 1945. 'By now I knew I didn't want to be an industrial chemist and when a job as a teacher in my old school in Northern Ireland was advertised, I decided to try teaching. And I loved it, from the beginning.'[62]

The *Manchester Guardian* heralded the victory – and the opportunities that came with it – as being of a truly historic nature:

'It is the kind of progressive opportunity that comes only once in every few generations – in 1832, in 1868, in 1885, in 1906. These were internal revolutions; this is part of a European revolution. The British vote parallels the revulsion of feeling that has occurred throughout Europe against old regimes and old habits of thought. There is encouragement in this, for if our affairs are wisely managed we have a magnificent chance of exerting British leadership in a terribly troubled world.'[63]

The newspaper summed up the challenge that lay ahead for the new Labour government: 'No government has ever had a harder task before it in time of peace, but none has ever had a greater opportunity.'[64]

Chapter 5

The Potsdam Conference and the New Shape of Europe

'A desperately serious conference held to decide the future of a stricken continent'

Manchester Guardian[1]

Two months after the end of the war in Europe, the leaders of the three main Allied nations – the United States, the Soviet Union and Great Britain – came together to decide the future of the continent. Truman, Stalin and Churchill – the so-called Big Three – assembled at Potsdam, a city just outside Berlin, the day before the conference started on 17 July 1945. Churchill arrived from the Southwest of France where he had been on holiday, touring through the rubble of Berlin on 16 July before heading to the villa he had been allocated in the grounds of the Cecilienhof Palace, where the conference was to take place.

July 16 was a significant day in world history for quite another reason: it was the date of the first nuclear detonation in the Jornada del Muerto desert in New Mexico. Churchill recalled learning about it for the first time the following day when American Secretary of State for War Henry Stimson handed him a report on the detonation. The headline at the top of the page read: 'Babies satisfactorily born.' It meant that the test had been successful.

> 'The bomb, or its equivalent,' Churchill remembered reading, 'had been detonated at the top of a pylon one hundred feet high. Everyone had been cleared away for ten miles round, and the scientists and their staffs crouched behind massive concrete shields and shelters at that distance. The blast had been terrific. An enormous column of flame and smoke shot up to the fringe of the atmosphere of our poor earth. Devastation inside a one mile circle was absolute. Here then was a speedy end to the Second World War, and perhaps much else besides.'[2]

Churchill was impressed. For him it changed everything. But for Alan Brooke, Churchill was naïve in the extreme. 'He had absorbed all the minor American exaggerations, and as a result was completely carried away!' he wrote in his diary on 23 July. Paraphrasing the prime minister he wrote, 'It was now no longer necessary for the Russians to come in to the Japanese war, the new explosive alone was sufficient to settle the matter. Furthermore we now had something in our hands which would redress the balance with the Russians!' Brooke wrote that he 'tried to crush his over-optimism based on the results of our experiment, and was asked with contempt what reason I had for minimizing the results of these discoveries. I was trying to dispel his dreams and as usual he did not like it.'[3]

The detonation did cast the negotiations in Potsdam in a rather different light for the Americans and British. But the Soviets did not learn about it until 24 July. The talks in the meantime were both complex – it was not just the future of a nation (Germany) that was being decided, but the fate of many countries – and shrouded with distrust. Truman and Churchill feared that the Soviets would further extend their influence across Europe; Stalin was certain that the Allies were preparing to attack Russia. The previous conference between the three big powers, at Yalta in February 1945, with Roosevelt rather than Truman then as president, had decided a great deal, but there had been significant changes in the meantime. In particular, the Soviet Union had advanced across Europe at great speed in the spring of 1945 and now completely controlled Poland, Czechoslovakia, Hungary, Bulgaria, Romania and the Baltic states, as well as having a significant presence in Germany and Austria. This gave strength to their hand. The conference aimed to come to an agreement on what should be done about Germany in terms of punishment, reparations and administration, the definition of new European borders and what should be done with those people who effectively found themselves homeless and stateless because of the redrawing of boundaries. What about the Poles? And the Czechs? And the displaced Germans?

Richard Dimbleby was on hand for the BBC to describe the setting in which the conference would be held.

'Both the President and the Prime Minister have comfortable houses in which to live,' he reported on 16 July. 'Mr Churchill has a cool garden and a lake close at hand – a lake which is not polluted as are so many others around Berlin. President Truman has moved into a house furnished by the American Army from the house of the Nazi Gauleiter of Halle. This includes white maple furniture, paintings, carpets, rugs and specimens of fine earthenware. There were fourteen truckloads in all. The President's temporary White House in Berlin is in the uniform colour of brown and most of its furnishings are very modern. Ten minutes' car ride from the private compound where the two allied leaders will live and entertain during the Conference which, incidentally, most observers believe is going to be a long one, are the Conference headquarters in a fine two-storey building of the schloss or castle type. In the courtyard there's a perfect round flowerbed with a great red star grown in flowers. Only the cars of the big three themselves will be allowed to enter here, others must walk. A small hallway leads directly into the Conference Room and that is probably the most striking room in which such a meeting has ever been held. One end of the entire room is devoted to big windows looking out to the grounds. The Conference table is twelve feet in diameter, and is covered with a thick red plush cloth. Round it there are three main chairs each a foot higher than all the others, and adorned with golden cherub heads. Between them are twelve smaller chairs in batches of four. Two huge chandeliers light the room dazzlingly showing the high vaulted ceiling with its dark oak beams, and the dark panelling of the walls. […] American engineers have been carrying out major building conversions in the American compound, including the erection of brand new houses, the conversion of German houses into restaurants, and the laying and the clearing-up of the gardens. Potsdam was knocked about by Allied bombing and fighting, it's now become one of the most gleaming, spotless, luxurious garden suburbs in the world.'[4]

In austerity Europe, and in particular war-torn Germany, the conspicuous luxury enjoyed by the delegates brought to mind the phrase 'to the victors the spoils'. The *Manchester Guardian* reported that the United Sates Post Exchange Service was operating a shop at Potsdam that offered 'items such as cameras, films, wrist watches, alarm clocks, and fountain pens'. The visiting dignitaries also had the opportunity to purchase a

> 'full selection of women's handbags from Paris, men's leather travelling kits, perfumes from southern France, and novelty French lipsticks in perky umbrella-shape pink containers, in addition to more prosaic articles: playing cards, poker chips, checker and chess sets, and an ample supply of toilet articles and replenishments. The Exchange is stocked with large supplies of tobacco, all brands of cigarettes and cigars. It represents one of the most complete stores in the present war-time world.'

The newspaper also reported the fact that the talks would be conducted largely in secret with only official communiqués to inform the outside world of progress within the talks. 'If there is to be secrecy over quite such breathlessly lavish provisions for the delegates,' huffed the *Manchester Guardian*, 'it is perhaps as well.'

The same article compared the conditions within the conference 'campus' with those faced by the surviving inhabitants of the nearby streets of Berlin where 'the dominant emotion … is a simple anxiety rather than any particular hope or fear. The mechanics of living are so hard and difficult that most people are obsessed with their own immediate problems in keeping themselves alive. Many really do not seem to know what they have to hope for in the near future, and while they dread the thought of winter and are afraid that conditions may become worse, they are too war weary to be able to feel much interest in how their lives are to be ruled. At the back of their minds, however, is the knowledge that life in Germany must somehow go on and a profound although probably in most cases unformulated anxiety concerning what the future holds. It must be remembered that the present population of Berlin is made up largely of women and children, the elderly and the unfit. Yesterday one saw a woman collapse while crossing the road from fatigue and general under-nourishment, and this sight is by no means uncommon in Berlin, through whose streets hundreds of women trudge each day with their bundles, looking for a new home. Among such people formulated hopes for the future can scarcely be expected.'[5]

G. Bamber, the Mass Observation diarist based in Blackpool, had spent the weekend of 14 and 15 July out in the countryside away from the hordes of holiday-makers.

'I was on the fringe of the lovely hills,' she wrote in her diary, 'and there I found peace, solitude and the beauties of nature. Here one had an opportunity to attain that attitude of mind which enables one to know and understand God and the fundamental things in life. Here in matching one's strength against the hills and the elements one sees onself in true perspective and yet feels "part of the great stupendous whole, whose body nature is and God the soul."'[6]

Back in town on 16 July, she focused on the Potsdam Conference, but noticed that others were not so interested: 'The decisions taken at this meeting will be of paramount importance and yet not one person has mentioned the meeting to me today – people seem more interested in home affairs. What government are we going to have and when will things begin to get going here?'[7]

She was outraged at the pampered conditions in which the talks were taking place:

'When half Europe is starving (and this conference has to deal with this as one only of their problems) – the "delegates" are being fed on luxury foods brought from all over the world. When practically everyone in this country, not to mention others, is making do on thin, worn-out sheets, towels, etc. we hear of hundreds of dozens of pairs of linen sheets being flown there. Luxury conditions won't make it a good conference and in any case it is very bad tactics to boost this side of the matter. Yet the authorities won't issue any official news – not even information regarding the issue to be dealt with – so the newsmen fall back on trash.'[8]

Alan Brooke arrived from Northolt on 15 July.

'We had an excellent trip flying down the Thames, across to near Ostend, along Scheldt, crossing it just above Antwerp, over Venlo to the Rhine at Duisberg. On over Essen, Hamm, Hamelin, Braunschweig, Magdeburg to an aerodrome close to Potsdam. There we were met by a Guard of Honour of Navy, Army and Air Force with a Marine Band. After that a drive of some 20 minutes to our dwellings in Babelsberg! They consisted of a series of villas, all facing onto the lake, and very pleasant. We have a house for the three Chiefs of Staff, and have Jumbo with us. Attlee is next door on one side and Bridges [Cabinet secretary] beyond him and PM beyond that.'[9]

The conference was expected to last for at least ten days with the British general election result to be declared on 26 July. Clement Attlee accompanied Churchill so that he could be kept abreast of all the negotiations should it fall to him to take over after 26 July. It was said, too, in the British press at least, that Truman had many domestic issues that required his urgent attention and that he would have to leave the conference within ten days.

Before the leaders locked horns there were various pre-meetings. Brooke described how on the 16th, 'Monty came to see me at 12.30 and remained till after lunch. At 2.30 we had our first meeting with the Americans. Leahy, Marshall, King and Arnold were all there. An easy meeting with no controversial points!' He then set off for Berlin to meet with Churchill and tour the ruins of the city. He entered the Gestapo HQ and discovered

'in one part of the apartment masses of Iron Crosses on the floor and medal ribbons. On the way up I was handed a German decoration in its box by a Russian private soldier!! If I had been told a year ago that this would happen to me, I should have refused to believe it! In fact the whole afternoon seemed like a dream, and I found it hard to believe that after all these years' struggles I was driving through Berlin!'[10]

Brooke entertained himself between talks by fishing. 'We again caught a small number of small fish,' he recorded on 22 July, but the river was spoiled by countless American soldiers fishing with worms in every pool. As the German SS Division had also been fishing with hand grenades, the fishing had been badly spoilt.'[11]

Truman wrote in his rather antiseptic diary that '[Stalin] called on me as soon as he arrived [on the 17th]. It was about 11.00 am. He, Molotov, Vishinski and Pavlov stayed for lunch. We had a most pleasant conference and Stalin assured me that Russia intended to carry out the Yalta agreements and to enter the war against Japan in August.'[12] Stalin insisted on being called 'Generalissimo' by Truman in honour of his military victories. However, it was with Churchill that Stalin seemed to develop a genuine – or possibly calculated – rapport. Churchill's Foreign Secretary, Anthony Eden, despaired of the Prime Minister's susceptibility to Stalin's flattery at Potsdam. 'He is again under Stalin's spell,' wrote Eden. 'He kept repeating, "I like that man".'[13]

Churchill tells the story in his own memoirs of how he was charmed by Stalin at Potsdam. At the dinner that Churchill hosted at his villa on the night of 23 July, Stalin did an unusual thing:

'My formidable guest got up from his seat with the bill of fare card in his hand and went round the table collecting the signatures of many of those who were present. I never thought to see him as an autograph hunter! When he came back to me I wrote my name as he desired, and we both looked at each other and laughed. Stalin's eyes twinkled with mirth and good humour. I have mentioned before how the toasts at these banquets were always drunk by the Soviet representatives out of tiny glasses, and Stalin had never varied from this practice. But now I thought I would take him on a step. So I filled a small-sized claret glass with brandy for him and another for myself. I looked at him significantly. We both drained our glasses at a stroke and gazed approvingly at one another.'[14]

Nonetheless, Churchill retained his suspicion of Soviet intentions in Eastern Europe and beyond. But Stalin held all the trump cards and played a clever, inscrutable game with his allies. According to Eden, 'Marshal Stalin as a negotiator was the toughest proposition of all. Indeed, after something like thirty years' experience of international conferences of one kind and another, if I had to pick a team for going into a conference room, Stalin would be my first choice. Of course the man was ruthless and of course he knew his purpose. He never wasted a word. He never stormed, he was seldom even irritated.'[15]

Montgomery went to Potsdam immediately before the start of the conference to brief the Prime Minister on the situation in Germany, which was his own main concern. He suggested that if Germany were to be treated as a single country with a unified administration and economy, then a number of important points would have to be accepted by the three big powers. These included the 'free circulation of Allied nationals between all zones' and a 'common policy regarding the reconstruction of industries, wage rates and price controls'.[16]

The first day of negotiations between the Big Three focused on Germany. Disarmament was a key priority, the Nazi Party was to be destroyed and there would be war crimes trials. Truman suggested that a Council of Foreign Ministers meet quarterly to ensure good communication between the main powers. The Allied Control Council would jointly administer Germany. These points were agreed. The first real bargaining was over the fate of the German fleet. Churchill suggested that it be sunk; Stalin replied that Churchill was entitled to sink his share of the German fleet, but he would prefer to keep his.

The following day, the vexed question of how to define Germany was broached by the three. The borders of Germany had changed significantly before and during the war. Should Austria and the Sudetenland (in Czechoslovakia) be counted as part of Germany? Stalin wanted Königsberg in East Prussia to become a Soviet city and made a big play for it at the Conference. Some of the most horrendous atrocities committed by Red Army soldiers had been carried out in that city, and once Stalin had won the concession from Truman and Churchill, the ethnic cleansing of Germans continued unabated. Of the 73,000 Königsbergers alive in June 1945, only 25,000 would survive.[17] A German doctor, Hans Graf von Lehndorff, was in the city that summer. He had never been a Nazi, but as an ethnic German he was treated in the same way as all other Germans by the Red Army invaders. 'Does this still have anything to do with natural wildness,' he wondered in his diary, 'or is it vengeance? Vengeance, probably.'[18]

Poland's borders also had to be discussed, and Stalin was keen to do so. This question had mainly been decided in Yalta earlier in the year, but again, the Red Army occupation meant that Stalin was now in the position to dictate terms. He proposed that Russia take some of what had been Poland before the war (in the east), but that Poland also claim territory that had been German before 1939 (in the north, the west and the south). This included the cities of Breslau and Gdansk and the important industrial region of Silesia. In total, Poland's surface area was reduced by around 20 per cent.

By this time, Poland was already in effect a satellite state of the Soviet Union with a puppet government that had been foisted on the country in rigged elections. Germany lost around a quarter of its pre-1937 extent – both to Poland and to Russia. There seemed to be little humanitarian concern for the more than 8 million Germans who were displaced by this, nor for Poles, Ukrainians and Jews who were also affected by the redrawing of these borders and who would also be on the move – hungry, homeless and vulnerable. Churchill's main worry, it seemed, was that the British should not have to take responsibility for feeding more Germans heading west from the Soviet-occupied zones. However, he had previously shown some sympathy for the plight of German refugees – for example, in February 1945 he wrote to his wife that 'my heart is saddened by the tales of the masses of German women and children flying along the roads everywhere in 40 mile long columns before the advancing armies. I am clearly convinced that they deserve it; but that does not remove it from one's gaze. The misery of the whole world appals me and I fear increasingly that new struggles may rise out of those we are successfully ending.'[19]

On the last day that Churchill attended the conference – on 25 July – he remembered in his memoirs that 'I urged once more that Poland's western frontier could not be settled without taking into account the million and a quarter Germans who were still in the area ... I said that if the Poles were allowed to assume the position of a fifth occupying power without arrangements being made for spreading food produced in Germany equally over the whole German population, and without our agreeing about reparations or war booty, the conference would have failed.'[20] But Stalin's proposal was not that Poland became a fifth occupying power – rather it was that parts of Germany simply became Polish – and he presented it as a *fait accompli.* Stalin seemed to be winning all the concessions that he asked for. It had been the German invasion of Poland that had been the reason for Britain's declaration of war in 1939, but they had failed to protect Poland then. And now, in the post-war settlement, it seemed to many Poles that were being betrayed by the West once again.

The show-trial of sixteen members of the Polish Underground State – after they had all been offered immunity by the Soviet authorities – took place between 18 and 21 June 1945, just a few weeks before the Potsdam Conference. On 6 July, the US and the British governments withdrew their support for the Polish government in exile, which had been based in London since 1940. The Poles were being left to fend for themselves with Stalin. In practical terms, there was little else the Americans and British could do.

At this stage in the negotiations, Churchill had to leave the conference to return to Britain for the election result.

'No one in our conference delegation had the slightest doubt that he would be re-elected,' remembered Admiral Kuznetsov, the Soviet Admiral of the Fleet. 'I hope to be back,' said Churchill by way of parting.[21][22] But he did not return. He lost the election to the surprise of almost everybody at Potsdam. According to Montgomery, 'The decisive defeat of the Churchill government came as a great surprise to all, and the formation of a new government caused a slight delay in the return of a British delegation to Potsdam. There was not unnaturally some uncertainty about the effect that the change of government would have on the deliberations of the conference.'[23]

G. Bamber wrote on the 27th, 'Mr Churchill has refused the invitation to go to Potsdam – in a liaison capacity. I hope this is not indicative of the "co-operation" which may be expected from other resigning ministers. The announcement of the Labour cabinet is eagerly awaited.'[24]

Kathleen Tipper wrote the following day,

'Some of Mr Atlee's new cabinet are already chosen, and as expected Mr Bevin is Foreign Secretary. There couldn't be two more contrasting men than Mr Eden and Mr Bevin, so foreign diplomats are in for a shock I think. Mr B has great confidence in his powers to settle foreign countries' troubles and disputes judging from some of his utterances, so now is his chance to do his strong man act with Stalin and Truman. Actually his appointment doesn't bring forth great opposition from the Beaverbrook press, I think they are too relieved that Sir Stafford Crips hasn't got that job, they seem rather frightened of his revolutionary ideas.'[25]

The right-wing press certainly didn't have to fear that the new Labour representatives would cosy up to the Soviets – in fact, Bevin thought Churchill had been too soft with Stalin. Stalin had wryly said of Attlee that 'he does not look like a greedy man',[26] but Attlee's portrait of Stalin was rather more direct; he said Stalin 'reminded me of the Renaissance despots – no principles, any methods but no flowery language – always Yes or No, though you could only count on it if it was No'.[27]

G. Bamber wrote on the 30th, 'The next news we can look forward for is from the Potsdam Conference – I wonder how things are gong there and what difference the change in our "team" will make.'[28] The truth was that for all of Attlee and Bevin's undoubted competence – Montgomery wrote that 'these two grasped the problems with both hands and created a very good impression on everyone' – they achieved no more concessions than Churchill could and the Americans did little to help.[29] At the same time that the Americans opposed Soviet power, they were also keen to dent any continuation of Britain's ambitions as a great empire. One of the key factors in this equation was the enormous amount of debt that Britain owed to the United States.

The change of personnel was significant in at least one major respect: it meant that Stalin was the sole survivor of the original triumvirate that had included Roosevelt and Churchill. Now Roosevelt was replaced with Truman and Churchill with Attlee. Yet Stalin kept going. However, he was ill for much of the last few days of the conference and his Foreign Minister, Molotov, took his place at the table. The nature of the agreements that they came to would cement the conditions for the Cold War – the underlying basis for which ran along the lines of what the then counsellor in the

US Embassy in Moscow, George Kennan, defined as dividing 'Europe frankly into spheres of influence – keep ourselves out of the Russians sphere and the Russians out of ours'.[30] That an iron curtain had descended across Europe was not a new idea – it had been around since at least 1920 to describe the barrier between the Soviet Union and the outside world. In the context of Soviet territorial claims across the Continent, though, the idea gained currency in writings during the war by prominent Nazis, including Goebbels. But the concept of the iron curtain is most famously, though wrongly, attributed to Churchill, who first used the term in a telegram he wrote to Truman on 12 May.

> 'Meanwhile what is to happen about Russia? I have always worked for friendship with Russia, but, like you, I feel deep anxiety because of their misrepresentation of the Yalta decisions, their attitude towards Poland, their overwhelming influence in the Balkans, excepting Greece, the difficulties they make about Vienna, the combination of Russian power and territories under their control or occupied, coupled with Communist technique in so many other countries, and above all their power to maintain very large armies in the field for a long time. [...] An iron curtain is drawn down upon their front. We do not know what is going on behind. There seems little doubt that the whole of the regions east of the line Lübeck–Trieste– Corfu will soon be completely in their hands.'[31]

Given the context, it was probably unrealistic to expect that the talks at Potsdam would change the wider situation in terms of relations between East and West and the issues at the heart of the conflict between the two. According to Churchill,

> 'It is difficult to see what more we could have done. For five months the Soviets had fought every inch of the road. They had gained their object by delay. [...] All the Polish parties, except their own Communist puppets, were in a hopeless minority in the new recognised Polish Provisional Government. We were as far as ever from any real and fair attempt to obtain the will of the Polish nation by free elections.'[32]

Only force would remove the Soviets from Poland and the rest of Eastern Europe and neither the United States nor Britain was willing to enter a new 'hot' war. The Cold War had not quite begun – and conviviality at Potsdam was conspicuous – but all the evidence indicated that the complete deterioration of relations between the Soviet Union and the West was simply a matter of time. The issue of reparations from Germany was another issue that looked designed to test the relationship between the major powers – including France – to the limit. As Montgomery had requested of Churchill at the start of the Potsdam Conference, it was agreed that Germany would remain as a single administrative and economic entity. But the different way that reparations worked within the respective individual zones meant that Germany remained effectively divided – especially between the Russian zone and the other three zones, between which there was no exchange of any sort, and this created arguments that would rumble on for the next few years.

For people in Britain and America, the agreements reached at Potsdam did not attract widespread interest – the major points were not seen as being relevant to their lives and much of the detail seemed technical and geographically obscure. For people in Germany, Poland and other Eastern European countries, the agreements certainly were important. Potsdam demanded a more orderly resettlement of displaced people – Germans, Poles and others. But for people like Hans Graf von Lehndorff, the doctor from Königsberg, the preoccupation with the simple act of survival against the odds – and helping others survive – continued regardless of what had been agreed at the conference. At the end of June, he was facing a dilemma with many patients he came across – they were suffering from starvation, but their legs were bloated by oedema. The only option was to amputate. But how could a starving person with no legs survive in such a hostile environment especially when they were German?[33]

In Czechoslovakia, the situation was also terrible in the months after the German capitulation. Edvard Beneš, previously the Czech President, lived in exile in London during the war years. In a radio broadcast in 1945, he warned: 'Woe, woe, woe, thrice woe to the Germans, we will liquidate you!'[34] The threat was carried out by vigilante groups, aided by legislation devised by Beneš and his political allies that stripped ethnic Germans of property and citizenship. A woman called Else was held at the country estate of a Prince von Lobkowitz in Czechoslovakia after being rounded up in Prague. She described how she was forced to work 'from early morning into the night' for thirteen months. She said,

'Food was available in the pig troughs. ... We were so starving that we even ate the poisoned rodent bait we were supposed to put around the potato sacks. One old man went to get a tin can from the garbage pile and was caught by a guard. We all had to line up and watch as the old man was made to strip to the waist, stand on one leg with his arms raised and shout: We thank our Führer – all the while he was whipped until, covered with blood, he collapsed.'[35]

In Czechoslovakia, three-quarters of a million Germans had been chased out of the country even before the expulsion had been legitimised at the Potsdam Conference. For many, the Conference was too late; for many others, it made no difference anyway. The Czechs, the Russians and others had been pricked until they had bled; wronged by Nazi aggression, they would have their revenge regardless of far-off politicking, agreements, doodles on maps and compromises. Just as an enormous bonfire takes a long time to stop burning, so the violence of the Second World War did not end immediately, but fizzled out slowly through a long summer of rape, revenge, pillage, death marches, deliberate starvation and expulsion from homes and countries. It took a while for all this 'hot' anger to dissipate and only once it had would the Cold War begin.

Hitler, shortly before his death, made a prescient statement in which he predicted the post-war order:

'With the defeat of the Reich and pending the emergence of the Asiatic, the African, and perhaps the South American nationalisms, there will remain in the world only two Great Powers capable of confronting each other – the United States and Soviet Russia. The laws of both history and geography will compel these two powers to a trial of strength, either military or in the fields of economics and ideology. These same laws make it inevitable that both powers should become enemies of Europe. And it is equally certain that both these Powers will sooner or later find it desirable to seek the support of the sole surviving great nation in Europe, the German people.'[36]

The Potsdam Conference, which took place three months after his death, did little to contradict his analysis.

above: Devastated Dresden in early 1945. © *Deutsche Fotothek/dpa/CORBIS*

above: Field Marshal Alan Brooke, Chief
of the Imperial General Staff (1941– 45).
© *Popperfoto/Getty Images*

below: Iris Murdoch celebrated VE Day
in London. © *SNAP/REX*

above: Richard Dimbleby, the first Allied
reporter to enter both Bergen-Belsen and Berlin
© *Leonard McCombe/Stringer/Getty Images*

below: Simone de Beauvoir.
© *Roger Viollet Collection/Getty Images*

above: German General Anton Dostler moments before his execution for war crimes.
© AP/Press Association Images

above: Celebrations in Trafalgar Square on VE Day.
© *Massecar T G/IWM*

below: Enthusiastic VE Day celebrations in London.
© *Picture Post/Stringer/Getty Images*

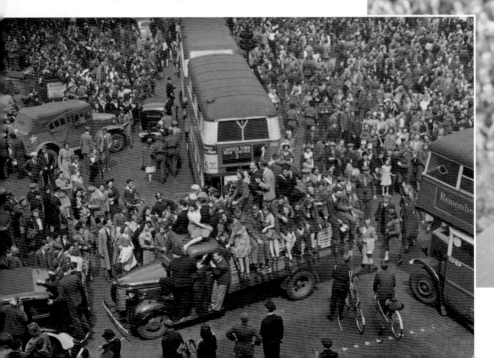

above: Churchill addresses the crowds on 8 May. © *IWM/Getty Images*

left: American soldiers climbing high in Paris. © *Photo 12/Getty Images*

below: In London, some threw caution to the wind.
© *Popperfoto/Getty Images*

above: VE Day in Moscow. © *Heritage Images/Getty Images*

below: The Soviet flag hoisted above the Reichstag. © *Sovfoto/Getty Images*

above: Clement Attlee on the campaign trail. © *Popperfoto/Getty Images*

right: Churchill struggled to engage with the electorate in the run up to the election on 5 July and in some places he was even booed.
© Popperfoto/Getty Images

left: Clement Attlee shares his moment of victory with King George VI.
© Keystone/Stringer/Getty Images

right: The three week interval between polling day and the result was made so that all the overseas services votes could be counted.
© No 1 Army Film & Photographic Unit/ Trevor J Hawkins (Sergeant)/IWM

left: A guard at Bergen-Belsen concentration camp is forced to bury bodies.
© *George Rodger/ Getty Images*

below: Two emaciated Allied prisoners-of-war in Japan.
© *AP/Press Association Images*

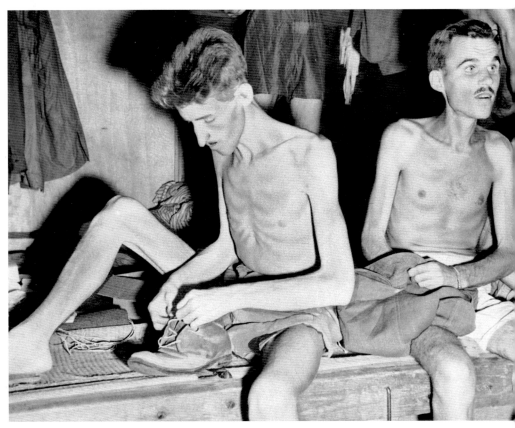

right: Jewish survivors heading for Palestine.
© *GPO/Handout/Getty Images*

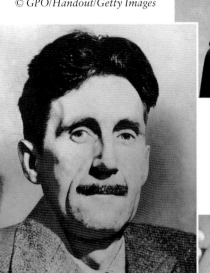

left: 'If you want a vision of the future, imagine a boot stamping on a human face – forever.' George Orwell started writing his most famous novel – *1984* – in the summer of 1945.
© *Hulton Archive/Stringer/Getty Images*

right: He 'makes one think of his wax effigy in the Grevin museum'. Marshal Petain on trial.
© *Bettmann/CORBIS*

right: Colonel Paul Tibbets stands in front of the Enola Gay aircraft which was used to drop the first atom bomb on Hiroshima.
© *Universal History Archive/Universal Images Group/REX*

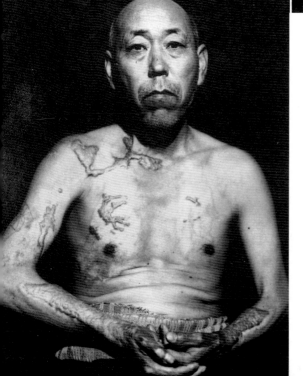

left: A survivor of the Hiroshima blast showing characteristic scars on his body. © *AP/Press Association Images*

above: Hiroshima in December 1945, a bleak and blackened landscape.
© *Alfred Eisenstaedt/Getty Images*

above: Churchill, Truman and Stalin in a jovial mood at Potsdam.
© Popperfoto/Getty Images

left: Senior
Nazis sit in
the dock at
Nuremburg.
© Keystone-France/
Getty Images

above: The Royal Family wave to the crowds from the balcony at Buckingham Palace on VJ Day. © *Keystone/Stringer/Getty Images*

right: Crowds celebrating victory over Japan on 15 August 1945, in Albert Square, Manchester.

© *Mirrorpix*

above: The famous VJ Day kiss in Times Square, New York was not as romantic as it perhaps at first seemed. © *Lt. Victor Jorgensen/Getty Images*

Chapter 6

From Belsen to Vichy

Justice and Revenge

'In the shade of some trees lay a great collection of
bodies. I walked round them, trying to count – there
were perhaps 150, flung down on each other. All
naked, all so thin that their yellow skins glistened like
stretched rubber on their bones.'

Richard Dimbleby, broadcasting from Bergen–Belsen[1]

While justice is generally held up as a civilised response to
wrongdoing, revenge is its barbaric and unrestrained cousin.
As Nazi crimes were uncovered, so there was a desire for
those responsible to be brought to justice. As the Germans
lost the war, so there was a desire for those who had been
oppressed by Nazi rule and war making to exact their own
revenge. Both revenge and justice belonged in the summer
of 1945 to the victorious. Churchill wrote in his memoirs:

'Crimes were committed by the Germans under the
Hitlerite domination to which they allowed themselves
to be subjected which find no equal in scale and
wickedness with any that have darkened the human
record. The wholesale massacre by systematised
processes of six or seven millions of men, women, and

155

children in the German execution camps exceeds in horror the rough-and-ready butcheries of Genghis Khan, and in scale reduces them to pigmy proportions. Deliberate extermination of whole populations was contemplated and pursued by both Germany and Russia in the eastern war.'[2]

Churchill includes Russia, who was Britain's ally, in this assessment of war crimes but they were never brought to task in any international court for the crimes they committed. And any alleged war crimes that other allies may also have been accused of – from unrestricted submarine warfare to the bombing, and deaths, of tens of thousands of civilians in cities such as Dresden and Cologne (not to mention Hiroshima and Nagasaki) – were also never tried. Instead, they were simply ignored. In this sense, the justice meted out *was* that of the victors. Hermann Göring wrote on his court documents when he was accused of war crimes that 'the victor will always be the judge and the vanquished the accused'.[3] However, there was at least legal process, something which at first Churchill – and others – had insisted was not necessary. The US Secretary of State Cordell Hull, for instance, had said to his British and Soviet counterparts that he would 'take Hitler and Mussolini and Tojo and their arch-accomplices and bring them before a drumhead court martial. And at sunrise the following day there would occur a historic incident'.[4] Anthony Eden, who was the British foreign minister during the war, wrote a memo that stated his opposition to trials of senior Nazis because 'the guilt of such individuals is so black that they fall outside … any judicial process'.[5] Churchill suggested merely that they be lined up and shot.[6] Clearly, there is a much thinner line between summary justice of the kind suggested by many senior allies and simple revenge than when a full and transparent judicial process is used. The Nuremberg Trials did not begin until November 1945, but the preparation for them was done in the summer of that year and the deliberations that took place in the months immediately after the end of the war are therefore relevant to this book. In the meantime, there were other trials, such as those of Marshal Pétain and Pierre Laval in France. But, in the main, there was a more atavistic and vicious kind of justice that was handed out across Europe and Asia that summer: summary justice against collaborators and women who had slept with Nazis and Japanese soldiers; and pure and simple revenge – everywhere there was revenge.

In April 1945, the so-called 'atrocity films' were shown in British and American cinemas. They depicted Bergen–Belsen concentration camp in northern Germany, which had been liberated by the British Army on 15 April. The reactions to the footage varied enormously. Most people were shocked – 'the film is pure horror' – and one woman in London said, 'I hear that some of the most hopeless cases are just being quietly put to sleep – there's nothing else to be done with the poor wretches.'[7] Edmund Wilson, the American writer touring Europe in 1945, suggested that the film was Allied propaganda designed to inure people to the suffering of German people. 'Goebbels hardly used a different technique in working up the Germans to a point at which it seemed to them quite natural to attempt to exterminate the Poles and the Jews,' he wrote. 'And our efforts have been equally successful. We can contemplate now with equanimity, with a cheerful self-satisfaction, a kind of warfare that crushes whole cities and that brings down agony and death on thousands of women and children.'[8] In France, the sight of the first deportees and prisoners to come back from German-run camps had already shocked the nation. When people were shown film footage of the newly liberated camps, it caused further outrage. Pierre-Henri Teitgen, the Minister of Justice, noted that crowds stormed two jails – in Dinan and Cusset – and lynched collaborators there.[9]

But at least one fifty-year-old Christian man in London still believed in the decency of most Germans:

> 'I find this present official attitude of blaming the local peasantry round the concentration camps for not interfering very absurd. Once the Nazi Party had the arms they could only be opposed by force of arms. The peasants were helpless, and it's very muddled thinking to hold them responsible. I don't like this phase of righteous indignation. And not a word of blame for the people here and in America who backed Hitler. Another thing I feel strongly against is the orders against fraternisation. You can't occupy a country for years and not fraternise at least with the frightened but decent few – and I still believe there are some. As a matter of fact, I'm very glad I'm going to Germany on an essentially Christian work.'[10]

Across Europe, many people did not have the same sympathy for ordinary German people or – in previously occupied countries – for their fellow countrymen who had fraternised with Germans during the Occupation. Instead, where they could, people sought to take revenge against their most hated enemy. And almost certainly they also dressed up the opportunity to obtain the spoils of war – be that loot or women – as an act of revenge. The Soviets had withstood one of the most savage attacks in military history. Not only had it been a military campaign, it had also resulted in the death of millions of Soviet civilians. The Germans had first advanced into the Soviet Union in the summer of 1941, and the ensuing conflict for almost the next four years was ferocious, sustained and unrelenting. And it was mainly fought on Soviet soil. The Nazis treated the Slavs as *untermenschen* (subhumans) and Soviet POWs died in their millions in open-air camps. More than one million Soviet Jews died in extermination camps and on death marches. The SS *Einsatzgrüppen* extermination squads assassinated hundreds of thousands of Jews and political prisoners on the Eastern Front. So when, towards the end of 1944, the Soviets began to fight on German soil for the first time – in East Prussia – it was inevitable that they would not only kill as many German soldiers as possible, but also retaliate against German civilians, too – with rape, looting and murder. This was exacerbated by the ferocity of the resistance that the Red Army faced as they advanced westwards. It was clearly Hitler's intention to fight to the very last, and in East Prussia in October 1944 Himmler gave instructions to a unit of *Volkssturm* – a form of home guard or national militia made up of males between the ages of 13 and 60 – instructing them to do so:

> 'Our opponents must know that every kilometre that they want to advance into our country will cost them rivers of blood. They will step onto a field of living mines consisting of fanatical uncompromising fighters. Every block of flats in a city, every village, every

farmstead, every forest will be defended by men, boys and old men and, if need be, by women and girls. Furthermore, in the territory that they believe they have conquered, the German determination to resist will rise up behind them and, like werewolves, fearless volunteers will do damage to the enemy and cut off his lifelines.'[11]

The fighting would continue to be intense and Hitler had no interest in preserving or protecting the German people. For him, the war was all or nothing. And if defeat was the fate of Germany, then it would be total defeat; he would not surrender; he would let the German people be overrun and killed if necessary.

'If the war is lost,' Hitler told Albert Speer in March 1945, 'the people will be lost also. It is not necessary to worry about what the German people will need for elementary survival. On the contrary, it is best for us to destroy even these things. For the nation has proved to be the weaker, and the future belongs solely to the stronger eastern nation. In any case only those who are inferior will remain after this struggle, for the good have already been killed.'[12]

In this climate, the millions of invading Red Army soldiers were ready to unleash as much violence as they could hand out; the self-proclaimed 'master race' was on its knees. 'Woe to the land of the murderers,' warned Red Army Marshal Zhukov in an order in January 1945. 'We will get our terrible revenge for everything.'[13] Revenge was not just bad discipline on the part of Red Army soldiers, it seemed tantamount to official policy, enforced by propaganda such as this piece called 'Woe to Germany' written by novelist Ilya Ehrenburg: 'We are coming to Germany, having left behind us the Ukraine, Belorussia, the ashes of our cities, the blood of our children. Woe to the country of the assassins! Not only our troops, the shadows of the slain too, have come to the borders of Germany. Who is hammering at the gates of Prussia? The slaughtered old men from Trostyanets; the children from the Babi Yar ravine: the martyrs of Slavuta.'[14]

There were orders against rape and looting – even from Stalin himself – but these were seldom enforced. Once an army has been whipped up into a frenzy of hatred and blood lust, at what point do their officers tell them that enough is enough? The Germans were the enemy of Red Army soldiers in every respect: they were capitalists and fascists; they had invaded their country and humiliated and killed millions of Russians. And for many of the soldiers, the conditions they encountered as they ran into Germany represented a kind luxury that they had never seen before, which also offended them. It conformed to the ideas that they had been fed in Soviet propaganda of bourgeois capitalist decadence.

One of the first incursions by the Red Army onto German soil in October 1944 gave a dire warning to Germans of what was to follow. Nemmersdorf (now known as Mayakovskoye) fell to the advancing Russians and they raped females between the ages of eight and eighty-four and killed more than seventy women and children as well as one elderly man. Some of the victims were crucified, though precise details remain disputed. The Russian advance into Germany began in earnest in January 1945, and the capital of East Prussia, Königsberg (now known as Kalingrad), was soon under siege. It was captured in April, and the destruction and the rape began. The Russian writer Alexander Solzhenitsyn, who was serving in the Red Army at the time, later wrote a poem called 'Prussian Nights' while he was in captivity in a Soviet gulag.

> The little daughter's on the mattress,
> Dead. How many have been on it
> A platoon, a company perhaps?
> A girl's been turned into a woman,
> A woman turned into a corpse.
> It's all come down to simple phrases:
> Do not forget! Do not forgive!
> Blood for blood! A tooth for a tooth![15]

Many women, according to Doctor Hans Graf Von Lehndorff, begged to be shot, but most were not given that privilege, at least not until they had been raped multiple times.[16] Hundreds of thousands of Germans attempted to flee west to escape the Russians; many others committed suicide.

The violence continued unabated as the Russians swept through Germany and into the heart of the Third Reich. In Berlin, a city mainly populated by that time by women, children and old men, the ordeal of rape was so ubiquitous and such a shared experience that in some sense it had lost the horrendous power that it might have in other conditions. The anonymous woman in Berlin wrote in her diary that:

> 'I have a good look at this sixteen-year-old girl [janitor's daughter], the only one I know to have lost her virginity to the Russians. She has the same, stupid, self-satisfied expression that she always had. I try to imagine how I'd feel if sexual experience had come to me for

the first time in this way. But I have to dismiss the thought; I cannot imagine it. But one thing is certain: had this girl been raped in peacetime by some stray man, had it been followed by the usual proceedings of denunciation, of police reports, investigation, indeed of arrest and confrontation, newspaper reports, and local gossip – then the girl would have reacted differently, have suffered a very different kind of shock. But this is a question of a collective experience, anticipated, feared for some time – something which is happening to women all around us, an inevitable part of our present existence.'[17]

The woman in Berlin, as many German women attempted to do, sought the protection of a Russian officer – in her case a major – who would keep all the other soldiers away. After the initial frenzy of rape, it was a tactic that worked effectively for her. Many other women were not so lucky.

Cities across Germany and other parts of German-speaking Europe were ravaged in the Red Army onslaught – from Vienna to Breslau, Danzig (now known as Gdansk) to Gleiwitz (Gliwice) in Silesia. Prague, which had been occupied by the Germans since 1939, contained almost 250,000 ethnic Germans in 1945.[18] The Prague uprising by the Czech Resistance against their German occupiers began on 5 May. The uprising was suppressed by the Germans three days later, but on 9 May the Red Army arrived and the Czechs were able to take out their anger on the Germans who still remained in the city. Barricades that were still in the streets prevented the Red Army from driving their tanks through the city and so civilian Germans were organised by Czech mobs to clear the barricades away. At the same time, they were beaten and made to run over broken glass. Women were forced to eat pictures of Hitler and had their hair cut with the blades of bayonets. The actress Margarete Schell was rounded up along with other women and made to clear rubble from the railway station. At the same time, the crowd around them kicked and hit them. And there was much worse happening as well: while the Czechs were not as ready to rape Germans as the Russian soldiers, they did murder large numbers of them – thousands were mown down by machine guns in the football stadium for sport; suspected SS men were hanged from lampposts and set on fire; and teenage German boys who had been in the Hitler Youth were sometimes beaten to death and sometimes shot at random.[19]

Margarete Schell was sent to a slave labour camp, where she was whipped and beaten. She was not released until March the following year. One of her overseers during her time in captivity treated her especially well. He was a Jewish man who had been in one of the concentration camps. 'Having spent five years in a concentration camp, he said, where he lost both his parents and his sisters, he didn't wish to abuse anyone. He knew what being a prisoner was like. Although he had a perfectly sound reason to hate all Germans, he didn't take it out on us.'[20]

Those Germans who were not killed in Czechoslovakia were expelled from the country, sometimes on marches across the border to Germany or Austria, sometimes by train.

Other Eastern European countries also joined in with their revenge against the Germans – the Poles in Silesia and East Prussia, for example, formed militias that robbed, detained, beat up, murdered and expelled ethnic Germans. One Pole from Katowice, who had been a prisoner in both

Auschwitz and Buchenwald, spoke to the Jewish American intelligence officer Saul Padover: 'He raised his arms and cried out to God to bring down His vengeance upon the German nation; to exterminate every German man, woman and child; to strike to death every living German being; to cleanse the earth of all German blood unto eternity. I was tempted to say Amen, and I felt like crying.'[21] Hungarians, Romanians and Yugoslavs all expelled their German populations from May 1945 onwards, often after they had been stripped of all their possessions first.

Vengeance and atrocities were not limited to the east, though. The French Army was accused of mass rape in a number of places, including Freudenstadt, Bruschal and Constance in southwest Germany. One account of the Freudenstadt incident mentioned that more than 500 women had reported being raped and that the French soldiers responsible also committed acts of arson while allegedly chanting 'We are the avengers, the SS of the French army'.[22] France, like Russia, had endured years of German occupation and had been humiliated by their neighbours. Once the French had been allocated their occupation zone (nicknamed the brassiere because of its shape) in the rich border region of the Rhine, they administered it in a much harsher fashion than the Americans and the British administered their zones, restricting rations to 800 calories per German adult – just 200 more than the amount that had been given to prisoners in Dachau. They shipped natural resources such as coal back to France and used German prisoners as labourers. They widely anticipated that they would be able to annexe certain areas of their occupation zone and incorporate them into French territory. In March 1946, Phillipe Livry-Level said in a National Assembly debate that 'we have here a land for us to exploit'.[23] In 1945–46, eighty-nine per cent of exports from the French Occupation Zone went to France.

The Americans and the British, who had not been occupied, were nonetheless also guilty of raping German women, though on a much lesser scale than the other Allied nations. However, 487 American soldiers were tried for rapes allegedly committed in March and April 1945.[24]

Some British and American soldiers were certainly not averse to a little of their own summary justice; against German camp guards, for example, after they had come across the concentration camps. They were not just directly responsible, on at least two notable instances, but also on these occasions enabled the newly liberated prisoners to take revenge against their now ex-guards. Given the conditions that they encountered, the desire to administer what they saw as justice was perhaps understandable.

Just as many people in Britain were outraged when the atrocity films made at Bergen–Belsen were shown, so, even more so, were the soldiers who first entered the camp on 15 April 1945 and were confronted with sights and smells that would haunt them for the rest of their lives. BBC correspondent Richard Dimbleby was also there. 'I passed through the barrier and found myself in the world of a nightmare,' he said in his broadcast.

> 'Dead bodies, some of them in decay, lay strewn about the road and along the rutted track. On each side of the road were brown wooden huts. There were faces at the windows, the bony emaciated faces of starving women too weak to come outside, propping themselves against the glass to see the light before they died. And

they *were* dying, every hour, every minute. I *saw* a man, wandering dazedly along the road, stagger and fall. Someone else looked down at him, took him by the heels and dragged him to the side of the road to join the other bodies lying unburied there. No-one else took the slightest bit of notice – they didn't even trouble to turn their heads.'

As Dimbleby walked further into the camp, he was continually shocked by what he saw:

'In the shade of some trees lay a great collection of bodies. I walked round them, trying to count – there were perhaps 150, flung down on each other. All naked, all so thin that their yellow skins glistened like stretched rubber on their bones. Some of the poor, starved creatures whose bodies were there looked so utterly unreal and inhuman that I could have imagined they had never lived. They were like polished skeletons – the skeletons that medical students like to play practical jokes with. At one end of the pile a cluster of men and women were gathered round a fire. They were using rags and old shoes taken from the bodies to keep it alight and were heating soup on it.'

Belsen was not an extermination camp, but as its numbers swelled in the last few months of the war with an influx of various prisoners – Jews, Russians, Poles, gypsies and others – from the east, the food and medical supplies were insufficient for the camp population. In April, there were around 60,000 prisoners in the camp. It seems likely that Anne Frank had died in the camp a few weeks before it was liberated. There was an outbreak of typhus in March and starvation was commonplace to such an extent that cannibalism of dead bodies was taking place. Dimbleby reported this when he observed the large pit of bodies in one corner of the camp:

'It is fifteen feet deep and it is piled to the very top with naked bodies that have been tumbled in one on top of the other. Like this must have been the plague pits in England, only nowadays we can help by digging them quicker with bulldozers and already there's a bulldozer at work at Belsen. Our army doctors examining some of the bodies, found in their sides a long slit, apparently made by someone with surgical knowledge. They made enquiries and established beyond doubt that in the frenzy of their starvation, the people of Belsen had taken the wasted bodies of their fellow prisoners and removed from them the only remaining flesh – the liver and the kidneys – to eat.'[25]

Preparing to make his broadcast, Dimbleby broke down. According to his son, Jonathan, the BBC in London at first refused to broadcast it until it had been independently verified, but Dimbleby insisted that it be transmitted at once.[26] The Camp Commandant Josef Kramer – later nicknamed 'The Beast of Belsen' – was immediately arrested at the camp by the British. He and forty-four others were tried in November 1945 at a British military tribunal. Eleven of the forty-five, including Kramer, were sentenced to death. Fourteen were acquitted altogether. At the time of liberation, some British soldiers were complicit in some of the survivors taking revenge on the Hungarian overseers – the *kapos*[27]

– when some of them were murdered. The British also organised the remaining SS men and women at the camp into burial squads that collected bodies and cleaned the camp. When German nurses entered the camp on the invitation of the British army to try to nurse some of the liberated prisoners back to health, they were attacked. The first attempts at medical intervention by the British were ineffectual, survivors were fed food that was too rich for their emaciated, malnourished bodies and people continued to die there in there thousands.

The Americans liberated Dachau concentration camp in Bavaria on 29 April, when around 30,000 prisoners were still in the camp. According to one US Army sergeant, who first visited Dachau on 3 May,

'The air [...] was filled with the smell of lime and the unforgettable smell of the dead. Facing us was a big grey building with a grey wall, about 10 feet high, all around it. To the left of this building and wall were fifty rail cars. [...] In at least 40 of the cars including the four open ones, there were dead, starved, emaciated bodies lying in every conceivable position. They wore striped suits (prisoner's uniform) parts of which seem to have been torn from their bodies in their death throes, thus revealing that wax-like skin of the dead. In a plot of grass, opposite the train, were three dead SS guards, evidently beaten to death, because there were terrific bruises all over their bodies.'[28]

The sights that the liberating soldiers were confronted with at Dachau were so horrendous that many of the soldiers wanted to take immediate revenge against the camp guards. The details of exactly what happened immediately after the liberation of Dachau are disputed, but more than one account details the fact that many SS guards were executed with machine guns by American troops. Other guards were handed to the prisoners for them to exact their own retribution. According to Jack Hallett, who was one of the American soldiers who liberated the camp on 29 April:

'Control was gone after the sights we saw, and the men were deliberately wounding guards that were available and then turned them over to prisoners and allowing them to take revenge on them. And, in fact, you've seen the picture where one of the soldiers gave one of the inmates a bayonet and watched him behead the man. It was a pretty gory mess. A lot of the guards were shot in the legs so that they couldn't move and … and that's about all I can say.'[29]

In France, as in other previously occupied countries, including Holland and Belgium, revenge and summary justice was meted out to those identified as being collaborators with the enemy. The crime of *collaboration horizontale* – French women having sex with German soldiers – made the perpetrators guilty of *indignité nationale* – in other words, they had affronted the national dignity. Although this most commonly resulted in the unpleasant punishment of a shaved head and other public humiliations – being spat upon, tarred and feathered, for instance – many women were also executed. They included prostitutes who had done business with German soldiers as well as women whose husbands had been in POW camps and who had consorted with German soldiers merely to try and feed themselves and their families. This 'justice' was administered from the liberation of France onwards, but continued throughout the summer of 1945. According to historian Ian Buruma,

> 'The most enthusiastic persecutors of *filles de Boches* were usually not people who had distinguished themselves in acts of courage during the war. Once liberation came to formerly occupied countries, all kinds of men managed to present themselves as members of resistance groups, strutting around with newly acquired armbands and sten guns, disporting themselves as heroes as they hunted for traitors and bad women.'[30]

In Italy, there was a similar hunt for fascists. Mussolini and his mistress had been shot by partisans in Milan in April, but they were the tip of the iceberg. Many thousands of suspected fascists were killed in the summer of 1945. Sometimes, they were executed without trial; on other occasions, kangaroo courts were hastily convened in town squares to try the accused. Edmund Wilson observed gangs of teenagers with guns cruising around Milan looking for fascists to shoot when he was there in May. He also saw the aftermath of the Mussolini killing: 'Over the whole city hung the stink of the killing of Mussolini and his followers, the exhibition of their bodies in public and the defilement of them by the crowd. Italians would stop you in bars and show you photographs they had taken of it.' The photos were not a pleasant sight – after he had been shot, Mussolini had been hung upside down and his face beaten until it was virtually unrecognisable as a human form.[31]

Public executions were also a feature in Malaya in the summer of 1945 as the Japanese retreated and the anti-Japanese resistance took vengeance on collaborators. For others, in Asia, like the Vietnamese at the start of September 1945, the war offered an opportunity to take revenge on their colonial masters – in this case the French. French homes were attacked and looted by violent mobs; waiters in Hanoi's best hotel attacked the French guests. It took two weeks for the French to control the violence.

Formal court proceedings *were* instituted in France against the man who was seen by many as the main collaborator with the Nazis – Marshal Pétain – along with one of his most senior ministers, Pierre Laval. By the end of the Second World War, when he was put on trial for treason, Pétain – a war hero from the First World War – was eighty-nine years old. During the German Occupation, he became the head of government, which moved from Paris to Vichy, and then, after the liberation of France, was relocated by the Germans to the Sigmaringen enclave in Germany. There, the Vichy government became a government in exile, but Pétain refused to participate in it. When proceedings started against Pétain in his absence at the start of April 1945, he wrote to Ribbentrop that he wished to return to France to face his accusers. He did not get a reply, but a few weeks later he was taken to the Swiss border. From Switzerland, he made his way to Paris by train. As he crossed the border into France at Pontarlier, a crowd of two thousand threw stones at the train carriages and screamed out, 'Shoot the old traitor! Pétain for the firing squad.'[32]

Pétain's full trial began on 23 July in the Palais de Justice in Paris. The trial was an enormously popular event in Paris with thousands queuing to get into the public galleries. There was actually only space for six hundred of them.

Pétain was never going to get a fair hearing at the trial; in part because the original jury of twenty-four comprised twelve members of the Resistance and twelve members of the National Assembly who had all voted to refuse powers to Pétain in 1940. De Gaulle later criticised the atmosphere and content of the trial in his memoirs: 'Too often, the discussions took on the appearance of a partisan trial, sometimes even a settling of accounts, when the whole affair should have been treated only from the standpoint of national defence and independence.'[33]

Pétain wore his immaculate uniform and a single medal. He was an old man and he looked like it – one of the bystanders at the court mentioned that his face looked like the wax effigy that existed of him in the Musée Grévin.[34] But he read out a statement to the court in a clear voice in which he stated that everything he had done had been in France's best interests. A lot of political speeches followed, which were largely irrelevant to Pétain's guilt or innocence. Kathleen Tipper, the diarist in South London, wrote that 'although we have nothing but contempt for the old man, the way these other French politicians are turning on him in attempts to whiten their own foul characters, is rather revolting'. But it did emerge that Pétain had known about the deportation of Jewish people from Germany who had sought refuge in France, including children. He had not ordered the deportations, but neither had he done anything to stop them. Pétain's guilt was a foregone conclusion anyway, and he was sentenced to death. However, this was later commuted to life imprisonment as reported in the *Daily Telegraph* on 18 August: 'Despite a campaign in the

Communist Press for the execution of Pétain his death sentence was today commuted to life imprisonment in a fortress.'

Pierre Laval was not so fortunate. He had also participated in deportations of Jewish citizens to Germany. The once handsome man was a shadow of his former self according to Janet Flanner, writing for the *New Yorker*. 'The fact of his face is now gone. His oily, Moorish hair is now dry and gray and his moustache is the color of tobacco juice. His crooked, stained teeth make a dark cavernous background for his large lips … [His] rumpled gray-and-white striped suit was so large for his frame that it looked borrowed.'[35]

He was sentenced to death, which inspired a little rhyme that was popular in France at the time: 'Pétain, to sleep / Laval to the stake / de Gaulle to work.'[36] Before he could be shot, Laval tried to poison himself using a phial that had been sewn into his jacket, but the poison was so old that it failed to kill him. He was made well enough to walk to the stake in October 1945 where he was tied and shot. His last words were '*Vive la France!*'[37]

Although various trials, such as that of the camp staff at Bergen–Belsen, were already being put in process in the summer of 1945, the principal focus was to bring the major Nazi war criminals to justice at what would become the Nuremberg trials. Discussions took place between the Allied Nations throughout the summer of 1945, and in August a four-power agreement was signed. According to the *Manchester Guardian*, on 9 August:

'The discussions, which have been taking place in London between the representatives of the United Kingdom, the United States, Russia, and France concerning the prosecution and punishment of major war criminals have now been completed, and yesterday the representatives of the four Powers signed an agreement establishing an international military tribunal before which the major war criminals of the European Axis will be tried. The agreement is supplemented by a charter, setting out the constitution of the tribunal and the principles governing its operations.'[38]

Twenty-three senior Nazis were scheduled to be tried at Nuremburg, including Hermann Göring, Joachim von Ribbentrop, Albert Speer and Julius Streicher. In reality, the figure was twenty-one, as Martin Bormann was tried in his absence and Robert Ley managed to commit suicide at the start of the trial. There were also a dozen subsequent military tribunals at Nuremberg between 1946 and 1949, including the trial of members of the notorious *Einsatzgrüppen* execution squads. And various other trials, including the first Auschwitz trial in Poland in 1946 and the Dachau trials (held in situ at what had been Dachau concentration camp), administered by the US military, were also held following the main Nuremburg trials.

However, given the scale of the atrocities, remarkably few people were ever brought to justice and some – such as Klaus Barbie, 'the butcher of Lyon' – were scandalously saved from justice by Allied intelligence services.[39] Only a tiny number of the *Einsatzgrüppen*, responsible for the deaths of hundreds of thousands of Jews, were ever charged. The initial *Einsatzgrüppen* trial in Nuremburg featured just twenty-four defendants.

Tom Bower's book *Blind Eye to Murder: Britain, America and the Purging of Nazi Germany – A Pledge Betrayed* provides an angry and impassioned account of how the Allied nations failed to bring large numbers of war criminals to justice. He is far from alone in his assessment. Ian Kershaw, for example, wrote that 'many implicated in crimes against humanity escaped lightly'.[40] Bower tells the story of Colonel Clio E. Straight, who before the war had been a lawyer in Iowa, and who was appointed to run the American war crimes prosecutions. On VE Day, Colonel Straight was at the Hotel Majestic in Paris, not in Germany where he needed to be in order to start bringing war criminals in the country to justice. He had no trained staff, no headquarters and no plans. At that stage, he had not yet made contact with his British counterpart. By contrast, an American operation to secure 9,000 top level German scientists and engineers, called Project Paperclip, according to Bower showed 'just what could be achieved, even amid the ruins of a defeated nation, given careful planning, well-researched information, resources and a sense of urgency'.[41]

Colonel Straight did not get from Paris to Germany until July, missing vital weeks in which he and his small team could have collected evidence and begun the process of apprehending suspects. In the meantime, prominent war criminals, including Gustav Wagner, who was a notoriously brutal staff sergeant variously nicknamed 'The Beast' and 'Wolf' at Sobibor extermination camp in Poland, had already evaded capture. As well as being responsible for helping to carry out mass exterminations within the camp, Wagner also perpetrated many acts of sadistic violence and humiliation against the inmates of the camp. He was held in an internment camp in Bavaria, questioned and released. He managed to escape to Brazil, where he lived until his death in 1980.

Klaus Barbie, who was personally responsible for the torture, death and deportation of thousands of Jews and suspected Resistance members in Lyon during the war, evaded capture immediately after it. In 1947, he was recruited by the American Counter Intelligence Corps (CIC) which used him as part of their fight against Soviet influence in Europe. In 1949, he fled to Bolivia, where he lived until 1983, when he was deported back to France to stand trial. In 1987, he was convicted and sentenced to life imprisonment. He died in 1991, aged seventy-seven.[42]

Heinrich Himmler – perhaps the single individual with the greatest responsibility for the Holocaust – was arrested by the British near Lüneburg in northern Germany on 23 May. But he committed suicide by biting on a cyanide capsule while in custody and so evaded justice.

Colonel Straight later said that the early stages of investigating war criminals were 'marked by a substantial lack of national policy as to punishment of those who committed war crimes, broad restrictions on trials of war criminals and almost a complete lack of appreciation of the magnitude of the impending problem ... During most of this phase it was still not appreciated that war crimes had been committed on an extremely vast scale.'[43]

Given that many of the concentration camps had been liberated before the end of the war, and that extermination camps liberated by the Russians, such as Auschwitz and Sobibor, were also known about by the Western Allies, it is hard to find this part of Colonel Straight's statement credible. As well as the failures in strategy and leadership that Straight mentions here, he also pointed out the administrative confusion involved in bringing war criminals to justice: 'It does not appear that steps were taken by the Commands to implement even the directives to arrest war criminals. Responsibility for apprehension and detention was just assigned indiscriminately to one or more agencies in addition to their normal function.'[44]

On the British side, Colonel Gerald Draper, a lawyer who would later become a renowned human rights judge, was a member of the Judge Advocate General (JAG) team working on the Belsen case. He realised that they had inadequate resources to deal with the case:

> 'The evidence flowed in like a deluge and we were submerged by it … Our efforts then and later were like a man standing at the edge of the sea dropping lumps of sugar into it, and saying: "Behold it is sweet." We were failing because the wave of criminality was so great and our resources were so inadequate. When Belsen was discovered it was decided in a hurried manner that the Judge Advocate-General's office should handle war crimes. We were not geared, or trained or qualified or had enough resources to do the job. It was a makeshift, hurried ad hoc decision and we had to do the best we could.'[45]

Viscount Bridgeman was appointed to lead the Adjutant General's war crimes branch (AG3) in May 1945. He later explained to Tom Bower that, on his appointment, he was told that he should ensure that British commitment to war crimes was 'not to be bigger than absolutely necessary'. This was because, he said, 'Everyone in the War Office felt that war crimes would be expensive, unrewarding work, which would not be popular with the public.'[46]

The public was reassured in the summer of 1945 that the most important members of the Third Reich had been captured and would be brought to justice, but meanwhile the criminality perpetrated by thousands of others was going unpunished. In the face of revenge, rape, looting and execution, the rule of law struggled to gain a foothold. Legal process seemed reassuring to some and unnecessary to others. After the ferocity of war, perhaps the sobriety of law was too great a change in tempo. According to Tom Bower, 'those who fought for justice were betrayed by their own side; worse still, the rhetoric of their leaders concealed a reluctance, often a refusal, to see their pledges put into effect when the time came'.[47] The wild times of a continent at war were not over yet. And in Asia, where the war continued into August, revenge in many forms was just as widespread and brutal and would continue for some time to come, as much against the colonial West as against their local enemies.

Chapter 7

Demob Happy

The Pleasures and Pains of Civilian Life in Britain

'Where our efforts have all gone toward destruction, we have been able to build nothing at home to fall back on amidst our own ruin.'

Edmund Wilson[1]

Demobilisation may, strictly speaking, describe the process of service men and women returning to civilian life, but the end of the war also 'demobilised' many civilians too – from the last evacuated children returning to the cities to people working in what had started off as an unfamiliar field preparing to return to their former jobs or to a domestic life. Fred Aiken decided to change his profession from an industrial scientist working in an explosives factory to a school science teacher. He had got married in March 1945 and was preparing for a new life.[2] Schoolboy Tony Bray returned to his home in bombed out Gosport.[3] Civil servant G. Bamber wanted more than anything to return to living in a home, 'rather than a billet', again: 'Then I should believe that the war was over.'[4] Soldier Sid Verrier had returned from Germany and, by August 1945, he was in barracks in Wiltshire, looking forward to being demobilised as soon as possible: 'Believe me when I write that I have never been as happy as I am now, and when I get that so long awaited "Boot from the Kate", whether I'm a private or a Tin Hat Bloody Shield-Nobody, with all the Red Tape and Brass Bands, I mean to get on the path in civvy street and make the best of the early years, and look back contentedly in the later years, and I'm sure I can manage it.'[5]

For many, the overwhelming feeling in the first days and weeks after VE Day was a flat dullness, as though, without the constant developments and news of the war, they were suddenly under-stimulated. The American writer Edmund Wilson wrote:

'How empty, how sickish, how senseless, everything suddenly seems the moment the war is over! We are left flat with the impoverished and humiliating life that the drive against the enemy kept our minds off. Where our efforts have all gone toward destruction, we have been able to build nothing at home to fall back on amidst our own ruin. Where the enemy are roofless and starving, where we have reduced their cities to rubble, we get now not even useful plunder or readily exploitable empire, but merely an extension, a more wearisome load, of harassing demands and duties.

'The novelist Graham Greene said to me the other day that they sometimes thought to themselves, now that the war was over: "If one could only hear the hum of a robot bomb!" Life had been dramatic because dangerous. Everything one did was pointed up, was lived with a special awareness, because it might be the last thing one did, and now they missed this: life was safe but blank. No doubt Greene's rather saturnine nature, his addiction to the peculiar excitements of pursuit and persecution, count for something in his nostalgia for the buzz of the V-Is; but then, Greene himself and his themes are partly products of the conditions of this period, of which a fundamental insecurity has been so much a permanent feature that, once having adjusted themselves to it, the English do not know how to live without it.'[6]

Part of the problem was that Britain itself was broke and broken, tatty and weary, drab and dreary; many of its cities had been smashed by Luftwaffe bombs and V-Is. There had been no internal investment because everything had been directed towards the war effort. Housing was insufficient. Food and clothing was in short supply. Even beer was not always available.

One soldier who had already been demobbed in the summer of 1945 wrote to a member of his battery that was still serving in Germany on VJ Day:

'I am enclosing a small article on shopping difficulties in civvy street which I am sure will enlighten the chaps who are expecting to be released during the next few months. I am still taking things easy with an occasional rugby scrum for a few drinks. I have been very surprised to find such a great shortage of clothing and other necessaries to build up even a small wardrobe. I don't suppose being VJ Day will make any great difference to the Battery, here great bonfires are ready and gay lights everywhere. It is a wet dreary day but I do not suppose it will dampen the spirits of those set out to enjoy the "Fruits of Victory", such as they are. The biggest joke around these parts – the pubs have an hour's extension but not one in twenty are open, I am sure the eight marks a barrel stuff would be welcome to say nothing of schnapps, which I miss. Whiskey is only for the Yanks, who are still here, at treble the market price.'[7]

Tony Bray, who as a boy had been evacuated with his family from Gosport to Rottingdean, just outside Brighton, noticed the difference immediately after VE Day: 'In the days that followed we were not used to the stillness that arrived, no more convoys grinding up and down the hills, no aircraft rushing about at low level, even the guns on the training ranges "over the back" had stopped, and the houses in the village which had been army billets were once again empty.' He remembered:

'the plan was for me, Bob and Pop to go ahead and put the place in order before Mum and Nick arrived. So, came the day, a Naval lorry arrived at Soundings, with a Wren driving it, 3 beds and some other sticks of furniture were loaded on, we said goodbye to all our friends, Pop climbed in the cab, Bob and I in the back, and we were off.

'I must admit I was very sorry to be leaving Rottingdean and Brighton, for in spite of six long years of war, and being right in the front line on the South Coast, the whole area had escaped relatively lightly from the Blitzes in the early years, and not a lot of damage from the "hit and run" raids and doodlebugs later on.'

Gosport, he recalled, was 'careworn and run down, the scars of bombing were still very much in evidence'. But with the war still going on in the Far East, Portsmouth Harbour was still full of ships coming and going. They settled back into their old house and decorated it with a new coat of paint. Later that summer, after VJ Day, Tony went on his bike with his friend Dicky Barton to Stokes Bay, immediately southwest of Gosport: 'It was the end of summer, but in spite of this, there was no-one there, the Army had pulled out, leaving behind all the detritus of war. There were lots of broken down cannibalized lorries, several large invasion barges moored alongside jetties, the remains of the great Mulberry Harbours, tool and rubbish strewn about everywhere, and a general air of desolation, with not a soul to be seen.'[8]

More rationing was introduced in Britain in May with less cooking fat (reduced from two ounces to one) and less bacon (from four ounces to three). Less meat was available in 1945 than there had been in 1944. But Kathleen Tipper discovered on a trip to Kensington that 'those people with money can live very well indeed still'.[9] The only positive news for the general population was that there would be more fish because the trawlers could now sail the seas without fear. But the outlook for the future of food was generally bleak. The headline in the *Evening Standard* on 9 August 1945 was 'Food problem is more acute'. The article went on to explain: 'Because of a marked deterioration in the world food position, the entire outlook for the 1945–46 crop year at the moment can only be viewed with "grave misgivings" and the sugar situation is expected to be the most critical of any year since the outbreak of war.'[10]

Edmund Wilson was surprised to find one shop in Holborn, Central London, selling an unusual item: 'rows and rows of dead crows. That was apparently all they sold in

185

that shop.'[11] He rented a room in Mayfair, and every night, as he walked back to his lodgings, he 'ran the gauntlet of the innumerable prostitutes that lined Piccadilly and Green Park. They would brush with "Come heah, sweetie!" or a simple "Hullo!" in their low quiet London voices that, with their pale dimly-looming forms, made them seem a part of the night like moths.'[12]

When he returned to America after a few months in Europe, Wilson found the contrast startling: 'I noticed characteristics of the Americans of which I had not been conscious when I left. They were much larger than Europeans – enormous, they looked to me now; their faces were insufficiently focussed and their personalities lacking in flavor; they were doing a good many things expertly, but in a way which made them seem rather uninteresting.'[13]

For others, the idea of going home was not a straightforward one. Kathleen Tipper volunteered in the evening at her local YMCA in South London where many foreign service men socialised, especially Australians, New Zealanders and Canadians. One of her regulars was nervous about sailing home. On 20 August, she wrote in her diary:

> 'At the Club this evening discovered Geoffrey who was due to go home some weeks ago. He confessed that he had been out merrymaking and didn't get the telegram which put forward the sailing, so now he is waiting for the next ship. I don't think he was sorry and I suspect that he is a little afraid of going home – he wonders if he will be able to pick up his work and married life after five years away. This is a common enough problem, but it makes me miserable because G is such a nice fellow, who has really led an

exemplary life here, and obviously his wife is the same sort, yet he is frightened to go home.'[14]

Captain I. A. Wallace had been serving in Burma and remembered his long trip home back to Britain:

'Suddenly my repatriation orders came through. The rain was now deluging down every day, but the main road to Rangoon was just passable. I took ship from Rangoon to Calcutta. There I spent a spell in hospital as a jungle sore had developed into an abscess and had to be excised. From Calcutta I had a remarkable train journey to Deolali with an alcoholic Australian, an Anglo-Indian woman with a small baby and a very upstage nurse who lived in Park Lane. Then a very over-crowded troopship back to Southampton via the Suez Canal.'[15]

The idea of resuming their previous lives again was enormously appealing to many soldiers, sailors and airmen, especially, no doubt, if their previous lives had been as a film star. This did not apply to many in the forces, but it did apply to David Niven, though he was also rather nervous about whether he could remember how to be an actor:

'The British Army gave me:
    1 suit, worsted grey
    1 hat, Homburg, brown
    2 shorts, poplin, with collars
    1 tie, striped
    1 pair shoes, walking, black –
    and above all my FREEDOM.

'Such was the stringency of the clothing rationing that Major General Robert Laycock, DSO, Chief of Combined Operations, asked me if I could spare him my discarded khaki shirts.

'It was an unbelievable feeling to be free again. Primmie was due to have the second baby in November so we took little David and treated ourselves to a holiday of luxury at the Ferryboat Inn on the Helford River. Then I cabled Goldwyn to the effect that I was "available".

'Goldwyn generously replied that he was giving me a new five-year contract at a mouth-watering figure and that in the meanwhile he was loaning me out to Michael Powell and Emeric Pressburger to star in *A Matter of Life and Death* (*Stairway to Heaven* in the US).

'This was a huge relief because although I had been disguising it from Primmie, I was extremely nervous about my future. Six months is too long for an actor to be out of business – six years is almost certain disaster.

'A whole new breed of stars had taken over the movie audiences and at thirty-five I had good reason to be worried. I was also highly apprehensive lest I had forgotten how to do it.'[16]

Tony Benn, who was not yet twenty-one, was keen to resume his education reading Philosophy, Politics and Economics at New College, Oxford, where he had already spent three terms before joining the RAF in 1943. However, he first had a short spell with the Fleet Air Arm (the flying arm of the Royal Navy):

'At about that time, when the European war was over,' he recalls in his memoirs, 'and RAF pilots were being made redundant, I applied to transfer to the Fleet Air Arm in order to be posted to the Far East and was sent to the Royal Naval College for a "knife and fork" course, so-called because the Navy did not believe that the RAF were gentlemen, and had to be trained as such if they were to be acceptable in the Senior Service.'[17]

He was soon given a class B release to return to university, which he did that autumn. He noted: 'Post-war Oxford was quite unlike the university in pre-war years, for there was a telescoping of generations, servicemen who had served, and some of whom were wounded in the war rubbing shoulders with youngsters straight from school.'[18]

In total, there were approximately four million service men and women that needed demobilising. Ernest Bevin, who at the start of the summer was the Minister of Labour in the coalition government, had initially planned for a gradual demobilisation programme over a period of two years which would take place between the defeat of Germany and that of Japan. However, this was soon speeded up when the British realised that the war against Japan would be over much sooner than initially anticipated. A week after VE Day, on 16 May, Bevin announced that releases would begin on 18 June, with the initial forecast to demobilise three-quarters of a million by the end of the year. Immediately after VJ Day, though, that estimate was increased so that more people could come out of the services more quickly. An article in the *Daily Telegraph* on 18 August reported that there would be '1,100,000 Out of Forces by End of Year', that the 'Speed-up plan will free 100,000 women', and that the engineering industries would be given top priority for making use of demobilised men:

'This news was contained last night in the first official government announcement about rate of demobilisation since Mr Bevin, then Minister of Labour, first set the target on May 16. It declared:

> '"The following statement is given by the Ministry of Labour and National Service tonight in response to inquiries arising out of the Prime Minister's announcement in the debate in the address in the House of Commons yesterday that the rate of release of men and women from the Forces and auxiliary services would be accelerated.
>
> '"Steps have now been taken to increase the rate of release, and from the first provisional estimates it appears that by the end of the year the number of men and women released [in class A alone] will not be far short of 1,000,000, of which about 100,000 will be women."'[19]

The two classes of demobilisation defined priority. Class B were priority releases – people who needed to be released to start building houses, for instance, or those, like Tony Benn, who wanted to start the new university term. The one clause in their release was that they could be recalled if they left the trade or university course to which they had been allocated. Class A releases meant everybody else, but after the debacle of demobilisation at the end of the First World War, where the men with the longest service records were most often the last to be demobilised, a new system was worked out. Age and length of service together were taken into account with two months of service equal to a year of age, meaning that young men who had done a lot of service would be treated equally with older men (who were more likely to have families) who had done less service. Young men with a short service record would generally be the last to be demobilised and for some it did take a long time.

It took Norman Longmate 764 days to make his way home from the Army.[20] Major T. C. Howes faced months of boredom in Greece before he was demobbed in 1946:

> 'Demobilisation plans were published. Each man was given a release number, dependent on age and length of service. Among the officers in the battalion only Tom Blackwell, the quartermaster, and Harvey Draper had a lower release number than me. I was Group 22. "Other ranks" of that number were released n September 1945. Officers were declared to be "operationally vital" and our releases were postponed.
>
> 'It became a pretty dull existence. Our only job was to guard petrol supplies at the docks. The rest of the time was spent in parades, cricket and football. I started a photography class.'[21]

Every demobbed man in 1945 got eight weeks' pay on his release as well as £12 worth of civilian clothing, which at the time, amid great shortages of clothes, was highly prized. The double-breasted pinstripe three-piece suit looked rather gaudy to many civilians – a little like something out of a 1930s gangster movie – and they were often either too big or too small. As part of their clothing allowance, demobbed men also got two shirts, a tie, shoes, a raincoat and a hat – either a felt fedora or a flat cap. Some sold their new clothes for cash on the black market. J. B. Priestley's 1945 novel about three demobbed servicemen resuming their civilian lives was called *Three Men in New Suits.*

In the war industries, there was also an order of priority for who got released first: the first priority was housewives needed at home, the wives of demobbed servicemen, women over sixty and men over sixty-five.

Juliet Gardiner tells the story of Zelma Katin, who worked as a 'clippie' during the war (clipping people's tickets). Katin said that she

> 'was glad I have done this sort of war work ... like millions of men and women in uniform I cannot pretend I am liking it. Perhaps the sacrifice and hardship are giving us a strength which will enrich us in the future and toughen us for the struggle that lies ahead. I confess, I am not only thinking of a future for humanity but a future for myself. I want to lie in bed until eight o'clock, to eat a meal slowly, to sweep floors when they are dirty, to sit in front of the fire, to walk on the hills, to go shopping of an afternoon, to gossip at odd minutes.'[22]

There were certain rules that applied so that people – perhaps a male 'clippie' who had been serving in the army, for instance – could get jobs back that they had left behind to serve in the forces, as long as they had been in the role within four weeks of entering service. At the BBC, the number of people in 'acting grades' had grown enormously during the war as jobs were left open for people to return. By autumn, though, the corporation was still struggling to move people from acting into substantive roles. The Director General sent a memo to staff outlining the problems that he faced:

'Proposals for the establishment of unestablished staff cannot be brought forward until a number of factors are clearer than they are at present. But now that the war is over I feel an appreciable measure of unnecessary penalisation is being imposed upon established staff by the rigid adherence to nothing but acting grades for all appointments since 1939.

'It was undoubtedly necessary throughout the war to suspend substantive promotion for established staff. But the fact that the war lasted six years has meant that a large body of "acting grades" has accumulated. Some staff, it is true, have been fortunate as they have owed their promotion to the absence of their colleagues and to purely wartime conditions. But others have been unfortunate as the war has suspended for so long the substantive promotion they would otherwise undoubtedly have gained.'[23]

BBC war correspondent Richard Dimbleby found himself frozen out of the post-war BBC at the age of thirty-two: 'I am now a free man,' he wrote in the autumn of 1945, 'and in some ways not awfully happy about it. It's rather a wrench after nearly ten years.'[24] After six years covering some of the main developments in the war and seeing an incredible range of human tragedy and triumph, he had become a significant celebrity, and was looking forward to interesting work when he returned back from Germany. Instead, though, the BBC offered him his old job back and no increase in salary. According to his son Jonathan, Richard Dimbleby was the victim of a new editorial austerity in the newsroom; his flamboyance and occasional bursts of opinionated coverage – like that at

Belsen and Berlin – did not fit in with the new philosophy. Jonathan Dimbleby quotes a statement from the BBC: 'Now that the war is over and party politics have begun again the importance of objectivity in BBC News becomes more than ever apparent; the objectivity of BBC News involves a most rigid and absolute avoidance of expressions of editorial opinion, combined with an equally rigid refusal to omit or bowdlerize any news that is of sober public interest.'[25]

Leaflets were produced for servicemen and women to give them advice about how to reintegrate with society. Given what many in the services had been doing before the end of the war, it was going to be a dramatic transformation. Written with great precision, the leaflet explained:

'The purpose of this pamphlet is to help you in the change over from Service to Civilian life. It contains information on a number of Services and other matters which will be of importance to you in the period immediately following your release from the Forces.

'If you were in a job before joining up, it explains what steps you must take to safeguard your rights to reinstatement, or if you have no job to return to it tells you how to set about getting one.'

They were advised to keep their uniform: 'in case of an unforeseen National Emergency you may be recalled to the Colours and you will need them. It is particularly necessary for officers to keep their outfit in good order. In the event of their being called up the Government will not give another outfit allowance.'

Many men in the services had been abroad for long periods and in that time might have contracted venereal disease. In order to limit outbreaks of disease on their return, the leaflet gave advice on the subject: 'If you have ever suffered from any form of this disease be sure that you have completed the treatment and observations recommended by your medical officer; the observation period for gonorrhea is a minimum of three months and for syphilis two years. Remember that disappearance of signs and symptoms does not mean that you are cured.'[26]

There were Resettlement Advice Offices set up across the country in order to help people reintegrate into the community and these were overwhelmed with men asking for advice. Towards the end of 1945, more than 30,000 men a week would visit a Resettlement Advice Office where they could speak to an advisory officer: 'Whatever your problem (no matter how unusual it may be or how doubtful you feel about getting help from an "official" service) the Resettlement Advisory Officers will be ready to do everything in their power to help you solve your difficulties. These officers have been specially trained and many of them are ex-Servicemen and women.'[27]

Another guide for the recently demobbed – 'Call Me Mister' – warned: 'Coming out of the Forces into civilian life is rather like plunging into a tepid bath. One finds neither the icy, tingling invigoration of a cold shower enjoyed on first enlisting, nor the steamy, heart-warming glow of a hot bath enjoyed on leave.'[28]

The new government's commitment to full employment meant that almost everyone leaving the service did get a job as they returned to civilian life. But for those coming home, the vision of a New Jerusalem that the Labour Party was trying to build from the wreckage was not always obvious. The first bank holiday after VE Day – on Whit Monday, 21 May – offered a taste of what post-war holidays might be like. Brighton was full of tourists, but much of the beach was closed because of mines. Up to the end of May 1945, sixty men had died on southeast coastlines clearing the beaches of mines and other live ordinance. It was only in July that Brighton beach was completely cleared and safe again.[29] Many of the pubs, restaurants and hotels were closed. Even buckets and spades had to be hired because their manufacture had been stopped during the war. One positive development for day-trippers and other holidaymakers was that a petrol ration was reintroduced which meant those people with vehicles found find it easier drive to places like Brighton, if they wanted to go. It doesn't sound like it was a universally pleasant experience. One Mass Observation diarist described VJ Day in Bognor:

'It's raining heavily. The bus going to Bognor is packed with women carrying shopping baskets. At the various bus stops people stand in the pouring rain waiting to get on, but the conductress can only find room for a few and this gives cause for much ill-feeling. Snappily the bus conductress retorts:

"It's not my fault it's VJ Day today and the shops have to close early. The government should have thought of that."

'And there's much sympathy for the bus conductress.'[30]

On one section of the coast near Durham in May, where a beach had been opened for the public for just two hours, 'the population of the whole of that part of County Durham converged on that section, or so it seemed. To paddle in the shallow water it was necessary to find an empty space and defend it against all comers.'[31]

At Hoylake on 16 August, K. M. Carruthers was disappointed that 'there was no ice-cream to be had (due to recent government price control?) and the promenade café was packed to the doors'.[32]

Kathleen Tipper went to the seaside for the bank holiday at the start of August. 'This afternoon we tried Seaford,' she wrote in her diary, 'and found it absolutely deserted, not surprising when the rain began to fall again, and what is more miserable than the seaside on a wet day?' At her hotel, she noted a number of guests expressing dissatisfaction with the government:

> 'Some of the people in the hotel were having an amusing conversation this morning about politics, and naturally they took a poor view of our present government. They seem to find it necessary to talk in whispers, and are hoping all the worst for Britain during these next few years, in order that the Labour party may be discredited. Some of these people are quite nice, but so smug and selfish, they think only of themselves, and seemed terribly concerned that they be called upon to make no more sacrifices, for, as one lady said: "It is enough of a sacrifice that I have to spend a holiday in England, and at a place like this, when I have always been abroad, etc."'[33]

Yet there were many consolations of peacetime – both for day-trippers and others as well: London Zoo, Kew Gardens and Richmond Park were all reopened for the first time since the Blitz; high-level cricket resumed in the form of the Victory Test series between England and the Australian services; and important cultural works were once again being written, published, premiered and performed. In other words, public life of the kind that was known before the war was slowly being remembered and re-enacted.

After serving as a correspondent in Germany with the *Observer*, George Orwell returned to Britain to cover the election. In the summer, he resumed writing a novel that he had started the previous year: *Nineteen Eighty-Four*. Orwell's publisher, Frederic Warburg reported that on 25 June 1945 (Orwell's 42nd birthday), Orwell had 'written the first twelve pages of his new novel'.[34] Having seen the carnage in Germany first hand, witnessed the authoritarianism of the Soviet Union and the terrible aftermath of the war in Europe, lines from *Nineteen Eighty-Four* like 'If you want a picture of the future, imagine a boot stamping on a human face – forever', must have seemed particularly apposite to Orwell that summer and the central protagonist of his novel, Winston Smith, is thirty-nine years old in 1984, meaning that he must have been born in 1944 or 1945. He is a child of that age.[35]

Orwell's wife Eileen had died in March and he was left alone to look after their adopted son, Richard, who was a year old in May 1945. 'The next thing is to find a nurse for him which is next door to impossible,' Orwell wrote in a letter on 11 May.[36] Later that summer, as relations between the Soviet Union and the West continued to deteriorate, Orwell's satire of Stalin, *Animal Farm*, was published. Evelyn Waugh's novel *Brideshead Revisited* and Jean-Paul Sartre's novel *The Age of Reason* were also published for the first time in 1945. On 5 June, Benjamin Britten's opera *Peter Grimes* had its premiere at the newly reopened Sadler's Wells Theatre in London. It was an enormous critical and box-office success. Edmund Wilson went to see it later on in June and wrote that 'I felt the power of a musical gift and a dramatic imagination that woke my interest and commanded my attention'.[37]

Iris Murdoch wrote breathlessly on 1 June, not about music, but about paintings:

'They have brought back about 50 pictures to the National Gallery. Oh heavenly bliss! Sir Kenneth Clark's favourites, I suppose. Well, they're alright. The Van Eyck man & pregnant wife. Bellini & Mantegna Agobnies. Titian Noli me Tangere. Ruben's Bacchus & Ariadne. El Greco Agony, Rembrandt portraits of self & of an old lady. His small Woman Bathing (lovely!) A delicious Claude fading into blue blue blue – blue lake, mountains, sky. Incredible distances to breathe. Two Vermeers, so blue & lemon, honey stuff, girls at the Virginals. And then oh more Bellini & Rubens, & then the Ruisdaels the Hobbemas, & chaps like Cuyp that one had forgotten about. I still feel delirious with the first shock. It felt <u>really</u> like peace. And all the people wandering about looking dazed.'[38]

She mentions in the same diary entry that she had also just seen Denis Healey, then the Labour candidate for Pudsey (later, of course, Chancellor of the Exchequer 1974–79): 'He looked bronzed & sleek & tough & handsome & very pleased with himself. I was glad to see him.'[39]

Kathleen Tipper was very keen on cricket and went to Lord's a number of times during the summer of 1945 to watch the five Victory Tests between an England side and an

Australian Services XI. These were not given full Test status because the Australians did not feel that they had a full-strength side. However, the Australians were still extremely strong and much of their team were to become mainstays of the Australian test side in the post-war years, including the 1948 'invincibles' side. At the YMCA where she volunteered, Kathleen regularly talked to Australians, New Zealanders and South Africans about cricket. On 26 June, she wrote in her diary that she 'talked to some Aussies, ex POWs who were keen cricketers – they are off to Sheffield for the test next weekend. They were full of cricket, and were making me laugh with tales of their matches in camp 344, which was in Poland. One of them said, "rather a change playing cricket there after Brisbane."'[40]

Ten days earlier, she had been at one of the three Victory matches that were played at Lord's that summer. 'Not very promising this morning,' she wrote in her diary, 'but we gathered our things together and packed food, etc. and went off, getting to Lords around 10.45, to find the ground still practically empty. Actually the crowd never got very large, it must have been rather disappointing for the Australians, who certainly deserve a larger audience. Keith Miller, as usual, did well, but the day's honours went to Wyatt for a grand innings.'[41]

On 14 July, she was at Lord's once more, where she and her two companions 'got our favourite seats, and after covering them carefully with macs, retired as the rain came on. It rained till nearly 12, then we sat on our perfectly dry seats, the players came out and the thousands of people there settled down to a nice day.'[42] Two days' later, at the YMCA, she 'had some arguments with New Zealanders about their lovely country (I find myself supporting lovely Britain with fervour when they will keep calling their own wretched country "Eden"), with some sailors about the morals of girls in this country, and with some Australians about their cricketers.'[43]

The series was ultimately drawn with two wins a piece and one draw, but the momentum was with Australia and Keith Miller, at the age of twenty-six, was one of Australia's great finds and scored the most runs out of any batsmen in the series – 514 in total. The final match at Lord's drew a crowd of more than 90,000.

Reunions were often keenly anticipated, but there were also worries – had a bored wife at home taken another lover? Had a husband in the army changed so much because of what he had seen that he was no longer the same person that he was? Might a husband have brought back venereal disease or have fathered a child in France or Germany? And then there were the children who could barely remember their fathers. These men, when they did come home, were now strangers to them, just as they often were to their wives as well. For Ella Glen in Beeston, seeing her husband again, who had been injured in action in Italy serving with the Coldstream Guards, was an immensely happy moment for her. But she soon realised, as did many other wives with their husbands, that her husband did not want to talk about the war or have anything else to do with it. 'I kept all my husband's letters that he sent to me during the war,' she told me. 'There were suitcases full of them. But when we moved house my husband took the whole case out and burned it – everything to do with the war he wanted to destroy; he wasn't a military man.'[44]

According to Juliet Gardiner, more than two million women had lived without their husbands during the war; many had also learned to look after their children on their own.[45] They had become independent and so a man moving back into the house required an enormous adjustment. For men coming home expecting tea on the table, roast dinners on a Sunday and everything to be the same as it had been before the war, it was generally a disappointment.

One of the things that was essential in trying to build harmony into marriages that had been resumed after a long hiatus, was decent housing. This was a commitment of the new Labour government in 1945 and Ernest Bevin, speaking in 1943, had stated that it was a basic need that had to be fulfilled: 'The one essential thing if you are going to stop moral disaster after the war is to enable these young folk to start off under reasonable conditions of home life as quickly as possible.'[46] However, the houses that were promised were not built as quickly as planned and young families remained marooned on waiting lists for many years.

There were also many instances of happy homecomings. Mary Tisdall had celebrated VE Day so boisterously because she was happy about the thought of the man she wanted to be with coming home. He was in the RAF. The following year, they married and remained together until his death.[47] Sergeant Ron Owen returned from Palestine on VJ Day and arranged to meet his sweetheart Eileen under the clock at Waterloo station. They had not seen one another for six years. He remembered that he hid at first so that she could not see him – 'I wanted to check that she hadn't got fat' – but he was reassured when he saw her. They got married ten days' later and went on honeymoon for a few days in Fowey in Cornwall.[48]

Most evacuees had already returned home by the summer of 1945 as the final threat to British civilians of V-I flying bombs had receded in the late winter. But for some, it wasn't until late 1945 that they headed home. Patricia Negin Berger was sent to boarding schools outside London – first in Essex and then in Wales – from the age of six. She remembered: 'Returning to London after the war the train seemed to be saying "I'm going home, I'm going home", instead of "clickety clack clickety clack". It wasn't what I'd dreamed it would be: from 1939 to 1945 I hadn't been home nor was my mother used to having three children to deal with.'[49]

Other evacuees had come from further afield – an operation to airlift 732 Holocaust survivors is described by Martin Gilbert in his book *The Boys*. On 14 August 1945, Lancaster Bombers brought 300 young Jewish boys and girls from Prague to Crosby-on-Eden, near Lancaster. They were then taken to a hostel at Windermere in the Lake District. Sixteen-year-old Arek Hersh, a survivor of a number of camps including Auschwitz and Buchenwald, remembered:

> 'After several days our clothes came and we all got fitted out in the proper sized suits. With all the good food, plenty of fresh milk and physical exercise, I was soon aware that I was growing taller. I used to love to swim in the lake but the water was ice-cold. We even had a football team and our rabbi was "in goal". I would go for long walks exploring the local countryside which was so beautiful, and we were taken on coach rides to the seaside.'[50]

Life in post-war Britain may have been challenging in many respects, but the existence of these survivors among the British people was a reminder that the consolations of peace in Britain – however austere – were almost always preferable to the terrible consequences of war.

Chapter 8

Little Boy and Fat Man

Two Bombs that Changed the World

'We knew the world would not be the same. Few people laughed, few people cried, most people were silent. I remembered the line from the Hindu scripture, the Bhagavad-Gita. Vishnu is trying to persuade the Prince that he should do his duty and to impress him takes on his multi-armed form and says, "Now I am become Death, the destroyer of worlds." I suppose we all thought that, one way or another.'[1]

Robert Oppenheimer

'At 8:15 am, I saw a bluish-white flash like a magnesium flare outside the window. I remember the sensation of floating in the air. As I regained consciousness in the total silence and darkness, I realised I was pinned in the ruins of the collapsed building.'[2]

Satsuko Thurlow

Many of the people of Hiroshima woke on the morning of 6 August as they had on previous mornings that summer. It was a hot, sunny and humid day. But around a third of the city's population would never wake again. For every other person who was in the city that day and survived the initial blast, their lives would be changed forever and many thousands more amongst them would die by the end of the year as a direct result of the bomb. The most destructive weapon that the world had ever seen – codenamed Little Boy – was dropped above the city at 8.15 am – the first time that an atomic bomb had been used in warfare and only the second time that one had ever been detonated. Just three days later another was dropped on Nagasaki.

Dr Michihiko Hachiya was Director of the Hiroshima Communications Hospital and was lying exhausted on his living-room floor in his home not far from the hospital on the morning of 6 August, having spent the night on duty as the hospital air warden.[3] Setsuko Nakamura was a thirteen-year-old schoolgirl, one of 30 schoolgirls who had been assigned to help at the army headquarters in Hiroshima.[4] At 8.15 am, they were just about to receive instructions on what they would be asked to do that day. Father Wilhelm Kleinsorge, a German priest, was sitting down to read a magazine on the top floor of the three-storey mission house where he lived, after having breakfast with the other priests who lived in the mission house with him.[5] Yoshitaka Kawamoto was also thirteen years old; he was in his classroom when the bomb was dropped.

All that most of them were aware of in the next few moments was a bright flash of light. And after that everything was different. Dr Hachiya remembered:

'Suddenly, a strong flash of light startled me – and then another. So well does one recall little things that I remember vividly how a stone lantern in the garden became brilliantly lit and I debated whether this light

206

was caused by a magnesium flare or sparks from a passing trolley.

'Garden shadows disappeared. The view where a moment before had been so bright and sunny was now dark and hazy. Through swirling dust I could barely discern a wooden column that had supported one corner of my house. It was leaning crazily and the roof sagged dangerously.

'Moving instinctively, I tried to escape, but rubble and fallen timbers barred the way. By picking my way cautiously I managed to reach the *roka* [an outside hallway] and stepped down into my garden. A profound weakness overcame me, so I stopped to regain my strength. To my surprise I discovered that I was completely naked. How odd! Where were my drawers and undershirt?

'What had happened?

'All over the right side of my body I was cut and bleeding. A large splinter was protruding from a mangled wound in my thigh, and something warm trickled into my mouth. My cheek was torn, I discovered as I felt it gingerly, with the lower lip laid wide open. Embedded in my neck was a sizable fragment of glass which I matter-of-factly dislodged, and with the detachment of one stunned and shocked I studied it and my blood-stained hand.

'Where was my wife?

'Suddenly thoroughly alarmed, I began to yell for her: "Yaeko-san! Yaeko-san! Where are you?" Blood began to spurt. Had my carotid artery been cut? Would I bleed to death? Frightened and irrational, I called out again "It's a five-hundred-ton bomb!

Yaeko-san, where are you? A five-hundred-ton bomb has fallen!"

'Yaeko-san, pale and frightened, her clothes torn and blood stained, emerged from the ruins of our house holding her elbow. Seeing her, I was reassured. My own panic assuaged, I tried to reassure her.

'"We'll be all right," I exclaimed. "Only let's get out of here as fast as we can."

'She nodded, and I motioned for her to follow me.'[6]

Yoshitaka Kawamoto, who had just arrived at school that morning, saw a little more than most – he got a glimpse of the Enola Gay bomber far above the city before the weapon that the airplane dropped was unleashed on Hiroshima's unsuspecting inhabitants. He wrote,

'One of my classmates, I think his name is Fujimoto … muttered something and pointed outside the window, saying, "A B-29 is coming." He pointed outside with his finger. So I began to get up from my chair and asked him, "Where is it?" Looking in the direction that he was pointing towards, I got up on my feet, but I was not yet in an upright position when it happened. All I can remember was a pale lightning flash for two or three seconds. Then, I collapsed. I don't know much time passed before I came to. It was awful, awful. The smoke was coming in from somewhere above the debris. Sandy dust was flying around. I was trapped under the debris and I was in terrible pain and that's probably why I came to. I couldn't move, not even an inch. Then, I heard about ten of my surviving classmates singing our school song. I remember that.

I could hear sobs. Someone was calling his mother. But those who were still alive were singing the school song for as long as they could. I think I joined the chorus. We thought that someone would come and help us out. That's why we were singing a school song so loud. But nobody came to help, and we stopped singing one by one. In the end, I was singing alone.'[7]

Satsuko Nakamura, who later married in Canada and changed her name to Thurlow, remembered:

'At 8:15am, I saw a bluish-white flash like a magnesium flare outside the window. I remember the sensation of floating in the air. As I regained consciousness in the total silence and darkness, I realised I was pinned in the ruins of the collapsed building. I could not move. I knew I was faced with death. Strangely the feeling I had was not panic but serenity. Gradually I began to hear my classmates' faint cries for help, "Mother, help me!", "God, help me!" Then suddenly, I felt hands touching me and loosening the timbers that pinned me. A man's voice said, "Don't give up! I'm trying to free you! Keep moving! See the light coming through that opening. Crawl toward it and try to get out!" By the time I got out, the ruins were on fire. This meant that most of my classmates who were with me in the same room were burned alive. A solider ordered me and a few surviving girls to escape to the nearby hills.'[8]

In his book *Hiroshima*, John Hersey described how Father Kleinsgorge never properly remembered how he got out of the house that he had been in when the explosion happened:

'The next things he was conscious of were that he was wandering around in the mission's vegetable garden in his underwear, bleeding slightly from small cuts along his left flank; that all the buildings round about had fallen down except the Jesuits' mission house, which had long before been braced and double-braced by a priest named Gropper who was terrified of earthquakes; that the day had turned dark; and that Murata-*san*, the housekeeper, was nearby, crying over and over, "*Shu Jesusu, awaremi tamai!* Our Lord Jesus, have pity on us!"'[9]

At around 31,000 feet above the city, and already some miles away after they had turned sharply to escape the force of the explosion, the twelve crew members of the Enola Gay Boeing B-29 Superfortress bomber watched as a cloud rose from below. It was not, according to the pilot that day, Colonel Paul Tibbets, a mushroom cloud of the type customarily associated with atomic explosions. Instead, he described it as 'a stringer. It just came up. It was black as hell, and it had light and colours and white in it and grey colour in it and the top was like a folded-up Christmas tree'.[10] The Enola Gay was named after Tibbets' mother, who in turn was named after a character in an obscure novel by Mary Young Ridenbaugh called *Enola; or, Her Fatal Mistake*. The book is introduced with a poem:

Oh, fatal day – oh, day of sorrow,
It was no trouble she could borrow;
But in the future she could see
The clouds of infelicity.[11]

Tibbets, already a highly experienced pilot, was recruited to the Manhattan Project – the United States project to develop atomic weapons – in September 1944. He was asked to put together a crew to drop the new weapons on targets which at that time were yet to be decided, though according to Tibbets, in an interview with American writer Studs Terkel, an undesignated target in Europe was mentioned as a possibility at that point. He knew straightaway that some of the crew he had previously flown with in Europe would be coming with him, and among them were Tom Ferebee (bombardier), Theodore "Dutch" van Kirk (navigator) and Wyatt Duzenbury (flight engineer). They were all in the bomber on 6 August when the bomb was dropped.

> 'The shockwave was coming up at us after we turned,' remembered Tibbets in an interview in 2002, 'and the tailgunner said, "Here it comes." About the time he said that, we got this kick in the ass. I had accelerometers installed in all airplanes to record the magnitude of the bomb. It hit us with two and a half G. Next day, when we got figures from the scientists on what they had learned from all the things, they said, "When that bomb exploded, your airplane was 10 and half miles away from it."'[12]

Terkel asked Tibbets if he had any idea of what had taken place below them. He replied: 'Pandemonium! I think it's best stated by one of the historians, who said: "In one microsecond, the city of Hiroshima didn't exist."'[13]

After Setsuko Nakamura was dug out of the wreckage of the building that she had been in, she was able to start to take in the damage around her:

'I turned around and saw the outside world. Although it was morning, it looked like twilight because of the dust and smoke in the air. People at a distance saw the mushroom cloud and heard a thunderous roar. But I did not see the cloud because I was in it. I did not hear the roar, just the deadly silence broken only by the groans of the injured. Streams of stunned people were slowly shuffling from the city centre toward nearby hills. They were naked or tattered, burned, blackened and swollen. Eyes were swollen shut and some had eyeballs hanging out of their sockets. They were bleeding, ghostly figures like a slow-motion image from an old silent movie. Many held their hands above the level of their hearts to lessen the throbbing pain of their burns. Strips of skin and flesh hung like ribbons from their bones. Often these ghostly figures would collapse in heaps never to rise again. With a few surviving classmates I joined the procession carefully stepping over the dead and dying.

'At the foot of the hill was an army training ground about the size of two football fields. Literally every bit of it was covered with injured and dying who were desperately begging, often in faint whispers, "Water, water, please give me water". But we had no containers to carry water. We went to a nearby stream to wash the blood and dirt from our bodies. Then we tore off parts of our clothes, soaked them with water and hurried back to hold them to the mouths of the dying who desperately sucked the moisture. We kept busy at this task of giving some comfort to the dying all day. There were no medical supplies of any kind and we did not see any doctor or nurse. When darkness fell, we sat on the hillside, numbed by the massive scale of death and suffering we had witnessed, watching the entire city burn. In the background were the low rhythmic whispers from the swollen lips of the ghostly figures, still begging for water.'[14]

The force of the explosion had literally stripped the clothes from many people's bodies, leaving them entirely naked. Others had their clothes in shreds. On some people's skin, the heat of the explosion had left burn marks in the pattern of the clothes that they had been wearing: for many women wearing kimonos with flowers on them, the flowers had been imprinted on their skin. Dr Hachiya was naked as he and his wife tried to walk to the hospital where he worked. He remembered:

'We started out, but after twenty or thirty steps I had to stop. My breath became short, my heart pounded, and my legs gave way under me. An overpowering thirst seized me and I begged Yaeko-san to find me some water. But there was no water to be found. After a little my strength somewhat returned and we were able to go on.

'I was still naked, and although I did not feel the least bit of shame, I was disturbed to realise that modesty had deserted me. On rounding a corner we came upon a soldier standing idly in the street. He had a towel draped across his shoulder, and I asked if he would give it to me to cover my nakedness. The soldier surrendered the towel quite willingly but said not a word. A little later I lost the towel, and Yaeko-san took off her apron and tied it around my loins.

'Our progress towards the hospital was interminably slow, until finally, my legs, stiff from drying blood, refused to carry me farther. The strength, even the will, to go on deserted me, so I told my wife, who was almost as badly hurt as I, to go on alone. This she objected to, but there was no choice. She had to go ahead and try to find someone to come back for me.

'Yaeko-san looked into my face for a moment, and then, without saying a word, turned away and began running towards the hospital. Once, she looked back and waved and in a moment she was swallowed up in the gloom. It was quite dark now, and with my wife gone, a feeling of dreadful loneliness overcame me.

'I must have gone out of my head lying there in the road because the next thing I recall was discovering that the clot on my thigh had been dislodged and blood was again spurting from the wound.

'I pressed my hand to the bleeding area and after a while the bleeding stopped and I felt better.

'Could I go on?

'I tried. It was all a nightmare – my wounds, the darkness, the road ahead. My movements were ever so slow; only my mind was running at top speed.

'In time I came to an open space where the houses had been removed to make a fire lane. Through the dim light I could make out ahead of me the hazy outlines of the Communications Bureau's big concrete building, and beyond it the hospital. My spirits rose because I knew that now someone would find me; and if I should die, at least my body would be found. I paused to rest. Gradually things around me came into focus. There were the shadowy forms of people, some of whom looked like walking ghosts. Others moved as though in pain, like scarecrows, their arms held out from their bodies with forearms and hands dangling. These people puzzled me until I suddenly realised that they had been burned and were holding their arms out to prevent the painful friction of raw surfaces rubbing together. A naked woman carrying a naked baby came into view. I averted my gaze. Perhaps they had been in the bath. But then I saw a naked man, and it occurred to me that, like myself, some strange thing had deprived them of their clothes. An old woman lay near me with an expression of suffering on her face; but she made no sound. Indeed, one thing was common to everyone I saw – complete silence.'[15]

Father Kleinsorge was walking around the vegetable garden immediately after the explosion in a state of confusion and when the Father Superior approached him he asked, 'Where are the rest?'[16] All around them buildings were on fire. The two other priests that lived in the same mission house as Father Kleinsorge both emerged, although one of them, Father Schiffer, was seriously wounded with blood pouring from a head wound. The priests, along with thousands of other survivors, made their way to Asano Park. John Hersey described the scene:

'All day, people poured into Asano Park. This private estate was far enough away from the explosion so that its bamboos, pines, laurel, and maples were still alive, and the green place invited refugees – partly because they believed that if the Americans came back, they would bomb only buildings; partly because the foliage seemed a centre of coolness and life, and the estate's exquisitely precise rock gardens, with their quiet pools and arching bridges, were very Japanese, normal, secure; and also partly (according to some who were there) because of an irresistible, atavistic urge to hide under leaves.'[17]

Great hot winds scoured the people who were still alive. Father Kleinsorge saw a group of around twenty soldiers who were all in a terrible state, sitting in amongst some bushes. They were probably anti-aircraft personnel and had been looking up as the bomb exploded above the city so that the blast caught them square in their faces, producing profoundly shocking results. Their eye sockets were hollow, their eyeballs melted and the fluid from their melted eyes had rolled down their cheeks. They were unable to move their damaged mouths and so the priest cut straws for them from plant stems so that they could at least drink some water.[18]

Many of the survivors in the park – no doubt including these soldiers – would not live; people were badly burned and lots of them vomited for much of the day. They had radiation poisoning. Some died from this quite quickly. Others took weeks, months and even years to die. For young people who survived the bomb and lived into their old age, they were mostly beset with health problems for the rest of their lives. Father Kleinsgore was one of these, though he did also live for another thirty-two years after the bomb, dying in 1977. Dr Michihiko Hachiya lived until the age of seventy-seven, dying in 1980, while at the time of writing Setsuko Thurlow is still alive and living in Canada.

The degree of destruction did not just shock the people of Hiroshima; across the world, people were horrified, astounded and amazed by what had happened on 6 August. On 7 August, the *Daily Telegraph* was sketchy about the nature of the new technology when they wrote that 'President Truman has just described a startling new air weapon employed against Japan – an "atomic bomb". The conception of immense force derived from splitting the atom has long since haunted the imagination of science, but even in 1939 few thought it a possibility of the near future.'[19]

It took a couple of days for the details to emerge, but on 8 August, London's *Evening Standard* splashed the word 'OBLITERATION' across its front cover. It explained in a sub-headline: 'All living things, human and animal, seared to death.' The article described how 'photographs taken by Allied reconnaissance airplanes show that four square miles – or 60 per cent – of the built-up area of the city were completely wiped out'. The newspaper quoted General Spaatz as saying:

> 'The heart of the city had been wiped out with such awful thoroughness that it was as though some giant bulldozer had swept across the buildings and houses.
>
> 'The effect of the bomb was so terrific that several man-made firebreaks and seven streams failed to stop the fires.
>
> 'One fire spanned a firebreak three city blocks wide. Only a few concrete structures remain standing in the heart of the city. They are believed to be air-raid shelters.'[20]

The complete devastation of the city dwarfed anything else that had been seen in that war or any other war. President

Truman felt confident that it would bring the conflict against Japan to an end. Ever since the successful test in the desert of New Mexico, the ambition had been to use the atom bombs to prevent the need for an invasion of Japan. 'We were planning an invasion of Japan with the use of 2,000,000 men and the military had estimated the invasion might result in very heavy casualties,' wrote Truman later in his memoirs. 'General Marshall said in Potsdam that if the bomb worked we would save a quarter of a million American lives and probably save millions of Japanese.

'I gave careful thought to what my advisors had counseled. I wanted to weigh all the possibilities and implications. Here was the most powerful weapon of destruction ever devised and perhaps it was more than that.'[21]

Three days after the Hiroshima bomb, on 9 August, an even more powerful bomb – codenamed Fat Man, but measuring just 3 metres in length and 1.5 metres in diameter – was dropped above the city of Nagasaki on the island of Kyushu. Nagasaki was the secondary target, but weather conditions meant that the primary target of Kokura was dismissed on the day. This time, the B29 bomber that flew the mission was piloted by Major General Charles Sweeney. Remarkably, one man who had been in Hiroshima and survived the blast there was also in Nagasaki when Fat Man was detonated. Tsutomu Yamaguchi, who designed oil tankers for Mitsubishi Heavy Industries, was on a business trip to Hiroshima when he was caught in the first blast, which knocked him off his feet but did not seriously injure him. The next day, he made his way to the railway station and travelled home to Nagasaki, his burns covered in bandages. On 9 August, his family home was destroyed as the implosion-type plutonium bomb burst over Nagasaki. However, he, his wife and his son all survived. But it was not until 2009 that his special status as a survivor of both bombs was recognised in Japan.[22]

On 9 August, the London *Evening Standard* reported the destruction of another Japanese city.

'Although preliminary reports say that the raid was a great success,' wrote the report in the newspaper, 'the full measure of that success will not be known until the aircraft which carried the bomb gets back to its base, so that the crew can be interrogated.

'The world awaits the full tale of horror in Nagasaki that will soon be unfolded.

'If the Nagasaki bomb has had the same effect as Atom Bomb No 1 had on Hiroshima in Monday's raid it will have devastated more than four square miles of built-up area and will have killed and wounded an estimated total of 200,000 Japanese.'[23]

In fact, the bomb killed far fewer people than this because it was dropped in a valley in the city, thus shielding much of the rest of the city from the blast. However, it was still the most destructive weapon ever to have been used by mankind and the results were terrible.

That evening, President Truman made a broadcast to the nation. The *Manchester Guardian* reported on it the following day. Truman threatened that

'if Japan did not surrender atomic bombs would be dropped on her war industries and thousands of civilian lives would be lost. "I urge Japanese civilians to leave the industrial cities immediately and to save themselves from destruction," he added.

'"We shall continue to use the atomic bomb until we completely destroy Japan's power to make war. The atomic bomb is too dangerous to be let loose in a lawless world. That is why Great Britain and the United states, who have the secret of its production, do not intend to reveal the secret until means have been found to control the bomb so as to protect ourselves and the rest of the world from the danger of total destruction."'[24]

Truman had just returned from the Potsdam Conference and he took the opportunity to make a wider statement about America's post-war intentions in this broadcast.

'We also saw some of the terrible destruction which the war had brought to the occupied territories of Western Europe and to Britain. How glad I am to be home again. And how grateful to almighty God that this land of ours has been spared. We must do all we can to protect her from the ravages of any future breach of the peace. That is why, though the United States wants no territory or profit or selfish advantage out of this war, we are going to maintain the military bases necessary for the complete protection of our interests and of world peace.'[25]

He warned that a third world war was unimaginable given what had just unfolded: 'No one can foresee what another war would mean to our own cities and to our own people. What we are doing to Japan now, even with the new atomic bomb, is only a small fraction of what would happen to the world in a third world war.'

The newly formed United Nations, he said, would help to ensure that no other global war could ever happen again: 'We can never permit any aggressor in the future to be clever enough to divide us or strong enough to defeat us. That was the guiding spirit of the conferences at San Francisco and Berlin, and it will be the guiding spirit in the peace settlement to come.'[26]

Albert Einstein, who was not directly involved in the atomic weapons programme, but whose theoretical work formed an essential underpinning to it, co-wrote a letter to the *New York Times* along with other prominent figures in autumn 1945. 'The first atomic bomb destroyed more than the city of Hiroshima,' they wrote, 'It also exploded our inherited, outdated political ideas.'[27]

One of the main ideas that Einstein and his cosignatories were referring to was that of national sovereignty. They saw this moment in history as an opportunity for the United Nations to be at the heart of a new world order in which the conflicting desires of nation states could no longer lead to devastating consequences. 'We must aim at a Federal Constitution,' the letter urged, 'a working worldwide legal order, if we hope to prevent another atomic war.'[28]

John Hersey noted that 'a surprising number of people in Hiroshima remained more or less indifferent about the ethics of using the bomb'. He mentioned the argument that the concept of total war was widely subscribed to in Japan, 'that there was no difference between civilians and soldiers, and that the bomb itself was an effective force tending to end the bloodshed, warning Japan to surrender and thus to avoid total destruction'. But Hersey also recorded that there was widespread hatred for America and Americans, and that when war crimes trials started against the Japanese, there was a feeling amongst many in Hiroshima that Americans should also be facing trial for what they had done.[29]

Tokyo radio also expressed this opinion in the immediate aftermath of the Hiroshima bomb. One broadcast was quoted in the British press:

'The major part of Hiroshima is destroyed.

'The destructive force of the new weapon is indescribable as is the terrible devastation it has caused.

'The enemy has now completely thrown off the mask of humanity. He has used this new and brutal weapon to set off the superiority of the Japanese forces in Japan proper.

'In this way he hopes to end the Pacific war sooner by murdering innocent Japanese civilians.

'Hiroshima is a city of ruins, and dead are too numerous to be counted.

'Authorised Tokyo quarters recall that article 22 of the Hague convention makes it clear that attacks against open towns are unforgivable actions.

'The US ought to remember that they protested to Japan on numerous occasions in the name of humanity against the small scale Japanese raids on China.'[30]

In Britain, there was a wide range of views. First and foremost the bomb was seen in the context of the war. The Japanese were as unpopular as the Germans had been to the British public and there was not a widespread outpouring of sentimentality on behalf of the civilians who had lost their lives – six years of conflict had hardened many people's hearts and if the outcome was an end to the war against Japan, then that was a positive thing.

This comment is representative of this attitude:

'I could not feel any pity or sorrow for the Japanese dead and dying, partly because of the imperceptible hardening of my perspectives by the cumulative horrors of war, and also because distance deadens feeling. I felt that every allied life which it was possible to save by bombardment, no matter how devastating, should be saved. Pity and compassion mean nothing to the oriental mind. Japan was and is an ulcerated sore which needed lancet treatment and perhaps still needs it before peace can be established on dignity and fraternity in the Far East.'[31]

Lord Louis Mountbatten, the Supreme Allied Commander for South East Asia, told reporters that 'if the bomb kills Japanese and saves casualties on our side I am naturally not going to favour the killing of our people unnecessarily'.[32]

One fifty-year-old woman said: 'Well, it is a good thing. If we don't do it to them, they will do it to us. War is war, and they wouldn't consider us. It is a good thing Germany did not get it first.' She added, 'Once we use this bomb the Jap will soon give in, they will be so scared.'[33]

Kathleen Tipper wrote in her diary on 9 August, while she was on holiday on the south coast:

'A German refugee in a little restaurant in Alfriston began talking a great deal about the wickedness of the Allies in using the atom, and we let her know our views on this subject very firmly. I said that my only regret was that we didn't use them on the Germans, then we would have had no German problem (not my real opinion, but these well-dressed German refugees make me sick, and this one was wearing a pair of shoes I have been trying to buy for years!). I understand nothing about the atom, but I cannot see that it is more wicked to drop one of these bombs, than it is to drop an ordinary bomb, and it certainly is less costly in lives of pilots.'[34]

Fred Aiken, though, remembered: 'We were in Wales with my new in-laws when Hiroshima was atom bombed. The news was horrific – we were shocked. The power of the new bomb should have been demonstrated to the Japanese as a warning about what would happen if they didn't admit defeat.'[35]

Some were ecstatic about the new scientific discovery, like this twenty-five-year-old woman: 'I read about it in the paper this morning. I think it's marvellous. It's just what we want, isn't it?'[36] Some – mainly, but not all, men – like the research chemist E. Van Someren, were merely curious about the mechanics of the weapon – 'I am eager for technical information about it,' he wrote in his diary.[37] Another man was fascinated by the fact that the bomb was so small yet so powerful: 'I can't get over the size of it. They say it's only the size of a ball, and it has such an explosion.'[38] G. Bamber suggested that 'with this power applied and used we should probably only need to work 2–3 hours a day'.[39]

However, there were also many more humanitarian attitudes in evidence. In a country cottage in Kent, ten people – six adults and four children – spontaneously collected around the radio on 6 August to hear the

Six O'Clock News. One of them was a Mass Observation investigator who recorded what happened next. At about two minutes to six one of the women said, 'It would be funny if there were a world-shaking announcement, with all of us gathered around the wireless like this. You might think we expected one.'

The group then listened 'aghast and in silence' to the announcement about Hiroshima on the radio. At the end of the announcement, some of them murmured, 'God!' 'Good Lord how awful'. One of the men said, 'I watched all your faces the whole time and I could see nothing but dismay. One would think it was the Japs that had invented it.'

Everyone then talked at once; some said that it was 'frightful news and they hoped no more will be dropped': and 'surely this will make the Japs surrender. Anyway it sounds too awful: it must mean either the end of the world, or else the end of all war. Nobody seems particularly hopeful that it means the latter.' One of the women said, 'Well, nobody on earth can be so stupid that they can't see the issue now.' The woman writing the report down told a story 'of a young friend who has been talking of chalking up all over London the slogan: SHOOT ALL SCIENTISTS.' One of the other women said: 'We're not fit to have it – we'll only blow the planet to bits.' The children remained silent, watching the faces of the adults. After some time one of the boys, who was fifteen, and 'of very pessimistic temperament at any time', said, 'I don't think I'll put my name down for hop-picking now – it's not worthwhile.' He then picked up the book that he had been reading – *The Four Feathers* by A. E. W. Mason – and carried on reading it.

One of the men said to him ironically that 'I should think it's hardly worthwhile to finish *The Four Feathers*.'

On the following day – 7 August – a newspaper arrived at the cottage and everyone rushed to read it. One of the men said, 'Looks as if they decided it at Potsdam. You can imagine how it went – Truman and Attlee very frightened and tentative, standing first on one leg and then the other, saying "Shall we or shan't we" and Stalin saying "Don't be such fools – if you've really got it, then get on with it and finish the war."'

One of the women said, 'How much did Russia know? That's what's interesting.'

The fifteen-year-old boy: 'If they've got it too, they'll be bombing us.'

One of the men: 'We're not at war with Russia – yet!'

A twelve-year-old girl: 'Well, I don't feel sorry for the Japs – I hate the Japs – I hate them more than the Germans – they're the cruellest people on earth – I don't care how many they kill.'

One of the women, her mother, perhaps: 'A lot of them are no more cruel than you or I are – women and little children that hate the war just as we do.'

The girl replied, 'I think they're awful – they're like insects – ugh!'[40]

This exchange clearly shows that people – even within a group of relatively similar people – had varying responses to the bombs. Many in Britain, though, were simply completely horrified, like this (anonymous) person quoted in a Mass Observation report:

'When I first heard about the atomic bomb I felt a rather sick, horrible feeling; I felt that it was a dreadful thing that man had such terrific power to bring destruction to other men. I was not inclined to think that men would be wise enough to use the power given by the application of atomic energy. In the past every discovery of man's has been used to the detriment of mankind, as well as for his benefit. And the means of bringing death on a large scale has become increasingly effective as the years roll by.'[41]

A large number of people who were asked in the Mass Observation questioning said that the atom bomb represented a pivotal point in the evolution of the human race; in some ways, it was one of the most important historical moments in the history of humanity.

'I feel, too,' said one anonymous contributor, 'that the whole thing is so horrible and carries such a threat to the continuance of the human race that if the nations of the earth have yet a glimmer of sanity the effect of these bombs should give them pause and make them more inclined to forebearance and tolerance – otherwise we are all doomed to extinction in a very short time. I really don't understand a single thing about the scientific side of the bomb, but I presume it is the same as every other scientific discovery – it can be used for good or evil. Let us hope that the nations choose the narrow path.'[42]

Japan surrendered soon after the Nagasaki bomb and the war was over. Parliament reconvened on 15 August, which was also declared as VJ Day, and the following day Churchill, now the Leader of the Opposition, spoke to the House about something that he had known about for longer than anyone else in Parliament. He said, 'Success beyond all dreams crowned this sombre, magnificent venture of our American allies' and that the idea that the atom bomb should never have been used in the war against Japan was a wrongheaded one:

> 'If the Germans and Japanese had discovered it they would have used it on us to our complete destruction with the utmost alacrity.
>
> 'The bomb brought peace; but men alone can keep it. The secret of the bomb should not be imparted to other countries.
>
> 'I am surprised that very worthy people – but people who in most cases had no intention of proceeding to the Japanese front themselves – should adopt the position that rather than throw this bomb we should have sacrificed a million American and a quarter of a million British lives in the desperate battles and massacres of an invasion of Japan.'[43]

It had been a dramatic month in world history at terrible human cost. Whether atomic weapons are a force for good or evil remains a contentious point. In 1945, people across the world were trying to digest the nature of the new world in which they existed: an atomic world, in which whole cities could be destroyed by a bomb the size of a small car dropped from a plane flying so high in the sky that it could barely be seen, a world in which it was possible to envisage the destruction of entire nations and, perhaps, even, all human life. Hundreds of millions of people living through the war felt that it had been frightening enough; as the war ended, though, the world suddenly seemed an even scarier, more perilous place in which to live. And for tens of thousands of people in Hiroshima and Nagasaki who had escaped death in August 1945, the terrible sickness caused by radiation would come and cut them down long after the debris of their stricken cities had been removed.

Chapter 9

VJ Day – The End of the War
Ticker-tape, Kisses and Queues

'I think it's a disgrace to our serving men. They should have fished up some entertainment of some sort. Good lord, a little bit of a sing-song wouldn't do anybody any harm. It was heaps livelier on VE Day. They did have a band playing then.'[1]

An unnamed woman in Bognor, 15 August 1945

'Suddenly, I was grabbed by a sailor. It wasn't that much of a kiss. I felt that he was very strong. He was just holding me tight. I'm not sure about the kiss … it was just somebody celebrating. It wasn't a romantic event.'[2]

Greta Friedman, New York

The atom bombs in Hiroshima and Nagasaki – and also the fact that in August the Russians had joined the fight against Japan – meant that the Japanese surrender was seen as inevitable everywhere from Sydney to Washington and from London to Nanking. People were tuned to their wirelesses and rushed out to buy every newspaper that was printed, expectant of news at any moment. Rumours were rife that the Japanese were about to give up. By 10 August, the

Japanese had made an offer to surrender to the Americans. Truman wrote in his diary that day: 'Ate lunch at my desk and discussed the Japanese offer to surrender which came in a couple of hours earlier. They wanted to make a condition precedent to the surrender. Our terms were "unconditional". They wanted to keep the Emperor. We told them we would make the terms.'[3]

When news of the offer emerged, it was enough immediately to set celebrations in motion in London's West End without any form of official confirmation. The *Daily Telegraph* reported on 11 August that 'the most joyful people in the crowds congregated around Piccadilly were the American and Australian Service men. The end of the war in Japan meant that they could go home with no thought of more years of service in the Far East.'[4]

It was not until the night of 14 August, though, that the formal offer of Japanese surrender finally did come through. It was announced in a radio broadcast by President Truman at 7.00 pm local time that evening. Truman said in his broadcast that the war would not be truly over until Japan had also formally signed the surrender document, along the lines of the Potsdam Declaration. The signing ceremony did not actually happen until the start of September and the United States formally recognises 2 September as the date of VJ Day, but for Americans, the celebrations that the war was finally over began immediately and two days of holiday were declared for 15 and 16 August. They celebrated in New York on the night of 14 August and all day on 15 August. Truman had said that up to two million United States soldiers might have been committed to a land invasion of Japan and, given the high mortality rates seen in Pacific battles such as Iwo Jima and the ferocity of Japanese resistance, ordinary

American soldiers, sailors and air force men and women were relieved that they would not be needed.

The *Manchester Guardian* reported that on the night of 14 August there had been an 'all night celebration in New York' and that on 15 August

> 'Americans continued ... to celebrate the victory over Japan with undiminished vigour. The rejoicing, which began last night at seven o'clock when President Truman announced the Japanese acceptance of the Allied terms, continued all night and is still going on.
>
> 'President Truman declared today and tomorrow to be holidays for all employees of the Federal Government. Business houses throughout the nation closed today and probably many of them will do the same tomorrow.
>
> 'New York's Times Square, the traditional scene of great celebrations, was packed all night last night by a great crowd. They cheered, sang and waved flags, and pretty girls were kissed by complete strangers and took it good-naturedly. Throughout the city motor-cars roared through the streets with horns sounding and the occupants shouting, while tons of torn paper floated down from sky-scraper windows in spite of preliminary pleas by officials that paper is still scarce and should not be wasted.
>
> 'Numerous premature reports that the war was over and several spontaneous celebrations had not diminished the enthusiasm of the crowds when the official news finally came. The demonstrations were much larger than when Germany capitulated. In Washington huge crowds gathered before the

Whitehouse. Mr Truman and his wife appeared in the portico and greeted the throng.'[5]

In New York, the celebrations were especially energetic. The streets of the city were filled with the biggest crowds the city had ever seen; they were covered in ticker tape, torn paper and cloth thrown from the windows of buildings. People drank and danced in the street. One of the most famous of all American photographs from the Second World War – and the single most iconic picture of VJ Day – was taken in Times Square on 15 August by Alfred Eisenstaedt. It shows a sailor kissing a nurse. The sailor was George Mendonsa, who at the time, aged twenty-two, was on his first date with the woman who would later be his wife. The nurse was not that woman. Her name was Greta Friedman and she was a dental nurse. Mendonsa, who had served in the Pacific, was drunk and had grabbed Friedman and pulled her close to him. 'I felt that he was very strong,' she later said. 'He was just holding me tight. I'm not sure about the kiss … it was just somebody celebrating. It wasn't a romantic event.' He said later that he did not even remember doing it as he was so drunk at the time.[6]

In San Francisco, the celebrations turned into a riot. 'A looting, smashing crowd is tearing up Market Street tonight,' *San Francisco Chronicle* reporter Stanton Delaplane wrote at 8 am on the night of 14 August. '... this crowd is out of hand. You couldn't stop it if you tried, not short of tear gas and fire hoses.' Most of the rioters were young soldiers and sailors who got drunk and caused carnage: shop windows were smashed, women were raped and more than thirty of San Francisco's famous streetcars were trashed. Eleven people were killed and over a thousand injured. 'If you pull all restraints off and add liquor, that's what happens,' said Kevin Mullen, a former deputy police chief. 'Everybody went nuts. These were not veterans, they were young people who hadn't been in the war. They were not warriors.'[7]

In Australia, VJ Day was widely known as VP Day – Victory in the Pacific. The Prime Minister, Ben Chifley, announced the news at 9.30 am local time on 15 August. ABC Reporter Talbot Duckmanton was in Martin Place in central Sydney that morning and described the scenes in a live broadcast with great cheers and other rowdy crowd noise in the background:

> 'There are thousands and thousands of people – honestly I've never seen so many people in Martin Place before. They're packed tight from above Castlereagh Street all the way down across Pitt Street, past the cenotaph and way down here to the George Street end of Martin Place where we have the mobile studio parked. There are men, women and girls – lovely girls too – hundreds and hundreds of them, they've got paper hats on their heads, waving streamers, flags: Union Jacks, Stars and Stripes, they've got whistles, those gas alarm rattlers and they're just having one whale of a time. It's about an hour since the official news came through and of course most of these young people are on their way to the offices and so they've just stayed in town. I heard someone down below, say that they stayed in just for the fun of it and there's certainly plenty of fun here in this part of Sydney this morning. Over on my right in one of the buildings at the back someone has hung out a big dummy of Adolf Hitler with a great swastika on the back of it. And with

great cheers from the crowd he was lowered down from the top of the building and duly hung.'[8]

In New Zealand, some of the celebrations on 15 August got out of hand in a similar way to those in San Francisco. In Auckland, the familiar city scenes of drinking and dancing in the street got rowdier; windows were smashed and dozens of injured people were taken to hospital. One merchant seaman remembered that on 'VJ Day we actually had arrived the night before in Auckland. And if I remember right, well the whole city went bloody mad. The following morning it was reputed that they swept up five ton of broken bottles. They went nuts ... I had a cousin who was in the navy, fell off a tram and nearly killed himself, pissed.'[9]

In Britain, Clement Attlee announced the peace in a broadcast at 11.45 pm on 14 August. Most people were in bed and those who were awake, like Norman Longmate who listened with his fellow soldiers in overseas billets, were not inspired by Attlee's oration.

'Japan has today surrendered,' said Attlee. 'The last of our enemies is laid low. ... Here at home you have earned respite from the unceasing exertions which you have borne without flinching or complaint for so many dark years. ... For the moment let all relax and enjoy themselves in the knowledge of work well done. Peace has once again come to the world. ... Long live the King!'[10]

The King made his own speech, which was broadcast the following day. He told listeners: 'The war is over. You know, I think, that those four words have for The Queen and myself the same significance, simple yet immense, that they have for you. Our hearts are full to overflowing, as are your own. Yet there is not one of us who has experienced this terrible

war who does not realise that we shall feel its inevitable
consequences long after we have all forgotten our rejoicings
of today.'[11]

Many people did rejoice but others, like on VE Day,
grumbled about what they saw as the government's ineptitude
at the timing of the announcement. On 15 August, K. M.
Carruthers, in Heswall, Merseyside wrote:

'Woke up ... at about 7.10 hearing the national
anthem. Thought I was still dreaming until my mother
shouted to me that the Japs had surrendered. No-one
had any bunting out and everywhere was very quiet. At
8 o'clock I saw Mr Clark, a neighbour, who said:
  "The government mucked it up again. I got ready to
go to work and I'd have been on the bus if Williams
hadn't put his head out of the window and asked me
where I was going. This was at 5 to 7, so most of the
men will have turned up at Laird's this morning –
those that didn't hear the news at midnight."'[12]

It was a common problem: many people had woken up on
15 August not knowing that it was a bank holiday or that the
war was officially over. Kathleen Tipper wrote in her diary
that she 'Got up at the usual time as Joyce and Pop are going
in to work and it seems that most people are up as few seemed
to have heard Atlee last night'.[13]

G. Bamber, living away from home in Blackpool, wrote
that she

'was staggered to hear on the 8 am news that VJ was
declared on the midnight news. The 9 pm news gave
no indication it was as near. Rather a swizz this for

workers who leave home before the BBC news and it made it difficult for housewives and shops, as far as food was concerned.

'For myself, and for many like me, who are away from home and friends, and who travelled to be with their loved ones on such occasions, it deprived one of some very precious time.'[14]

One woman in Corfe Castle wrote in her diary:

'Slept rather late and missed 8 o'clock news (I don't get a paper sent here, as it's too remote: I generally call for mine some time during the afternoon, at a small shop about a quarter of a mile away on the main road). I turned on the wireless about 10 – & just as they were playing the usual programme I concluded that nothing had happened; so I tidied up the house and got some painting materials and picnic things ready for a day's sketching. On my way out I called in at my old gardener's cottage to see if he was coming over – I said to him, "Can you come tomorrow afternoon, as tomorrow morning I shall be going to the market?" to which he replied, "I don't think there will be any market, tomorrow." I asked him whether tomorrow would be Victory Day and he said, "It's today!" So that was how I heard that the war had ended.'[15]

Another diarist in Bognor wrote on 15 August:

'Mr G has arranged to go to London today. At 7am he switches on for the news and in his usual tone calls "It's over – today and tomorrow are public holidays."

'Mrs G calls "Come on L. We've got to go to Bognor food queuing – it's VJ Day. The only excitement comes from the children; on hearing the news they shout out "whoopee" and turn somersaults…'

'7.45am – Mr G isn't going to London after all. Mrs G thinks housewives should have been given more consideration. The government should have declared tomorrow VJ Day in which case there wouldn't have been such a run on the shops. Mr G pooh-poohs this idea, saying this was impracticable, that you could never get people to work when they once knew that the war was officially over. The result would be people would have three days off work instead of the official two.'[16]

Up and down the country, queuing was a major theme of VJ Day. Kathleen Tipper went shopping in south London where she 'sallied forth to buy some food for us on this public holiday and luckily got some fish with little trouble, but bread queues were dreadful and I gave up'.[17] The following day – also a public holiday – she headed out again: 'Had to spend a few more hours in the fish queue this morning, much to my horror, but we must eat, and with four people at home and nothing at all in the cupboard there was no other alternative. Had a pleasant chat with a very nice woman in the queue (I know now why so many women really enjoy queuing) then came out with herrings for lunch, shrimps for tea and kippers for breakfast.'[18]

K. M. Carruthers wrote:

'A large crowd waited for the Co-op stores to open, at 8.30 am, and later, larger droves of women wandered between the village and the lower village, with empty baskets. The question every time was "Is so-and-so open? Well do you know where I can get some bread and cakes?"

'My father was sent to the nearest pub to get something for us to celebrate on. He came back with the empty bottle: "Today's beer hasn't arrived yet, and nothing can be taken out. They're keeping it all for tonight."'[19]

In Hampstead, one housewife noted that there was

'Definitely much less excitement than on VE Day. The predominant feeling encountered among housewives at least in the early part of the day was annoyance at the shopping difficulties involved. By 09.30 am enormous queues (30 and 40 people) were lined up outside bakers and greengrocers. This was a feature of VE day also, but then there was an excitement and elation about the queues that was almost entirely absent this time.'[20]

The sense of fatigue and a lack of excitement was certainly evident amongst many more people than a few months earlier on VE Day. One woman in Bognor said: 'We're relieved it's over. Everybody is for that matter, but we haven't quite got the same thrill we had as when we heard that the war with Germany was over. The war with Japan's been too far away and as far as we're concerned the war was over when the bombing stopped. Of course we can't feel the same as we did on VE day – you never get the same kind of thrill a second time.'[21]

G. Bamber, a Londoner living in Blackpool, had gone to meet up with family in Wolverhampton. She wrote, 'I should love to have been in London for the celebrations – anywhere in the provinces seems very "flat" to a Londoner.'[22] According to Norman Longmate, 'It was a muddled, unsatisfactory beginning to the two-day holiday. The weather, too, was not kind: rain fell in many places about midday, though there were sunny periods, especially in the West of England. The speeches, the fancy dress parades, the bonfires, all had the jaded feeling of being a repeat performance and the crowds were generally smaller and quieter.'[23]

As day turned into evening in Heswall, Merseyside,

'… the gentle voices of young drunks were heard, and fireworks began to go off. The children were still enjoying the fun at midnight, but the older people took the day quietly and kept indoors.

'The glow of fires, together with searchlights roaming the night sky (the s/l unit at Bidston making merry), made it all look like another blitz night. Across the Dee estuary, north Wales was a flashing tiara of bonfires.

'Although this is the end of the world war, the celebrations here were not as hearty as on May 8th. Perhaps people were remembering those who were left in the Burmese jungles. Perhaps the rigours of peace – unemployment, lack of this and that – have put a damper on rejoicings.'[24]

In Bognor, one woman thought that the lack of organised celebrations was 'a disgrace to our serving men. They should have fished up some entertainment of some sort. Good lord, a little bit of a sing-song wouldn't do anybody any harm. It was heaps livelier on VE Day. They did have a band playing then. Bognor's very conservative. Last week in the Picturedrome they were showing Churchill's photo on the screen and everybody clapped. And then they showed Atlee's and only two poor devils in the audience had the courage to clap. That's typical. Everybody I know voted for Joynson-Hicks (Conservative candidate at General Election).'[25]

However, in the main metropolitan centres and amongst people in their late teens and twenties, the celebrations were just as wild and uninhibited as they had been for VE Day. And for members of the armed forces who now knew that they would not be sent to fight against Japan, there was enormous relief. Private Sid Verrier, wrote a letter to his family on 11 August and told them:

'The peace coming news is marvellous and the thought of not having to go into action again certainly allows my tenseness, which the thought of going over again brings, to relax. When the actual and official news is announced I very much doubt if I will be allowed to come home. The travel limits will come down to within 20 miles of the camp, as it did on VE Day, according to the chaps who were here. But the celebrations don't bother us chaps, it is just good to know we have finished the rough times and maybe we will be demobbed sooner than we thought.'[26]

Plenty of the British troops who were in Germany wanted to celebrate. The Anti-Tank Regiment of the Argyll and Sutherland Highlanders were in Kiel, northern Germany. Desmond Flower described the scene in his history of the regiment:

'On that day 146 Battery were accorded the supreme honour of firing a royal salute of one hundred and one guns in the main square, before the Town Hall of the city of Kiel. Our twelve M.10s, drawn up in line and gleaming in new paint, thundered at solemn ten-second intervals before a huge crowd of silent Germans. On that morning, at the hour, guns were thundering wherever the armies of Britain stood upon captured soil. We fired on the day of triumph not only as a battery; we fired as well in memory of our comrades lying at rest beneath their white crosses, scattered from Normandy to the Baltic, for our comrades sick and wounded still in hospital ... for Scotland, for Britain, for victory, and, we hoped, as we thought of our children, for the end of the war.'[27]

In many provincial towns and villages, the young people headed for the nearest city to go and celebrate properly and leave the old people at home to grumble. 'I'm going to try to get to Liverpool this afternoon,' said one young women in Heswall, 'There'll be some real celebrating there.'[28] The *Manchester Guardian* reported that on VJ Day itself, the centre of Manchester 'surged with enthusiastic youth. The girls went round in circles. Sailors gave one another pick-a-back rides, flagpoles were climbed, and there was such a crowd in Albert Square that though you could hear the City Police

Band making music it was some time before you could see it.' The newspaper told the story of one old man trying to push through the crowd of revellers to get to his place of work. 'The world's gone mad,' he said.[29]

The celebrations had not started auspiciously in Manchester according to the newspaper:

'Manchester received the general circulation of the surrender news quietly, almost with phlegm. Many people, indeed, missed all the earlier announcements that the war had ended and went to work as usual. Probably the pleasantest part of VJ Day for most of these was to go home again at once. For some time the city presented the unusual spectacle of a "rush" hour at the wrong end of the day.

'But not everyone was pleased that VJ Day had taken them either unawares or unready for it. There were complaints of closed shops – and the closed shops of Manchester were a sobering spectacle yesterday – and the growth of queues at grocers and bakers, some people had some hard things to say about the way national celebrations are managed.

'Public relief that the years of war were at last really over did, eventually, of course, get the better of all this, and Manchester abandoned itself to a good and noisy time. Before the day was out there were queues for fireworks and for cigarettes; but, while there were fireworks, yesterday, of all days, found Greater Manchester without, apparently, a single "smoke" to be had.'[30]

The rain in the morning cleared up, though, and celebrations began in earnest in the afternoon: ticker tape fell onto the streets, Verey lights were fired into the sky, hawkers sold hats and flags, little groups danced in rings and sang joyful songs, firecrackers were let off amongst the crowd. In Salford, the night of 14 August had been noisier with 'ship's hooters, fireworks and rockets, impromptu street dance bands and singers all contributing', but on the 15th the city was much quieter.

In central London, large crowds congregated in the afternoon. One of the people that they saw was Field Marshal Montgomery, who was receiving the freedom of Lambeth. He said that day that if people wanted peace then they must be prepared to make the personal sacrifices demanded by their leaders:

> 'We can by no means sit back and relax because the war is over; we must work hard at the next task. Our task of reconstruction in England and in Europe and throughout the Empire calls for great energy and drive.
>
> 'I firmly believe that every enterprise which man undertakes, if it is to achieve any lasting success, must have a strong spiritual basis. If we attempt any great thing for solely material reasons the results cannot be good. Today we look to the churches to give us a clear and simple lead on those spiritual issues which are always important and over which we must never compromise.
>
> 'There is need in these days for clear-thinking, and especially on the subject of what we have been fighting to achieve and how we are able to secure it. Some say

we have been fighting for peace, but peace cannot automatically ensure justice and freedom which must first be established before peace can be secured.

'But we do not want only peace; we want prosperity, and we will win it for ourselves only by much hard work and by personal sacrifices on the part of us all.'[31]

Montgomery drove down Whitehall and through Parliament Square through dense crowds on his way to Lambeth. Crowds raced from Horse Guards Parade, Trafalgar Square and the Mall in order to see him and the crush around his car was intense. Streamers were thrown over the bonnet and flags waved at the windows.

One Mass Observation investigator recorded her impressions of the scene in the West End and Whitehall that afternoon: 'There are crowds in Parliament Square and lining Whitehall: a good many have got thermoses or bottles of milk or tea and other provisions in string kits or bulging out of shopping bags.' She went and spoke to some people sitting on a dustcart and the side of the road. 'Another lot of people declare they don't know why they are there. "We're not expecting anything – we're just joining in the throng."' She went to Westminster Abbey, where there were thanksgiving services at regular intervals throughout the afternoon and evening. She noted that at the service she attended 'a few women are openly in tears, and during the service there is some furtive dabbing of eyes with handkerchiefs, sniffing, throaty coughing, and during the last hymn (Praise, my soul, the King of Heaven) one or two strangled sobs can be heard'. After the service, she walked up to Trafalgar Square, where she noticed for the first time 'the cardboard hats which later are to be seen everywhere:

here, a group of young ATS are wearing them: they have inscriptions round the brim: ANY GUM, CHUM? WHOOPEE! I'LL HAVE TO ASK ME DAD, TAKE A CHANCE, YOU'VE HAD IT, CUDDLE ME AGAIN, KISS ME QUICK are the usual ones.'[32]

In Trafalgar Square, she watched as

'people keep letting off fireworks and there is a flight of pigeons into the air. "Pigeons don't 'arf get scared, do they?" says [an 18-year-old man]. At 7 pm the Metropolitan Police Band appear, and begin their programme with "Daisy, Daisy". Crowd takes it up and sings it. They follow on with "One of the Early Birds" and "Two lovely black eyes". Also sung by crowd, and half a dozen young people climb up on one of the fountains and dance hand in hand round its rim. A girl wearing a green paper bonnet with a yellow frill starts dancing by herself where the crowd is sparse, and several more people join her. They take hands and dance in two lines. "In the shade of the old apple tree," and "After the ball" are now played. A few people sing but there is no general singing. "Funny how you forget the words," says [a forty-year-old woman].

'The group is still dancing at the top of the fountain. The crowd bursts into laughter. "Look – he's slipped in," [a sixteen-year-old boy] remarks, "The old 'un would like to see this, eh?" to [a fourteen-year-old boy]. Band plays "Knees up Mother Brown" and knots of people all over the square start dancing. Group on top of fountain exaggerate their movements: laughter in crowd. "They'll do anything, won't they?" Three girls of about 18, all wearing cardboard hats with the slogan "CUDDLE UP!" start dancing and are joined by others.'[33]

When she got to Piccadilly Circus it was crowded with young people.

'Occasionally,' she wrote, 'a firework is let off, and the crowd scatters as far as it is able to. Sailors and young girls are marching down Piccadilly singing Land of Hope and Glory. At the two fountains in the wall by St James's Church there are two queues for water; girls try to drink out of their cupped hands; men splash their faces; some dabble their wrists for a moment and moisten their mouths. One or two boys put their head under the stream. Everybody seems very hot, very cheerful, very short of cigarettes – at a rough estimate, hardly one person in a hundred was smoking – and pretty short of food. There is also an air of slight bewilderment and pointlessness about it all: it lacks the joyful spontaneity of VE Day.'[34]

Kathleen Tipper had purposely gone into town not for the VJ Day celebrations but to see a play:

'Went up to town around 4.30 to meet Eileen, for we are going to see "Duet for two hands" at the Lyric. Joyce and Phil are off to see "Madame Louise", having booked only yesterday, and I consider it a most low show to see, but they should enjoy it on VJ night. The crowds were immense, perhaps not so dense as on VE night, but they seemed to stretch further afield than they did before. I also thought them less jolly, the people seemed much more noisy than they were before, in fact I didn't like the crowds tonight, but I did like the floodlighting which was beautiful. St Paul's looked lovely with two searchlights on the cross, and the lighting on the Thames side was most attractive. We enjoyed the play very much indeed, and the audience, despite noises from outside, was completely gripped the whole way through. John Mills was fine, a grand role for him of course, but I am now convinced that he is as fine a stage actor as he is film actor. The play whilst not being a masterpiece, I thought quite a brilliant one, and the atmosphere was most convincing.'[35]

The *Daily Telegraph* reported, 'All day crowds numbering many thousands waited outside Buckingham Palace. The King and Queen appeared on the Palace balcony six times, the last occasion being shortly after midnight.

'Late last night the two Princesses, who had accompanied their parents on four of their balcony appearances, left the palace, escorted by two police officers, and mingled with the crowd.'[36]

The *Manchester Guardian* praised the King's speech in its critique of the BBC coverage on VJ Day:

'The BBC's programmes for yesterday were not calculated so comprehensively for the occasion as were those for VE Day in May, but they covered the main events of the day, and they included two events which fell by the luck of coincidence to the London crowds, and so were extended to the people of the country. These were the passing of the King and

Queen down Whitehall to the opening of Parliament
and the arrival of Field Marshal Montgomery at
Lambeth Town Hall and his speech after receiving the
freedom. From both of these there was a vivid
commentary and a dramatic impression of great,
cheering crowds.'[37]

Richard Dimbleby was responsible for much of the outside
broadcasting for the BBC that day. He did not seem
particularly triumphant: 'When I look back tonight on the
horrors and misery and the cruelty and the death that I have
seen in the last six years, of the unforgettable experiences
I've had and how much older and tired they've made me, I
just want to go and sit in a corner and thank God it's all
ending.'[38]

The *Guardian*'s assessment of the BBC coverage was not
entirely uncritical: 'In the evening it was, one felt, a mistake
that the BBC did not announce the changes in the evening's
programmes during the *Six O'Clock News*. True, they had
been announced earlier in the day, but they should have
been repeated at the beginning of the evening.'

But overall, they felt as though the Corporation had done
a good job in reporting the day's events and that it was a
fitting end to wartime broadcasting:

'The introduction to the King's broadcast was
particularly well chosen. It was done by an infantryman
of the Fourteenth Army, who had just returned from
the Far East and whose home was in Blackburn,
Lancashire. It was simple, unaffected, and moving.
The King's Speech was, in the opinion of most
listeners, the best broadcast he has ever made; and it

was followed, after the news, by a stirring broadcast from outside Buckingham Palace, in which listeners once again heard the great crowd cheering the Royal Family while a commentator described the scene.'[39]

On the Mall, cheering the royal family that day, was Mary Tisdall, who had climbed a tree in St James's Park so that she could see what was going on: 'My husband-to-be's brother helped me to climb it. I remember feeling very insecure up in that tree but we managed to see pretty well from there.' Later on she recalled:

'I stayed up in town and I didn't go back to my digs all night; there was another girl who turned out to be a prostitute – I didn't realise at the time – she cottoned on to me and she took me back to her home. She said: "if you like listening to modern music I can find someone to take you out and buy you some tights – American soldiers you know" – and the following night I went there to see her. Anyway, I did go out with him – but I certainly didn't sleep with him – I was much too ignorant for that.'[40]

All over the country there were bonfires – in the middle of the cities as well as in the countryside. On her way back from the West End, the Mass Observation investigator who had earlier been to the service at Westminster Abbey, went to visit friends in Battersea:

'There were many more flags out in Battersea than in Chelsea: in one very poor street a "V" in coloured electric light bulbs had been rigged up outside the window of the ground floor. There were bonfires in almost every street, lovingly looked after by excited children: mother and father would come out for a while and look at the flames, and then go in again, while the children darted into blitzed houses and came out carrying more wood – plans, bits of window-frames, anything that would burn. In two [working class] streets a piano had been dragged out into the road and people were dancing to it, mainly round dances, or else in long lines dancing towards each other and back again. One street had a booth rigged up against the air raid shelter; two men were serving beer: a placard on the improvised counter said: "If you've paid, come on!" This street had organised a club for Final Victory Night and had been saving up their beer for it. Several streets where some soldier was expected home on leave were especially flagged and decorated, with lettering on white cardboard or cloth over the door: "WELCOME HOME TOM." There was far more genuine gaiety in Battersea than in the West End, or the more respectable districts like Chelsea and Kensington. However, it had an early end: [a 40-year-old woman] who drove through it with friends about midnight reported that not a soul was to be seen then, and nearly all the bonfires were out.'[41]

But in Bognor, even the municipal bonfire turned into an exercise in bureaucracy. Labourers had been building a new bonfire all day after the previous one, carefully assembled to be ready in time for Japanese surrender, was set alight by some drunken servicemen home on leave. As people assembled in the evening, an official went up to the labourers and said something to them, then drove away in his car. A Mass Observation investigator watched and recorded what happened.

A man asked one of the labourers who it was. 'One of them from the council,' the labourer replied, according to the investigator. 'What did he want?' asked the man. 'He says we're not to light up until after 9.20 pm when the King's speech would be over.'

'But there's no loudspeaker here, even if we wanted to listen.'

'Just a bit more red tape,' said a 50-year-old man, who looked like he might work in the city. 'That's what we've got to put up with all the time.'

Ten minutes later, the same man suggested that they all have a sing-a-long while they wait for the bonfire to be lit and he starts singing 'When You're Going Lambeth Way'.

The Mass Observation investigator noted:

'They sing in a very self-conscious way, as if they were surprised at their own actions, but very soon others took up the refrain and by the time the last "Oi" was sung the line has swollen to about fifty, although the numbers singing were about twice that number. And then fireworks went off amid great amusement.

'There's excited shrieks of "Look, they're putting the petrol on the bonfire" and the crowd edge closer.'

According to the investigator, the labourer said, 'We're waiting for the Surveyor to light the fire. He might make a speech but I doubt if he will. There was more larking about last time. After the bonfire had been going for some time we had to have the fire brigade to put it out because of the blackout regulations that were still on. The crowd enjoyed that part quite as much as the bonfire.'

At 9.20 pm, the Mass Observation investigator reported,

'A cheer goes up as Mr E. T. Bryant, the chairman of the council lights the fire and soon the wood is crackling and the flames soaring higher and higher and the crowd move further back because of the intense heat. People watch the glow in silence – fascinated by the sight, but soon some soldiers set up a sing-song and dance round the bonfire. And then the kiddies make their own circle, and a young fellow ... says "Youth leads the way, what ho!"

'And the crowd join in singing Tipperary, Oh, I do like to be beside the sea-side, You put your right foot out etc. people are singing and dancing and shrieking as fireworks explode near them.'

At around 10.30 pm, the investigator watched as people were already leaving to go home. A long line of cars tailed away. The last memory of the bonfire for the investigator was 'of soldiers and young girls singing and dancing around the dying embers of the bonfire; a line of young people walking arm in arm along the sandy beach singing "Auld Lang Syne"; the red glow of the may small bonfires burning up and down the beach and the reflection of fire in the water; the splutter of fireworks and from afar the roar of the incoming tide...'

On her way home, as she returned to the bungalow where she was staying a car passed her with a sign written in big letters on its windscreen. It said, 'PEACE ON EARTH.'[42]

The day after VJ Day was also a holiday and a fine sunny day across most of the country and many people who had not done so before took the opportunity to go the seaside or spend the day outdoors in some other way. E. Van Someren and his family spent much of the morning on the river punting: 'In the afternoon we had a picnic between cornfields at Broxbournebury, they were stacking the sheaves with a mechanical stacker and we got some gleanings afterwards for our hens. It was warm and breezy, not hot enough for bathing. A quiet evening and to bed early, our first evening without visitors for a long time.'[43]

K. M. Carruthers went to the seaside on 16 August. It was

'a beautiful day. Everyone in summer holiday mood. Troops of girl guides and hikers passed through the village, as we stood in queue for a bus to take us to Hoylake. It was a big queue and a packed bus. We passed other patient bus queues, all the way there.

'Hoylake is a modern "splendide" place of detached houses along a magnificent promenade. The open sea beyond the stretch of sand, the sun beating down on the shite swimming-baths – against this passed the colours of the rainbow, as holiday seekers in bright bathing costumes and summer dresses thronged the promenade.

'A group of WAAFs passed, caps in hand, careless of any official eyes. I did not envy their thick stockings, shoes, skirts, and tight collars on such a lovely day. The WAAFs looked "sweltered" and "browned-off".

'There was no ice-cream to be had (due to recent government price control?) and the promenade café was packed to the doors.

'At the end of the day, after baking beautifully in the sun, we walk one mile to the bus depot, to get a seat on the home-bound bus (again, we passed queues of people waiting for a bus home).

'People were making their way to the cinemas as if it were Saturday night. Someone remarked to us that it was a pity we didn't celebrate victory a bit more often.

'The night was quiet. The children had exhausted firework stocks, there was little firewood left from the last nights' bonfires.

'Everyone looked tired, dusty and very sunburnt.

'It's been a grand VJ Holiday.

'The pubs are all "closed; sold out" in these parts.'[44]

As the festivities ended and the final realisation that the war had ended set in, people were set to roll up their sleeves and embark on their post-war lives. For some, that meant opportunity – to make money, to have a career, to start a family, to get married, to follow interests and hobbies. For others, it meant grinding poverty, poor housing and rationing for years to come. But whatever the future held, there was no doubt that after war, atomic bombs and the birth of the welfare state, people were living in a very different world in 1945 than they had been in 1939.

Chapter 10

Epilogue
Beyond VJ Day

'Considering how likely we all are to be blown to pieces by it within the next five years, the atomic bomb has not roused so much discussion as might have been expected.'[1]

George Orwell

Amidst the ashes and the rubble that stretched across the world from Tokyo to Berlin and from Stalingrad to London in 1945, there were plenty of idealists and visionaries who saw the opportunity for a phoenix to rise: for long-lasting peace to leap from bitter war; for harmony amongst nations to spring from discord between them. At the heart of the global vision was the foundation of the United Nations and for most of the summer, as the events described in this book unfolded, a meeting in San Francisco defined exactly what this new body would look like. On 27 April 1945, five thousand delegates arrived in the city from fifty countries across the world to discuss how the United Nations would prevent a conflict on the scale of the Second World War from ever happening again. While the notion of a federalist country in the United States was a precarious enough idea, though, the concept of a federalist global state with a police force to stop a major war from breaking out was even more fragile. Previously colonised states with ambitions for independent nationhood, such as India, Syria and Vietnam, spent the summer of 1945 agitating for their status to be recognised. Other countries that had been occupied during the war, like China and France, did not now want to give up their hard-earned sovereign rights to a new global authority. The global superpowers were certainly not going to yield the power they had.

In the febrile climate of re-emerging nationalism, the internationalist idealism of people such as Albert Einstein and John F. Kennedy looked doomed to failure. Churchill claimed to have shared some of their idealism in his memoirs when he wrote, 'My idea as the end of the war approached was that the greatest minds and the greatest thoughts possessed by men should govern the world.'[2]

However, by 1946, this had been tempered by political realism: 'The United Nations Organisation was still very young, but already it was clear that its defects might prove grave enough to vitiate the purposes for which it was created. At any rate it could not provide quickly and effectively the union and the armed forces which Free Europe and the United States needed for self-preservation.'[3] Nonetheless, Truman said, 'The human race has been striving for peace ever since civilisation started. The United Nations represents the greatest organised attempt in the history of men to solve differences without war.'[4]

Kathleen Tipper wrote in her diary on 27 June:

'The World Security Charter was signed in San Francisco yesterday by representatives of 50 nations. This is a wonderful achievement and does give some hope for future peace. The only drawback as I see it is that these nations agree to this charter now, but as soon as a problem touches their own possessions, wealth or pride, some of that unity which they talk so grandly about, is liable to be brushed aside. France's recent trouble with Syria is a good example, whichever side was right. One can only hope that this time as America and Russia are parties to the agreement, we have a much better chance of a little peace.'[5]

Another nationalist movement began to gain ground in 1945. Jewish survivors from the concentration camps headed into Germany in their tens of thousands as soon as they were liberated. The British and, particularly, the American zones in Germany were seen by Jews as the safest place to be in Europe that summer, especially since there had been renewed violence against Jewish people, in Poland and Lithuania for instance. Many saw America as their new home. But there were also many others in the displaced person (DP) camps of Germany who dreamed of living in Palestine. The *Yishuv* was the Jewish settlement in Palestine. And the idea, advanced most strongly by Zionists, for the establishment of a Jewish homeland based around the *Yishuv* had been in existence for some time and had been the subject of been a British promise in 1917 – in the Balfour Declaration.

The key part of this Declaration reads:

'His Majesty's government view with favour the establishment in Palestine of a national home for the Jewish people, and will use their best endeavours to facilitate the achievement of this object, it being clearly understood that nothing shall be done which may prejudice the civil and religious rights of existing non-Jewish communities in Palestine, or the rights and political status enjoyed by Jews in any other country.'[6]

However, ever since the declaration, and in the face of strong Arab opposition to it, the British had failed to deliver on their promise and had severely restricted Jewish immigration into Palestine: a 1939 white paper limited immigration to fifteen thousand a year. And during the war, the British deported Jewish refugees who had arrived in Palestine from Nazi-occupied Europe. This was one of the reasons that more Jewish refugees sought protection in the American zone: approximately 90 per cent of the total in Germany and Austria were in American-run DP camps by the end of 1945.[7] Plus, the British were suspicious of the Jews in their DP camps; they thought that they had come into them only in order to seek deportation to Palestine. Zionism was certainly on the rise amongst the Jewish DPs and that hardly seems surprising after having survived a systematic genocide which none of the Allies had made any concerted effort to prevent or stop. Many Jews no longer felt that Europe could be their home – but how could they get to Palestine? And how realistic was the prospect of a state of Israel if they did manage to get there?

Churchill recalled later in his memoirs that in the years following the end of the war 'Great Britain was confronted with the tortuous problem of combining Jewish immigration to their national home and safeguarding the rights of the Arab inhabitants. Few of us could blame the Jewish people for their violent views on the subject. A race that has suffered the virtual extermination of its national existence cannot be expected to be entirely reasonable.'[8]

David Ben-Gurion, the single person most responsible for the foundation of Israel – and its first prime minister – had urged Jews to join the British Army during the war. In 1945, he was the leader of the Zionist movement in Palestine and after the war was over, he visited Europe with an appealing message to his fellow Jews. They should not think of themselves as victims and drown in despair; they still had the opportunity to create an heroic story for themselves. Ben-Gurion visited some of the concentration camps, including Dachau and Bergen–Belsen, and met survivors of the camps, who turned out to hear him speak in their thousands. In his book *Year Zero: A History of 1945*, Ian Buruma quotes Ben-Gurion's speech to camp survivors at a Benedictine monastery near Munich:

> 'I can tell you that a vibrant Jewish Palestine exists and that even if its gates are locked the *Yishuv* will break them open with its strong hands … Today we are the decisive power in Palestine … We have our own shops, our own factories, our own culture, and our own rifles … Hitler was not far from Palestine. There could have been terrible destruction there, but what happened in Poland could not happen in Palestine.'[9]

Rabbi Judah Nadich was the senior Jewish chaplain for the US Army in the European theatre during the war and became General Dwight Eisenhower's advisor on Jewish affairs and DP camps in 1945. He records that General George Patton was 'not sympathetic to the plight of the Jewish survivors'. However, he was also responsible for all the DP camps in Bavaria. Nadich reported to Eisenhower that the Bavarian DP camps were in an appalling condition. At around the same time, Patton said some rather dubious things about Nazism and Eisenhower soon relieved him of his duty. By the end of the year, Patton was dead after failing to recover from an injury that he sustained in what was an otherwise innocuous car accident.

Nadich accompanied Ben-Gurion on his tour of the concentration camps. Listening to him speak, he said that it was 'an unforgettable experience for Ben Gurion, for me, for the hundreds or thousands of Jews present'. For Nadich himself, the experience of the Holocaust challenged his faith in the most fundamental way. 'Where was God?' he asked.[10]

Truman intervened on behalf of the Zionists, urging the British to accept more Jews into Palestine, but the issue was complex. Even so, Jews made their way to Palestine in greater and greater numbers in 1946 and 1947. The British referred the issue to the United Nations, who set up the United Nations Special Committee on Palestine which recommended the partition of Palestine. This recommendation was accepted and, on 14 May 1948, the State of Israel was formally declared. On 15 May, the 1948 Arab-Israeli war began.

Those Nazis still alive who were considered to be most responsible for the Holocaust, as well as other war crimes and crimes against humanity, were placed on trial in Nuremberg from November 1945. The trial lasted for almost a year. Those who had the greatest responsibility for the final solution – especially Hitler, Himmler, Goebbels and Heydrich – were all dead. Of the twenty-one senior Nazis who were ultimately tried at Nuremburg, twelve were sentenced to death. Göring was one of those, but he committed suicide before the sentence could be carried out. During the trial, Göring noticed a group of Jews in the public gallery. He was heard to whisper, 'Look at them, nobody can say we have exterminated them all!'[11]

Ian Buruma tells the story of Ernst Michel, a young Jewish man who had survived Auschwitz, Buchenwald and a desperate march between the two camps as the Russians had advanced in the late winter of 1945. He was a reporter at the trial and wrote in his first piece: 'Often in those difficult hours in the camp I had been sustained by the faith that there would be a day when those responsible for this regime would be called before the bar. This faith gave me strength to keep going. Today this day is here. Today, only a few feet away from me, are the men who for all prisoners in the camps were symbols of destruction and who are now being tried for their deeds.'[12]

According to Tom Bower, though, the trials provided 'the comforting myth that Nuremberg somehow took care of the whole problem'. But he explains in his book *Blind Eye to Murder: Britain, America and the Purging of Nazi Germany – A Pledge Betrayed* that Nuremburg was, although just, effectively a show trial to persuade the world that the Nazis were being brought to justice when, in fact, many thousands who had planned and executed the Holocaust never were. Worse than that, he argues, the United States and Britain never allocated the resources nor expressed the political importance of catching these criminals, and so it was inevitable that so many would never go on trial. Instead, they vanished into the ether.

It was not until the end of 1945 that Bernd Koschland realised that he would never see his parents again. He had come to Britain on the *kindertransport* before the war as an eight-year-old. His last contact with his parents had been in March 1939 and he had since tried to contact them through the Red Cross without success. His elder sister met him from school one day and told him that their mother and father were dead. They had been deported from Bavaria to Riga and, according to Bernd Koschland, 'met their end somewhere near there'. He was fourteen when he found out, but 'life had to go on' he said.

Many other thousands of Jewish children in Britain faced the same horrendous experience as the full scale of the holocaust gradually became known. They now had to integrate into a new community in the knowledge that they were orphans. 'I lived in the countryside for quite a while during the war and this anglicised me a great deal – I became more English than the English,' recalled Koschland. 'I went to the grammar school in High Wycombe when I was old enough. Those experiences put down a certain curtain between me and what happened in the past. Lots of people did not talk about the camps until much later.'[13]

Nineteen-year-old Michael Etkind, who survived a death march and was liberated by American tanks on VE Day, came to Britain as part of the Prague airlift in August 1945. He wrote a poem about his experiences of Britain.

The rugged coastline of your lands
surrounded by the restless seas.
Your mist at night;
The steady drizzle overhead –
Your rolling fields with hedgerows
interspersed, divided into varying shades
of green.

The clumps of trees.
Your brooding past.

The feeble sun of your indifferent clime.
You made so few demands upon my
cunning and skill.
You never cared if I succeeded/failed,
Loved you or not.
England, you took me in your stride.[14]

In Britain, the wartime austerity stretched on into peacetime – the country, relative to its previously enormous wealth, had become poor and drab. Rationing continued in various forms until 1954. In some cases, the rationing got worse before it got better. After a poor wheat harvest in 1946, bread was rationed and would remain so for another two years. Potato rationing began in 1947. Rebuilding Britain's damaged housing was a slower process than had been planned and tens of thousand of people remained in inadequate homes. In *Austerity Britain, 1945–1951*, David Kynaston quotes a rehousing officer called George Beardmore who in 1946 wrote:

'Two wretched families have moved into one of our requisitioned mansions in Marsh Lane [in Stanmore, Middlesex] and are shortly to receive an injunction to leave. Have twice visited them officially and once unofficially, under pledge of secrecy, to give them some clothes and blankets Jean [his wife] has found for them. A scene of squalor and misery rare even in these days. A bus conductor, two women, and three schoolchildren, driven desperate for somewhere to live, camp out in a large dilapidated room without light, water and (yesterday at least) without fuel for a fire. Sullen and dirty faces swollen with colds, an orange-box scraped dry of all but coal-dust, two saucepans on an unmade bed, a spirit stove on which bacon was frying, and a green teapot shaped like a racing-car on a strip of newspaper many times ringed.'[15]

However, the Labour government was being run with a real sense of purpose and Alan Brooke admired the clear-headedness of Attlee's methods compared with how Churchill had run his administration. 'A wonderful transformation of the Cabinet,' he exclaimed in his diary on 7 August 1945. And in a later note on this diary entry, he wrote that he was 'very impressed by the efficiency with which Attlee ran his cabinet. There was not the same touch of genius as with Winston, but there were more business-like methods. We kept to the agenda, and he maintained complete order with a somewhat difficult crowd. Our work was quickly and efficiently completed.'[16]

But, of course, governments do not tend to get credit for the way that they run Cabinet meetings, and the Labour Party had an enormous mountain to climb with the challenges that lay in front of them and the country as a whole. As Churchill put it in his memoirs, 'Certainly those who were responsible in Great Britain for the direction of our affairs in the years that followed the war were beset by the most complex and malignant problems both at home and abroad.'[17]

Britain as an empire was a spent force in 1945 and, although the United States had been Britain's most important ally during the war, they had little time for the idea that Britain would continue to be a global player. In 1945, it was already clear that what had been the jewel of the British Empire – India – would gain independence. The devil, though, was in the detail, specifically in efforts to preserve Indian unity rather than adopting a two-state solution. Many ordinary people in Britain were indifferent to the fate of India. One diarist wrote after the breakdown of talks in Shimla in July 1945, 'Really, the Indians are hopeless. I wish we could just clear out and leave to fight it out amongst themselves.'[18] Churchill was critical of the Labour Party approach. 'They believed that the advantage lay in the granting of self-government within the shortest space of time,' he later wrote,

> 'And they gave it without hesitation – almost identifiably – to the forces which we had vanquished so easily. Within two years of the end of the war they had achieved their purpose. On the 18th of August, 1947, Indian independence was declared. All efforts to preserve the unity of India had broken down, and Pakistan became a separate state. Four hundred million inhabitants of the subcontinent, mainly divided between Moslem and Hindu, flung themselves at one another. Two centuries of British rule in India were followed by greater bloodshed and loss of life than had ever occurred during our ameliorating tenure.'[19]

The description of Britain's rule of India as 'ameliorating tenure' would not have met with much sympathy from India's first Prime Minister Jawaharlal Nehru, who in 1930 had written:

> 'We believe that it is the inalienable right of the Indian people, as of any other people, to have freedom and

to enjoy the fruits of their toil and have the necessities of life, so that they may have full opportunities of growth. We believe also that if any government deprives a people of these rights and oppresses them, the people have a further right to alter it or to abolish it. The British Government in India has not only deprived the Indian people of their freedom but has based itself on the exploitation of the masses, and has ruined India economically, politically, culturally, and spiritually. We believe, therefore, that India must sever the British connection and attain Purna Swaraj, or complete independence.'[20]

Burma, too, achieved independence from Britain in 1947. Along with India and the occupation of Germany, these were all major foreign policy challenges for Britain in an age in which the most important thing was to focus on domestic challenges.

But perhaps the greatest post-war foreign policy challenge for Britain and the United States was the relationship with the Soviet Union, which had turned from cordial to frosty through the summer of 1945. On VE Day in London, the Soviet flag had been hoisted high with the Stars and Stripes and the Union Jack, but by the time the Dynamo Moscow football team arrived in Britain in November 1945, the flag was notable by its absence as they were greeted – rather lukewarmly – at Croydon airport. Soviet communism was the new enemy. The meeting of the foreign ministers of Britain, the Soviet Union, the United States, France and China in London in September 1945 produced a conference characterised by confrontation, chicanery and distrust. They had come together to discuss peace treaties but ended up failing to find a peace between the five of them and the conference was abandoned. George Orwell wrote an article in October that mentioned the phrase 'cold war' for the first time. It is fair to say that it stuck:

'For forty or fifty years past, Mr. H. G. Wells and others have been warning us that man is in danger of destroying himself with his own weapons, leaving the ants or some other gregarious species to take over. Anyone who has seen the ruined cities of Germany will find this notion at least thinkable. Nevertheless, looking at the world as a whole, the drift for many decades has been not towards anarchy but towards the reimposition of slavery. We may be heading not for general breakdown but for an epoch as horribly stable as the slave empires of antiquity. James Burnham's theory has been much discussed, but few people have yet considered its ideological implications – that is, the kind of world-view, the kind of beliefs, and the social structure that would probably prevail in a state which was at once unconquerable and in a permanent state of "cold war" with its neighbours.

'Had the atomic bomb turned out to be something as cheap and easily manufactured as a bicycle or an alarm clock, it might well have plunged us back into barbarism, but it might, on the other hand, have meant the end of national sovereignty and of the highly-centralised police state. If, as seems to be the case, it is a rare and costly object as difficult to produce as a battleship, it is likelier to put an end to large-scale wars at the cost of prolonging indefinitely a "peace that is no peace".'[21]

The Cold War defined global politics for the next forty-five years and many of the wars – beginning with the Greek civil war in 1946 and those from Korea to Afghanistan – that were fought in this period were effectively proxy wars between the two global superpowers. The stage was set; the actors upon it moved in a strange new world with a new type of warfare. Nazism may have been defeated, but between them the victors were ready to play out a new form of ideological confrontation, consisting of propaganda, espionage and the widespread belief at least that virtually all humanity could be destroyed with the simple press of a button.

The voices of some of those who participated not just in the end of the war but in the post-war drama, too, have been featured in this book. This is the story of what they did next:

Fred Aiken
Fred married in March 1945 and began a career as a schoolteacher in Northern Ireland in September the same year. With his family, he later moved to Welwyn Garden City, where the old grammar school became one of the new comprehensive schools. He taught there for the rest of his working life.

Alan Brooke, 1st Viscount of Alanbrooke
Alan Brooke was made Baron AlanBrooke of Brookeborough in 1945 and Viscount Alanbrooke in 1946. He was also made a member of the order of Merit (OM) the same year. He remained passionate about ornithology for the rest of his life and was President of the Zoological Society of London from

1950 to 1954 and Vice-President of the Royal Society for the Protection of Birds.

The publication of his diaries in 1957 was a notable event in part because Alanbrooke had written in capital letters at the start of his wartime diary: 'ON NO ACCOUNT MUST THE CONTENTS OF THIS BOOK BE PUBLISHED.'[22] Yet he had been frustrated by the way other people's memoirs – and most notably Churchill's – had not, as he saw it, given due credit to the work of the Chiefs of Staff and him personally. There were many frank and scathing assessments of some of the most senior members of the Allied war effort in Alanbrooke's diaries – both British and American. Alanbrooke wrote of Mountbatten, who was the Supreme Allied Commander South East Asia Command from 1943 to 1946, 'Seldom has a supreme commander been more deficient of the attributes of a supreme commander than Dickie Mountbatten.' And of Montgomery: 'I had to haul him over the coals for his usual lack of tact and egotistical outlook which prevented him from appreciating other people's feelings.' But it was his criticism of Churchill that drew most attention. Churchill himself did not appreciate it and Norman Brook, the Cabinet Secretary, wrote: 'I could have wished that the book was not to be published in Sir Winston Churchill's lifetime. And I cannot refrain from asking what steps are to be taken to prepare him for the kind of publicity which (if I am not mistaken) it will receive.'[23] Yet the publication of the diaries, for all their unpopularity in certain quarters, did mean that he received a great deal more public recognition than he would otherwise have gained.

Tony Benn
Tony Benn returned to Oxford where he had started his degree during the war. He completed his studies and soon

gravitated towards where his real passion lay – politics. And on 30 November 1950, at the age of just twenty-five, he won the by-election for Bristol South-East and became a Labour MP. He did not make his maiden speech in the House of Commons until February 1951, when he spoke about the nationalisation of steel. 'The benches falling away from below me made me feel very tall and conspicuous,' he wrote in his diary.[24] It was the first of many speeches in parliament – he remained an MP for more than fifty years and died in 2014.

Sir Winston Churchill
Churchill moved out of Downing Street and into Claridge's Hotel after he lost the 1945 election. 'The rest of my life will be holidays,' he said then, and it must have felt extraordinarily deflating to have been at the centre of everything for six years and then to be at the centre of nothing. But he was the Leader of the Opposition and hung on to the leadership of his own party for another ten years. He remained preoccupied with global affairs and spoke in a famous speech in 1946 of the Iron Curtain that had been drawn across Europe:

'From Stettin in the Baltic to Trieste in the Adriatic, an iron curtain has descended across the Continent. Behind that line lie all the capitals of the ancient states of Central and Eastern Europe. Warsaw, Berlin, Prague, Vienna, Budapest, Belgrade, Bucharest, and Sofia, all these famous cities and the populations around them lie in what I must call the Soviet sphere, and all are subject in one form or another, not only to Soviet influence but to a very high and, in many cases, increasing measure of control from Moscow.'[25]

He was also a fierce critic of the government's policy on India. He lost another election in 1950, but returned to government in 1951 after Labour called an election after just twenty months in a bid to increase their majority. He remained Prime Minister until 1955 and was succeeded by Anthony Eden. His health, which had been poor even during the war, was in serious decline by the end of the 1940s. He suffered a stroke in 1949, another in 1953 and one more in 1956. However, he remained an MP until 1964 and died the following year in 1965 after a final, severe stroke. His funeral was a major international event with representatives attending from 112 countries.

Simone de Beauvoir

The journal *Les Temps Modernes* was founded by Simone de Beauvoir, Jean-Paul Sartre and a number of others in October, 1945. It was a literary magazine, focusing on philosophical and political criticism and publishing new writers. It is still published today. De Beauvoir published her most enduring work *The Second Sex* in 1949. It is widely regarded as one of the most influential works of feminism of the twentieth century.

Richard Dimbleby

After Dimbleby's falling out with the BBC at the end of the war, his prospects looked uncertain for a while, but he soon became a BBC fixture once again – this time on television. He became the go-to anchor for big occasions, including the coronation of Queen Elizabeth in 1953 and the funerals of Winston Churchill and John F. Kennedy. He had an intense work ethic and was the host of current affairs programme *Panorama,* as well as working on lighter programmes, such as *Down Your Way,* which he also hosted.

However, in 1960, he was diagnosed with cancer and five years later died as a result of it, working up until the last few weeks of his life. The then controller of BBC Television Programmes, Huw Weldon, wrote in tribute:

> 'He was the voice of the BBC on thousands of occasions, and on hundreds of occasions I think he was even the voice of the nation. To an extent I think incomparable in the history of radio or television so far as this country is concerned, he was the voice of our generation, and probably the most telling voice in BBC radio or television of any kind in this country so far. It is in this sense I feel he is irreplaceable.'[26]

Bernd Koschland

Bernd completed his education in Golder's Green, North London and soon after became a rabbi. However, he felt he lacked experience in spiritual matters and retrained as a teacher and taught for the rest of his working life. He retired in 1995, but still goes to schools to talk to children about the *kindertransport*. He told me that it took a long to come to terms with the death of his parents. In 1971, 'the curtain' started to rise for Bernd. Until that time, he had observed a ritualistic commemoration of his parents' deaths, but he had never really opened his heart to the idea of it. A conversation with a sixth-form pupil who wanted to learn about the Holocaust made him think about it further and gradually he became more involved in finding out about the *kindertransport* and the Holocaust himself.

'Life just goes on. I'm very pragmatic about it. I've got to live with the present and hope there is a future; there is nothing I can do about the past.

'I talk to a lot of children about the *kindertransport* but I don't like to leave them with a negative message. My theme is that we have the opportunity to make the world a better place, each of us, in a small way, and that is the positive message that I like to give to them.'[27]

Bernard Montgomery, 1st Viscount Montgomery of Alamein

Montgomery was made Viscount Montgomery of Alamein in 1946 and after a short tenure overseeing the British Zone in Germany stepped into Alanbrooke's shoes as Chief of the Imperial General Staff from 1946 to 1948. However, he had never been, as Alanbrooke had pointed out, a diplomatic man and the appointment was not a success. The publication of his memoirs in 1958 was also controversial and ended his friendship with Eisenhower.

Iris Murdoch

Iris Murdoch began working for UNRRA in 1944 and worked in various places across Europe, including Brussels, Innsbruck, Vienna and Graz in 1945 and 1946. In 1947, she studied philosophy as a postgraduate at Cambridge and, in 1948, became a fellow at Oxford. She taught philosophy there until 1963. But she was also a prolific writer of novels during this time, publishing seven in all between 1954 and 1963.

David Niven

Niven could not wait to resume his life as an actor, but had some concerns about whether he would remember how to do it. He did not have to worry. He had immense popular success for the rest of his career. His first film was the Powell and Pressburger romantic fantasy *A Matter of Life and Death* in 1946. The Nivens soon moved to California and threw a farewell party at Claridge's for 200 guests. When he eventually arrived in Hollywood after a difficult journey, he found a large banner across the gate at the studio. It said: 'WELCOME HOME DAVID!!'

George Orwell

It took another four years for Orwell's dystopian novel *Nineteen Eighty-Four* to be finished and published. In it, civil servant Winston Smith rewrites old newspaper articles for the Party as part of the wider effort to control what the population is thinking in a total-surveillance society. But in his small, personal rebellion against the Party, Winston finds that there is no escape from 'Big Brother', the leader of Oceania. One of the most influential British novels of the twentieth century, it spawned an entire vocabulary that seemed especially apposite in the Cold War years that followed the Second World War, and beyond into the modern era of CCTV and digital surveillance. Orwell spent some time on the island of Jura writing *Nineteen Eighty-Four* in 1946 and 1947, but his health was in serious decline following a diagnosis of tuberculosis. He died at the age of forty-six in hospital in London on 21 January 1950.

Mary Tisdall
After the war, Mary married her husband who was in the RAF. They lived in different places around the world with the RAF until they retired to Salisbury, Wiltshire.

President Harry Truman
Truman remained in office at the White House until 1953. In addition to the Cold War and the occupation of Japan, he presided over the Korean War between 1950 and 1953. Action against North Korea was sanctioned by the United Nations, but in reality it was one of the proxy wars between the United States and the Soviet Union. More than thirty thousand US soldiers were killed in the conflict. He was later quoted as saying: 'I hate war. War destroys individuals and whole generations. It throws civilisation into the dark ages. But there is only one kind of war the American people have any stomach for and that is war against hunger and pestilence and disease. Much as we have contributed to industrial and economic development, we have gotten even greater know-how in the saving and prolonging of human lives.'

Edmund Wilson
Edmund Wilson received some notoriety from his refusal to pay income tax between 1946 and 1955, which was later the subject of his book *The Cold War and the Income Tax*. Wilson objected both to the practices of the Internal Revenue Service (IRS) and the way the income gained from taxation was being used. In particular, he felt that the Cold War was a pretext for limiting freedom in the United States. He wrote:

'The accomplished, the intelligent, the well-informed go on in their useful professions that require high integrity and intellect, but they suffer more and more from the crowding of an often unavowed constraint which may prevent them from allowing themselves to become too intelligent and well-informed or may drive them to indulge their skills in gratuitous and futile exercises. One notices in the conversation of this professional class certain inhibitions on free expression, a tacit understanding that certain matters had better not be brought into discussion, which sometimes makes one feel in such talk a kind of fundamental frivolity.'[28]

Nonetheless, despite his disputes with the IRS, President Kennedy selected him to receive the Presidential Medal of Freedom. Kennedy was assassinated before he could make the award, and instead President Lyndon Johnson gave the medal to Wilson, who did not, in any case, attend the ceremony.

A Woman in Berlin

The author of the account of *A Woman in Berlin* was widely believed to be the German journalist Marta Hillers. She died in 2001, aged ninety. *A Woman in Berlin* was made into a film in 2009.

Notes

Introduction

1 Dickens, Charles, *A Tale of Two Cities*, Public Domain Books, Kindle edition, 2010.
2 *Life Magazine*, 28 March 1949, p.11.
3 Kaczynski, Richard, *Perdurabo: The Life of Aleister Crowley*, p.511.
4 Quoted in Hastings, Max, *His Finest Years: Churchill as Warlord 1940–45*, Harper-Collins, London, 2010, p.564.
5 Quoted in the *Guardian*, 24 April 2001, 'Price war offers cheer as the champagne bubble bursts'.
6 Quoted in Wilson, A. N., *After the Victorians*, Hutchinson, London, 2005, p.390.
7 Quoted in Gilbert, Martin, *The Day the War Ended*, Harper Collins, London, 1995, pp.209–10.
8 *Manchester Guardian*, 9 May 1945, 'The Victory', p.4.
9 Quoted in Longmate, Norman, *How we Lived Then: A History of Everyday Life During the Second World War*, Pimlico, London, 2002, p.502.
10 *The Times*, 9 May 1945.
11 Ibid, p.501.
12 Quoted in the *Manchester Guardian*, 9 May 1945.
13 MOA, File Report 2249: May 1945, 'Post VE Day Celebrations'.
14 'Japan WW2 soldier who refused to surrender Hiroo Onoda dies', retrieved from http://www.bbc.co.uk/news/world-asia-25772192, 8 Feb. 2015.

Chapter 1

1   Alanbrooke, Field Marshal Lord, *War Diaries: 1939–1945*, Ed. Alex Danchey and Daniel Todman, Phoenix Press, London, 2002, p.688.
2   MOA, TC49: Victory Celebrations and parades: 1945–46 (SxMOA1/2/49/1/C: 'VE Day and the Day After' 8 – 09.05.1945).
3   MOA, TC49: Victory Celebrations and parades: 1945–46 (SxMOA1/2/49/1/C: 'VE Day and the Day After' 8 – 09.05.1945).
4   Quoted in Schneider, Carl J. and Schneider, Dorothy, *World War II*, Facts on File, New York, p.394.
5   Gilbert, Martin, *The Day the War Ended*, Harper Collins, London, 1995, p.87.
6   Quoted in Gilbert (1995), p.95.
7   *Manchester Guardian*, 8 May 1945, p.2.
8   *Daily Telegraph*, 9 May 1945, p.5.
9   BBC Archive, Folder R34/920, 18 October 1943.
10 Ibid.
11 MOA, TC49: Victory Celebrations and Parades: 1945–46 (SxMOA1/2/49/1/A: 'Before VE Day: reactions to the end of the war').
12 *Manchester Guardian*, 9 May 1945, 'Weather forecasts again', p.5.
13 Ibid.
14 *Western Daily Press*, 9 May 1945.
15 IWM, Department of Documents 13624 'Private papers of Dr J. J. Beeston'.
16 MOA, TC49: Victory Celebrations and parades: 1945–46 (SxMOA1/2/49/1/C: 'VE Day and the Day After' 8 – 09.05.1945).
17 *Daily Telegraph*, 9 May 1945, 'London Day by Day', p.4.
18 MOA, Diarist 5216, 8 May 1945.
19 IWM Sound Archive 6221: Interview with William Ronald McGill.
20 Interview with author, 21 October 2014.
21 IWM, Department of Documents 14880, 'Private papers of A. Bray'.
22 BBC, WW2 People's War, Article ID A2756351.
23 Churchill, Winston S., *Memoirs of the Second World War*, Houghton Mifflin Company, Boston, 1959, p.966.
24 MOA, Diarist 5216, 8 May 1945.
25 MOA, TC49: Victory Celebrations and Parades (ScMOA 1/2/49/1/B).
26 MOA, TC49: Victory Celebrations and Parades: 1945–46 (SxMOA1/2/49/1/C: 'VE Day and the Day' After 8 – 09.05.1945).

27 Ibid.
28 Ibid.
29 IWM, Department of Documents 13624 'Private papers of Dr J J Beeston'.
30 Interview with author, 29 September 2014.
31 Quoted in Gilbert (1995), p.174.
32 MOA, TC49: Victory Celebrations and Parades: 1945–46 (SxMOA1/2/49/1/C: 'VE Day and the Day After' 8 – 09.05.1945).
33 Alanbrooke (2002), p.688.
34 Ibid.
35 Ibid.
36 Churchill (1959), p. 969.
37 *Manchester Guardian,* 9 May 1945, 'Memorable Commons scenes', p.5.
38 *Daily Telegraph,* 9 May 1945, 'London Day by Day', p.4.
39 MOA, TC49: Victory Celebrations and Parades: 1945–46 (SxMOA1/2/49/1/C: 'VE Day and the Day After' 8 – 09.05.1945).
40 Ibid.
41 Ibid.
42 Ibid.
43 Ibid.
44 Ibid.
45 *Manchester Guardian,* 9 May 1945, 'Manchester's victory day celebrations', p.3.
46 MOA, TC49: Victory Celebrations and Parades: 1945–46 (SxMOA1/2/49/1/C: 'VE Day and the Day After' 8 – 09.05.1945).
47 *Daily Telegraph,* 9 May 1945, 'London Revels in Glare of Floodlights', p.5.
48 http://www.royal.gov.uk/pdf/georgevi.pdf, p.3.
49 MOA, TC49: Victory Celebrations and Parades: 1945–46 (SxMOA1/2/49/1/C: 'VE Day and the Day After' 8 – 09.05.1945).
50 IWM, Department of Documents 15323, 'Private papers of C. L. R. Matthews'.
51 IWM, Department of Documents 13270, 'Private papers of F. Cowling'.
52 Murdoch, Iris, *A Writer at War: The Letters and Diaries of Iris Murdoch: 1939–1945,* Ed. Peter J. Conradi, Short Books, London, 2010, p.224.

53 Quoted in Longmate, Norman, *How We Lived Then*, Trafalgar Square, London, 2003, p.504.
54 Ibid, p.502.
55 Ibid.
56 BBC, WW2 People's War, Article ID A1112527.
57 MOA, TC49: Victory Celebrations and Parades: 1945–46 (SxMOA1/2/49/1/C: 'VE Day and the Day After') 8 – 09.05.1945.
58 Ibid.
59 MOA, TC49: Victory Celebrations and Parades: 1945–46 (ScMOA 1/2/49/1/D).
60 Interview with the author, 30 September 2014.
61 *Manchester Guardian*, 9 May 1945, 'Broadcasting review', p.8.
62 MOA, Diarist 5443, 8 May 1945.

Chapter 2

1   *Manchester Guardian*, 2 May 1945.
2   http://www.yadvashem.org/yv/en/holocaust/about/03/terezin.asp.
3   *Manchester Guardian*, 9 May 1945, 'End of thc Nazi salute', p.8.
4   Niven, David, *The Moon's a Balloon*, Hamish Hamilton, London, 1971, p.260.
5   IWM, Department of Documents 13159, 'Private papers of S. R. Verrier'.
6   IWM, Department of Documents 17648, 'Private papers of J. A. Lethi'.
7   This anonymous source is quoted in Gilbert (1995), p.244.
8   Quoted in Gilbert, Martin, *The Boys: Triumph over Adversity*, Weidenfeld & Nicholson, London, 1996, pp.242–3.
9   Anonymous, *A Woman in Berlin*, Secker and Warburg, London, 1955, p.169–70.
10 Ibid, p.173.
11 Ibid, p.174.
12 De Beauvoir, Simone, *Force of Circumstance*, Andre Deutsch Ltd. and Weidenfeld & Nicholson Ltd, London, 1965, p.28.
13 Ibid, p.30.
14 IWM, Department of Documents 19794, 'Private papers of J. E. Rhys'.
15 BBC, WW2 People's War, Article ID A2746695.

16 Wilson, Edmund, *Europe without Baedecker: Sketches Among the ruins of Italy, Greece and England*, Hogarth Press, London, 1986, p.217.

17 Quoted in Gilbert (1995), p.234.

18 Wilson (1986), p.201.

19 IWM, Department of Documents 13169, 'Private papers of Major T. C. Howes

20 Wilson (1986), pp.242–3.

21 BBC Archive, R34/920, memo from Director New Delhi Office to Senior Controller, London, 4 April 1945.

22 Benn, Tony, *Years of Hope: Diaries, Papers and Letters 1940–1962*, Ed. Ruth Winstone, Arrow Books, London, 1994, p.90.

23 IWM, Department of Documents 6985, 'Private papers of Captain I. A. Wallace'.

24 *Daily Telegraph*, 9 May 1945.

25 *New York Times*, 11 October 2009, 'Hitler's jaws of death, p. WK11.

26 *Observer*, 8 May 2005, 'Anguish of woman who held secret evidence of Hitler's identity': http://www.theguardian.com/world/2005/may/08/russia.secondworldwar.

27 Quoted in Kellock, Hon. Mr. Justice R. L., *Report on the Halifax Disorders, May 7th–8th, 1945*, Edmund Cloutier, Ottawa, 1945.

28 *New York Times*, 8 May 1945, 'The war in Europe is ended!', p.1.

29 *Manchester Guardian*, 9 May 1945, 'West is free, but east is still in bondage – President Truman', p.6.

30 *Daily Telegraph*, 9 May 1945, 'Our victory is only half won, says Mr Truman', p.5.

31 Quoted in *Kansas Historical Society*, Vol. 13, No. 7, August 1945, p.386.

32 *Melbourne Argus*, 11 May 1945, p. 7.

33 Quoted in Gilbert (1995), p.317.

34 *Canberra Times*, 8 May 1945, editorial, quoted on Australian War Memorial website: https://www.awm.gov.au/encyclopedia/ve_day/ on 3 Feb. 2015.

35 Australian War Memorial, NX6461, retrieved from https://www.awm.gov.au/collection/PAFU2014/153.01/ on 3 Feb. 2015.

Chapter 3

1 *Manchester Guardian*, 9 May 1945, 'The Victory', p.4

2 *Observer*, 8 April 1945, 'Future of a ruined Germany', retrieved from http://www.theguardian.com/books/1945/apr/08/georgeorwell. classics on 3 Feb. 2015.
3 BBC transcripts, 3 July 1945, Home Service.
4 Anonymous (1955), p.182.
5 Kershaw, Ian, *Hitler, 1936–45: Nemesis*, Allen Lane, London, 2000, p.784.
6 Quoted in Buruma, Ian, *Year Zero – A History of 1945*, Atlantic Books, London, 2013, p.79.
7 IWM, Department of Documents, 19794, 'Private papers of J. E. Rhys'.
8 Ibid.
9 *Observer*, 8 April 1945, 'Future of a ruined Germany', retrieved from http://www.theguardian.com/books/1945/apr/08/georgeorwell. classics on 3 Feb. 2015.
10 *Manchester Guardian*, 9 May 1945, 'The Victory', p.4.
11 Ibid.
12 Montgomery, Viscount Bernard, *The Memoirs of Field-Marshal Montgomery*, Pen & Sword Military, Barnsley, 2010, p.356.
13 Bach, Julian Jnr., *America's Germany: An Account of the Occupation*, New York: Random House, 1946, p.4.
14 Ibid, p.173
15 Quoted in Buruma (2013), pp.235–6.
16 Anonymous, (1955), pp.178–9.
17 BBC transcript, 4 July 1945.
18 Ibid, 16 July 1945.
19 Churchill (1959), p.979.
20 Alanbrooke (2003), p.705.
21 IWM, Department of Documents, 19794, 'Private papers of J. E. Rhys'.
22 Bach (1946), pp.18–19.
23 MOA, Diarist 5270, 8 April 1945.
24 Bach (1946), p.103
25 IWM, Department of Documents 13159, 'Private papers of S. R. Verrier'.
26 MOA, Diarist 5270, 8 April 1945.
27 IWM, Department of Documents 12628, 'Private papers of Major P. M. Barrington'.

28 IWM, Department of Documents 13159, 'Private papers of S. R. Verrier'.
29 Bach (1946), p.73.
30 Montgomery, (2010), p.358.
31 Anonymous, (1955), p.176.
32 MacDonogh, Giles, *After the Reich: From the Liberation of Vienna to the Berlin Airlift,* John Murray, London, 2008, p.236.
33 Ibid, p.76.
34 This is examined in more detail in the epilogue.
35 MacDonogh, (2008) and Buruma, (2013) both cover this.
36 Bach, (1946), p.88.
37 Montgomery, (2010), p.360.
38 Ibid, p.362.
39 Ibid, p.365.
40 Quoted in Bessel, Richard, *Germany 1945: From War to Peace*, Simon & Schuster, London, 2010, p.269.
41 Quoted in MacDonogh, (2008), p.229.
42 Quoted in Carruthers, Bob, *The SS On Trial: Evidence from Nuremberg*, Pen & Sword Books Ltd., Barnsley, 2013, p.13.
43 Quoted in Hillman, William, *Mr President: Personal Diaries, Private Letters, Papers, and Revealing Interviews of Harry S. Truman,* Hutchinson, London, 1952, p.98.
44 IWM, Department of Documents, 19794, 'Private papers of J. E. Rhys'.
45 IWM, Department of Documents 12628, 'Private papers of Major P. M. Barrington'.
46 BBC Transcript, 31 July 1945.
47 Montgomery, (2010), p.359.
48 Quoted in Buruma, (2013), p.73.

Chapter 4

1 Murdoch, (2010), p.233
2 *Manchester Guardian*, 9 May 1945, 'A general election?', p.4.
3 Bullock, Alan, *The Life and Times of Earnest Bevin*, Heinemann, London, 1960, p.382.
4 'A Future of Toil and Sweat: No Totalitarian System for England,' speech delivered by Winston Churchill on 15 March 1945 at the Conservative Party Conference, retrieved from http://www.ibiblio. org/pha/policy/1945/1945-03-15a.html on 3 Feb. 2015.

5   Jenkins, Roy, *Churchill* Macmillan, London, 2001, p.790.
6   *Manchester Guardian*, 9 May 1945, 'Memorable Commons scenes', p.5.
7   Quoted in Jenkins, (2001), p.791.
8   BBC Archives, folder R28/81/3: 'Overseas news department editorial directive: general elections'.
9   BBC Archives, folder R41/59, letter from J. T. Sharkey, 4 June 1945.
10 Ibid.
11 BBC Archives, folder R28/81/3: 'Overseas news department editorial directive: general elections'
12 Churchill, (1955), p.977.
13 Quoted in Buruma, (2013), p.250.
14 MOA Diarist 5243, 3 July 1945.
15 MOA Diarist 5443, 4 July 1945.
16 Quoted in *The Times*, 6 June 1945.
17 Benn, (1994), p.94.
18 Retrieved from http://www.conservative-party.net/ manifestos/1945/1945-conservative-manifesto.shtml on 3 Feb. 2015.
19 Benn, (1994), p.91.
20 MOA Diarist 5443, 18 June 1945.
21 Ibid, 20 June 1945.
22 Ibid, 27 June 1945.
23 Ibid, 21 June 1945.
24 Ibid, 25 June 1945.
25 Ibid, 3 July 1945.
26 Ibid, 29 June 1945.
27 MOA, Diarist 5243, 3 July 1945.
28 Ibid.
29 Ibid, 5 July 2015.
30 MOA Diarist 5443, 5 July 1945.
31 MOA Diarist 5216, 5 July 1945.
32 Alanbrooke, (2002), p.702.
33 IWM Department of Documents 12628, 'Private papers of Major P. M. Barrington'.
34 Churchill, (1955), p.977.
35 MOA, Diarist 5243, 6 July 1945.
36 *Evening Standard*, 26 July 1945, p.1.

37 Murdoch, (2010), p.233.
38 MOA Diarist 5443, 26 July 1945.
39 MOA Diarist 5243, 26 July 1945.
40 Ibid, 28–29 July 1945.
41 MOA Diarist 5216, 27 July 1945.
42 Longmate, Norman, *When We Won the War*, Hutchinson, London, 1977, pp.172–3.
43 Calder, Angus, *The People's War: Britain 1939–45*, Jonathan Cape, London, 1969, p.582.
44 Benn, (1994), p.91.
45 *Daily Telegraph*, 27 July 1945.
46 MOA Diarist 5443, 29 July 1945.
47 As mentioned in Gardiner, Juliet, *Wartime: Britain 1939–1945*, Headline, London, 2004, p.680.
48 Kynaston, David, *Austerity Britain 1945–1951*, Bloomsbury, London, 2007, p.75.
49 Churchill, (1955), p.990.
50 Ibid, p.991.
51 *Daily Telegraph*, 27 July 1945.
52 *Manchester Guardian*, 27 July 1945, 'Britain's revulsion against Tory rule'.
53 *Evening Standard*, 27 July 1945.
54 Alanbrooke, (2002), p.712.
55 Ibid.
56 BBC Archive, Folder R41/59.
57 MOA Diarist 5443, 18 June 1945.
58 MOA, Diarist 5243, 27 July 1945.
59 *Daily Telegraph*, 27 July 1945.
60 Quoted in Hastings, Max, *His Finest Years: Churchill as Warlord 1940–45*, Harper Collins, London, 2009, p.589.
61 *Manchester Guardian*, 27 July 1945.
62 Letter to author, 15 September 2015.
63 *Manchester Guardian*, 27 July 1945.
64 Ibid.

Chapter 5

1 *Manchester Guardian*, 18 July 1945.
2 Churchill, (1955), p.980.
3 Alanbrooke, (2002), p.709.

4   BBC Transcript, 16 July 1945.
5   *Manchester Guardian,* 18 July 1945.
6   MOA, Diarist 5243, 14–15 July 1945.
7   Ibid, 16 July 1945.
8   Ibid, 17–18 July.
9   Alanbrooke, (2002), p.705.
10 Ibid.
11 Ibid, p.708.
12 Hillman, (1952), p.106.
13 Hastings, (2009), p.502.
14 Churchill, (1955), p.985.
15 Quoted in Gellately, Robert, *Stalin's Curse: Battling for Communism in War and Cold War,* Oxford University Press, Oxford, 2013, p.103.
16 Montgomery, (2010), p.392.
17 MacDonogh, (2008), p.50.
18 Quoted in Buruma, (2013), p.82.
19 Hastings, (2009), p.551.
20 Churchill, (1955), p.986.
21 Kuznetsov is quoted in Hastings, (2009), p.589.
22 The remark attributed to Churchill is quoted in MacDonogh, (2008), p.489.
23 Montgomery, (2010), p.392.
24 MOA, Diarist 5243, 27 July 1945.
25 MOA Diarist 5443, 28 July 1945.
26 Quoted in MacDonogh, (2008), p.489.
27 Quoted in Bullock, Alan, *Hitler and Stalin: Parallel Lives,* Harper Collins, London, 1991, p.979.
28 MOA, 5243, 30 July 1945.
29 Montgomery, (2010), p.393.
30 Quoted in Bullock, (1991), p.976.
31 Churchill, (1955), p.971.
32 Ibid, p.973.
33 MacDonogh, (2008), p.167.
34 Quoted in Buruma, (2013), p.95.
35 Quoted in Spiegel Online article: 'A Time of retribution: paying with life and limb for the crimes of Nazi Germany', http://www.spiegel.de/international/germany/a-time-of-retribution-paying-with-life-and-limb-for-the-crimes-of-nazi-germany-a-759737-4.html retrieved 3 Feb. 2015.

36 Quoted in Bullock, (1991), p.955.

Chapter 6

1 Quoted in Dimbleby, Jonathan, *Richard Dimbleby: A Biography*, Hodder and Stoughton, London, 1975, p.191.
2 Churchill, (1955), p.12.
3 Quoted in 'Making Justice at Nuremberg, 1945–1946' by Professor Richard Overy, at http://www.bbc.co.uk/history/worldwars/wwtwo/war_crimes_trials_01.shtml retrieved on 3 Feb. 2015.
4 Quoted in Buruma, (2013), p.225.
5 Quoted by Overy, 'Making Justice at Nuremburg, 1945–1946'.
6 Quoted in Buruma, (2013), p.225.
7 MOA, TC49: Victory Celebrations and Parades: 1945–46, (SxMOA1/2/49/1/B)
8 Wilson, (1986), p.36.
9 Beevor, Anthony and Cooper, Artemis, *Paris After the Liberation, 1944–49*, Penguin, London, 1995, p.150.
10 MOA, TC49: Victory Celebrations and Parades: 1945–46, (SxMOA1/2/49/1/B)
11 Quoted in Bessel, Richard, *Germany 1945: From War to Peace*, (London: Simon & Schuster, 2010), p.16.
12 Bullock, (1991), p.956.
13 Quoted in Bessel, (2009), p.151.
14 Ibid, p.150.
15 Solzhenitsyn, Alexander, *Prussian Nights*, Farrar Straus Giroux, London, 1977.
16 MacDonogh, (2008), p.50.
17 Anonymous, (1955), p.168.
18 MacDonogh, (2008), p.132.
19 Ibid, pp132–5.
20 Buruma,(2013), pp.96–7.
21 Quoted in Bessel, (2009), p.165.
22 Ibid, p.158.
23 Ibid, p.382.
24 Ibid, p.161.
25 Quoted in Dimbleby, (1975), pp191–3.
26 Ibid, p.193.
27 MacDonogh, (2008), p.176.
28 Quoted in Bessel, (2009), p.162.

29 Ibid, p.164

30 Buruma, (2013), p.86.

31 Wilson, (1986), p.217.

32 Quoted in Beevor and Cooper, (1995), p.151.

33 De Gaulle, *Mémoires de guerre*, vol. 2, Pochet, 1983, pp.249–50.

34 Beevor and Cooper, (1995), p.153.

35 Quoted in ibid, p.156.

36 Quoted in Buruma, (2013), p.221.

37 Ibid, p.224.

38 *Manchester Guardian*, 9 August 1945, 'The trial of major war criminals'.

39 See Bower, Tom, *Klaus Barbie: Butcher of Lyons*, Corgi, London, 1985.

40 Kershaw, (2000), p.838.

41 Bower, Tom, *Blind Eye to Murder: Britain, America and the Purging of Nazi Germany – A Pledge Betrayed*, Granada, London, 1983, p.108.

42 See Bower, (1985).

43 Bower, (1983), p.122.

44 Ibid, p.123.

45 Ibid, p.129.

46 Ibid, p.130.

47 Ibid, p.xiv.

Chapter 7

1 Wilson, (1986), p.178.

2 Letter to author, 15 October 2014.

3 IWM, Department of Documents 14880, 'Private papers of A. Bray'.

4 MOA, Diarist 5243, 15 August 1945.

5 IWM, Department of Documents 13159, 'Private papers of S. R. Verrier', letter from 11 August 1945.

6 Wilson, (1986), p.178.

7 IWM, Department of Documents 9705.

8 IWM, Department of Documents 14880, 'Private papers of A. Bray'.

9 MOA, Diarist 5443, 15 June 1945.

10 *Evening Standard*, 9 August 1945, 'Food problem is more acute'.

11 Wilson, (1986), p.185.

12 Ibid, p.191.

13 Ibid, p.333.

14 MOA, Diarist 5443, 20 August 1945.

15 IWM, Department of Documents, 6985, 'Private papers of Captain I A Wallace'.

16 Niven, (1971), pp.261–2.

17 Benn, (1994), p.94.

18 Ibid.

19 *Daily Telegraph*, 18 August 1945, '1,100,000 out of forces by end of year,' p.1.

20 Longmate, (2002), p.507.

21 IWM, Department of Documents 13169, 'Private papers of Major T. C. Howes'.

22 Quoted in Gardiner, Juliet, *Wartime: Britain 1939–1945*, Headline, London, 2004, pp.685–6.

23 BBC Archive, Folder R1/81/1, 'Acting and Substantive Grades: Note by the Director General, 13/11/1945'.

24 Quoted in Dimbleby, (1975), p.204.

25 Ibid.

26 IWM Department of Documents, 'For your guidance – what to do on leaving the service, and how to do it'.

27 Calder, (1969), p.571.

28 Quoted in Turner, Barry and Rennell, Tony, *When Daddy Came Home: How War Changed Family Life Forever*, Hutchinson, London, 1995, p.1.

29 Longmate, (1977), p.160.

30 MOA, Victory Celebrations and Parades: 1945-46, (SxMOA1/2/49/1/B).

31 Quoted in Longmate, (1977), p.161.

32 MOA Diarist 5270, 16 August 1945.

33 MOA Diarist 5443, 11 August 1945.

34 Quoted in Orwell, George, *George Orwell Diaries*, Ed. Peter Davison, Harvill Secker, London, 2009, p.369.

35 Orwell, George, *Nineteen Eighty-Four*, Penguin, London, 2000, p.280.

36 Davison, Peter (Ed.), *George Orwell, A Life in Letters*, Harvill Secker, London, 2010.

37 Wilson, (1986), p.186.

38 Murdoch, (2010), p.227.

39 Ibid., p.228.

40 MOA Diarist 5443, 18 June 1945.

41 Ibid, 16 June 1945.

42 Ibid, 14 July 1945.

43 Ibid, 16 July 1945.
44 Interview with the author, 30 September 2014.
45 Gardiner, (2004), p.68
46 Quoted in Summer, Julie, *Stranger in the House: Women's Stories of Men Returning from the Second World War*, Simon & Schuster, London, 2008, p.8.
47 Interview with the author, 29 September 2014
48 Interview with the author
49 *Daily Telegraph*, 2 September 2009, 'WW2: Former Evacuees Look Back' – http://www.telegraph.co.uk/history/world-war-two/6122897/WW2-Former-evacuees-look-back.html retrieved 3 Feb. 2015.
50 Quoted in Gilbert, (1996), p.303.

Chapter 8

1 Quoted in Freed, Fred, *The Decision to Drop the Bomb*, Coward McCann, New York, 1965, p. 197.
2 The account of Setsuko Thurlow was retrieved from http://web.net/~cnanw/setsukostory.htm on 3 Feb. 2015.
3 Hachiya, Michihiko, *Hiroshima Diary*, University of North Carolina Press, Chapel Hill, 1955.
4 Thurlow, Op. cit.
5 See Hersey, John, *Hiroshima*, Penguin, London, 2001.
6 Hachiya, (1955), taken from 'Surviving the Atomic Attack on Hiroshima, 1945,' EyeWitness to History, www.eyewitnesstohistory.com (2001).
7 http://www.inicom.com/hibakusha/yoshitaka.html.
8 Thurlow, Op. Cit.
9 Hersey, (2001), p.18.
10 *Guardian*, 6 August 2002, 'One hell of a big bang'.
11 Ridenbaugh, Mary Young, *Enola: or, Her fatal mistake*, For the author, Saint Louis, 1886.
12 *Guardian*, 6 August 2002, 'One hell of a big bang'.
13 Ibid.
14 Thurlow, Op. cit.
15 Hachiya, Op. cit.
16 Hersey, (2001), p.29.
17 Ibid, p.47.
18 Ibid, p.68.

19   *Daily Telegraph*, 7 August 1945.

20   *Evening Standard*, 8 August 1945, p.1.

21   Hillman, (1952), pp.190–1.

22   *Guardian*, 25 March, 2009, 'A little deaf in one ear – meet the Japanese man who survived Hiroshima and Nagasaki'.

23   *Evening Standard*, 9 August 1945, p.1.

24   *Manchester Guardian*, 10 August 1945.

25   Ibid.

26   Ibid.

27   Quoted in Buruma, (2013), p.313.

28   Ibid.

29   Hersey, (2001), p.116–7.

30   Quoted in the *Derby Evening Telegraph*, 8 August 1945.

31   MOA File Report 2272: 'A Report on Public Attitudes to the Atom Bomb' (SxMOA 1/1/10/8/2).

32   *Manchester Guardian*, 10 August 1945, 'Use of atomic bombs: Lord Louis's views'.

33   MOA File Report 2272, Op. cit.

34   MOA Diarist 5443, 9 August 1945.

35   Letter to author, 15 September 2014.

36   MOA File Report 2272, Op. cit.

37   MOA Diarist 5216, 10 August 1945.

38   MOA File Report 2272, Op. cit.

39   MOA Diarist 5243, 7 August 1945.

40   MOA File Report 2272, Op. cit.

41   Ibid.

42   Ibid.

43   Hansard, *HC Deb* 16 August 1945, Vol. 413, cc70–133.

Chapter 9

1   MOA, Topic Collection 49, Op. cit.

2   Quoted in *Mother Jones*, 10 October 2012, 'The unromantic truth behind the VJ Day kiss photo', retrieved from http://www.motherjones.com/mixed-media/2012/10/unromantic-truth-vj-kiss-photo on 3 Feb. 2015.

3   Quoted in Hillman, (1952), p.108.

4   *Daily Telegraph*, 11 August 1945.

5   *Manchester Guardian*, 16 August 1945, 'Americans' Joy', p.8.

6   *Mother Jones*, Op. cit.

7   *SFGate*, 15 August 2005, 'The dark side of V-J Day: the story of the city's deadliest riot has largely been forgotten', retrieved from http://www.sfgate.com/bayarea/article/SAN-FRANCISCO-The-dark-side-of-V-J-Day-The-2647870.php on 3 Feb. 2015.

8   Transcript of broadcast from August 15 1945, ABC Radio, transcribed from http://sitesandsounds.net.au/soundings/martin-place-on-vp-day-1945/ on 3 Feb. 2015.

9   Merchant seaman Jim Blundell interviewed by Neill Atkinson, 2004, retrieved from http://www.nzhistory.net.nz/war/vj-day on 3 Feb. 2015.

10 Quoted in Longmate, (2002), p.507.

11 Historic royal speeches and writings: 'Broadcast, VJ (Victory over Japan) Day, 15 August 1945', retrieved from http://www.royal.gov.uk/pdf/georgevi.pdf on 3 Feb. 2015.

12 MOA Diarist 5270, 15 August 1945.

13 MOA Diarist 5443, 15 August 1945.

14 MOA Diarist 5243, 15 August 1945.

15 MOA, Topic Collection 49, Op. cit.

16 Ibid.

17 MOA Diarist 5443, Op. cit.

18 Ibid, 16 August 1945.

19 MOA Diarist 5270, op. cit.

20 MOA, Topic Collection 49, Op. cit.

21 Ibid.

22 MOA Diarist 5243, 15 August 1945.

23 Longmate, (2002), p.508.

24 MOA Diarist 5270, op. cit.

25 MOA, Topic Collection 49, Op. cit.

26 IWM, 'Private papers of S. R. Verrier'.

27 Quoted in Longmate, (1977), p.173.

28 MOA Diarist 5270, op. cit.

29 *Manchester Guardian*, 16 August 1945.

30 Ibid.

31 Ibid.

32 MOA, Topic Collection 49, Op. cit.

33 Ibid.

34 Ibid.

35 MOA Diarist 5443, 15 August 1945.

36 *Daily Telegraph*, 16 August 1945.

37 *Manchester Guardian*, 16 August 1945.
38 Dimbleby, (1975), p.201.
39 *Manchester Guardian*, 16 August 1945.
40 Interview with author, 29 September 2014.
41 MOA, Topic Collection 49, Op. cit.
42 Ibid.
43 MOA Diarist, 5216, 16 August 1945.
44 MOA Diarist 5270, 16 August 1945.

Chapter 10
1   *Tribune*, 19 October 1945, 'You and the atomic bomb'.
2   Churchill, Winston S., *Memoirs of the Second World War*, Houghton Mifflin, Boston, 1959, p.1015.
3   Ibid, p.1001.
4   Hillman, William, *Mr President: Personal diaries, private letters, papers, and revealing interviews of Harry S. Truman*, Hutchinson, London, 1952, p.188.
5   MOA Diarist 5443, 27 June 1945.
6   'The Balfour Declaration,' retrieved from http://news.bbc. co.uk/1/hi/in_depth/middle_east/israel_and_the_palestinians/ key_documents/1682961.stm on 8 Feb. 2015.
7   MacDonogh, Giles, *After the Reich: From the Liberation of Vienna to the Berlin Airlift*, John Murray, London, 2008, p.330.
8   Churchill, Op. Cit., p.1015.
9   Buruma, (2013), p.166.
10 United States Holocaust Memorial Museum Archives, Oral History Interviews of the Kean College of New Jersey Holocaust Resource Center, Interview with Judah Nadich March 15, 1990 RG-50.002*0044.
11 MacDonogh, (2008), p.445.
12 Buruma, (2013), p.232.
13 Interview with the author, 21 October 2014.
14 Gilbert, (1996), p.364.
15 Kynaston, p.102.
16 Alanbrooke, (2002), p.715.
17 Churchill, Op. cit., p.1009.
18 MOA Diarist 5338, 16 July 1945.
19 Churchill, Op. cit.

20 National Archives, 'Extracts from the Independence Day Resolution passed by the Indian National Congress in 1930', retrieved from http://www.nationalarchives.gov.uk/education/empire/transcript/g3cs3s2t.htm on 8 Feb. 2015.
21 *Tribune*, op. cit.
22 Alanbrooke, (2002), p.xi.
23 Ibid., p.xxiii.
24 Benn, Op. cit., p.138.
25 Churchill, Op. cit., p.997.
26 Dimbleby, (1975), cover.
27 Interview with the author, 21 October 2014.
28 Wilson, Edmund, *The Cold War and the Income Tax: A Protest*, W. H. Allen, London, 1964, p.26.

Bibliography

Books

Alanbrooke, Field Marshal Lord, *War Diaries: 1939–1945*, Ed. Alex Danchey and Daniel Todman, Phoenix Press, London, 2002

Anonymous, *A Woman in Berlin*, Secker and Warburg, London, 1955

Bach, Julian Jnr., *America's Germany: An Account of the Occupation*, Random House, New York, 1946

Beaton, Cecil, *The Happy Years. Diaries 1944–48*, Weidenfeld & Nicholson, London, 1972

Beevor, Anthony and Cooper, Artemis, *Paris After the Liberation, 1944–49*, Penguin, London, 1995

Benn, Tony, *Years of Hope: Diaries, Papers and Letters 1940–1962*, Ed. Ruth Winstone, Arrow Books, London, 1994

Bessel, Richard, *Germany 1945: From War to Peace*, Simon & Schuster, London, 2010

Bower, Tom, *Blind Eye to Murder: Britain, America and the Purging of Nazi Germany – A Pledge Betrayed*, Granada, London, 1983

Bullock, Alan, *The Life and Times of Earnest Bevin*, Heinemann, London, 1960

Bullock, Alan, *Hitler and Stalin: Parallel Lives*, Harper Collins, London, 1991

Bradford, Sarah, *George VI*, Fontana, London, 1991

Buruma, Ian, *Year Zero – A History of 1945*, Atlantic Books, London, 2013

Cabell, Craig and Richards, Allan, *VE Day: A Day to Remember*, Pen & Sword Books Ltd., Barnsley, 2005

Calder, Angus, *The People's War: Britain 1939–45*, Jonathan Cape, London, 1969

Carruthers, Bob, *The SS On Trial: Evidence from Nuremberg*, Pen & Sword Books Ltd., Barnsley, 2013

Chisholm, Ann and Davie, Michael, *Beaverbrook: A Life*, Pimlico, London, 1993

Channon, Sir Henry, *Chips – The Diaries of Sir Henry Channon*, Weidenfield & Nicolson, London, 1967

Churchill, Winston S., *Memoirs of the Second World War*, Houghton Mifflin Company, Boston, 1959

De Beauvoir, Simone, *Force of Circumstance*, Andre Deutsch Ltd. and Weidenfeld & Nicholson Ltd., London, 1965

Dimbleby, Jonathan, *Richard Dimbleby: A Biography*, Hodder and Stoughton, London, 1975

Flanner, Janet, *Paris Journal 1944–65*, Ed William Shawn, Gollanz, London, 1966

Friedrich, Ruth Andreas, *Battleground Berlin: Diaries 1945–48*, Latimer House, London, 1948

Gardiner, Juliet, *Wartime: Britain 1939–1945*, Headline, London, 2004

Gellately, Robert, *Stalin's Curse: Battling for Communism in War and Cold War*

Gilbert, Martin, *The Second World War*, Henry Holt and Company, London, 1989

Gilbert, Martin, *The Boys: Triumph over Adversity*, Weidenfeld & Nicholson, London, 1996

Gilbert, Martin, *The Day the War Ended*, Harper Collins, London, 1995

Gildea, Robert, *France Since 1945*, Oxford University Press, Oxford, 1996

Hastings, Max, *His Finest Years: Churchill as Warlord 1940–45*, Harper Collins, London, 2009

Hennessy, Peter, *Never Again*, Vintage, London, 1993

Hersey, John, *Hiroshima*, Penguin, London, 2001

Hillman, William, *Mr President: Personal Diaries, Private Letters, Papers, and Revealing Interviews of Harry S. Truman*, Hutchinson, London, 1952

Hills, Stuart, *By Tank into Normandy*, Cassell & Co, London, 2002

Howard, Norman, *A New Dawn:* The *General Election* of *1945*, Politico's, London, 2005

Jenkins, Roy, *Churchill*, Macmillan, London, 2001

Judt, Tony, *Postwar, A History of Europe Since 1945*, William Heinemann, London, 2005

Kershaw, Ian, *The End: Germany 1944–45*, Penguin, London, 2012

Kershaw, Ian, *Hitler, 1936 – 45: Nemesis*, Allen Lane, London, 2000

Kynaston, David, *Austerity Britain*, Bloomsbury, London, 2007

Longmate, Norman, *How We Lived Then*, Trafalgar Square, London, 2003

Longmate, Norman, *When We Won the War*, Hutchinson, London, 1977

Lowe, Keith, *Savage Continent: Europe in the Aftermath of World War II*, Viking, London, 2012

Márai, Sándor, *Memoir of Hungary 1944–1948*, Central European University Press, Budapest, 2005

Marr, Andrew, *The Making of Modern Britain: From Queen Victoria to V.E. Day*, Macmillan, London, 2009

MacDonogh, Giles, *After the Reich: From the Liberation of Vienna to the Berlin Airlift*, John Murray, London, 2008

Macmillan, Harold, *The Blast of War 1939–1945*, Macmillan, London, 1967

Miller, Russell and Miller, Renate, *VE Day: The People's Story*, Tempus, Stroud, 2007

Montgomery, Viscount Bernard, *The Memoirs of Field-Marshal Montgomery*, Pen & Sword Military, Barnsley, 2010

Murdoch, Iris, *A Writer at War: The Letters and Diaries of Iris Murdoch: 1939–1945*, Ed. Peter J. Conradi, Short Books, London, 2010

Niven, David, *The Moon's a Balloon*, Hamish Hamilton, London, 1971

Orwell, George, *George Orwell Diaries*, Ed. Peter Davison, Harvill Secker, London, 2009

Orwell, George, *Nineteen Eighty-Four*, Penguin, London, 2000

Shephard, Ben, *The Long Road Home: The Aftermath of the Second World War*, Vintage, London, 2011

Stafford, David, *Endgame 1945: Victory, Retribution, Liberation*, Little, Brown, London, 2007

Turner, Barry, *And The Policeman Smiled – 10,000 Children Escape from Nazi Europe*, Bloomsbury, London, 1990

Turner, Barry and Rennell, Tony, *When Daddy Came Home: How War Changed Family Life Forever*, Hutchinson, London, 1995

Vassiltchikov, Marie, *Berlin Diaries, 1940–1945*, Mandarin, London, 1990

Wilson, Edmund, *Europe without Baedecker: Sketches Among the Ruins of Italy, Greece and England*, Hogarth Press, London, 1986

BBC

Thank you to the BBC for access to their archives and permission to publish excerpts from them with special thanks to Kate O'Brien for her help in arranging this. Folders referred to:

R1/81/1
R28/81/3
R34/920
R34/923
R34/926
R34/928
R34/929
R34/ 931
R34/934
R34/937
R41/59

Imperial War Museum

Thanks both to the Trustees of the Imperial War Museum and to the individual copyright holders for allowing me access to the collections of papers held by the IWM, and for permission to publish extracts from them, with thanks also to Simon Offord for his help in arranging this.

IWM Department of Documents

Private papers of A. Bray, Documents.14880
Private papers of Major P. M. Barrington, Documents.12628
Private papers of Dr J. J. Beeston, Documents.13624
Private papers of Sub Lieutenant J. L. Clemens RNVR,
    Documents.13320
Private papers of F. Cowling, Documents.13270
Private papers of Major T. C. Howes, Documents.13169
Private papers of J. A. Lehtl, Documents.17648
Private papers of C. L. R. Matthews, Documents.15323
Private papers of S. R. Verrier, Documents.13159
Private papers of Captain I. A. Wallace, Documents.6985

IWM Sound Archive
Ronald William McGill, 6221

Mass Observation
All extracts from diaries, file reports and topic collections held at the Mass Observation Archive, University of Sussex have been reproduced with permission of Curtis Brown, London on behalf of The Trustees of the Mass Observation Archive.

Diarists
Mass Observation diarists are anonymous, though some explicitly declare their names in their diaries. Here I have given the diarist numbers and the names where applicable:

5199 – Walter Shipway
5201 – C. W. Smallbones
5216 – E. Van Someren
5243 – G. Bamber
5270 – K. M. Carruthers
5338
5443 – Kathleen Tipper
5460

File Reports
2249 – May 1945: Post-VE Day Celebrations
2263 – June 1945: Victory in Europe
2270 – August 1945: Report on the 1945 General Election
2272 – September 1945: Report on public attitudes to the atom bomb

Topic Collections
TC49: Victory celebrations, 1945–46

Newspapers and Magazines
Various dates have been looked at, as detailed in the Notes.

The *Aberdeen Journal*
The *Derby Evening Telegraph*

Bibliography

The *Gloucestershire Echo*
The *Daily Telegraph*
The *Evening Standard*
The *Manchester Guardian*
The *New York Times*
The *San Francisco Chronicle*
The Times
Time Magazine
The *Western Daily Press*

302

The *Gloucestershire Echo*
The *Daily Telegraph*
The *Evening Standard*
The *Manchester Guardian*
The *New York Times*
The *San Francisco Chronicle*
The Times
Time Magazine
The *Western Daily Press*

Index

von Ribbentrop, Rudolf 56

Wagner, Gustav 176
Wallace, I. A. 69–72, 187
Wilson, Edmund 63–6, 157, 171, 181, 182–3, 185–6, 277–8

Woman in Berlin, A 59–60, 82, 95–6, 278

Yamaguchi, Tsutomu 218

Zionists 259–62

Acknowledgements

Sam Harrison, then an editor at Aurum, first came up with the idea for a VE day oral history book to coincide with the seventieth anniversary of VE day. Thanks to him for getting the project off the ground. I decided that it would be even more interesting to focus on the entire period between VE Day and VJ Day. Given the time I had to pull it together, I needed all the help I could get. Sam played an important role in developing the early ideas about how this might work. As ever, my agent Andrew Gordon was also helpful and supportive both in the early days and right through to the completion of the project.

Iain McGregor, Charlotte Coulthard, Jennifer Barr and Vanessa Daubney have since played significant roles in getting this book published and I thank them all for their help.

I am indebted to the authors of many books on this period of history, some of which I have made specific reference to in the text. Others have helped me in a more general way to form an understanding of events, issues and the people who were part of them. These texts are detailed in the bibliography. I have looked at a lot of primary material, but secondary material was also an essential part of telling the stories in this book.

Thanks also to the trustees of the Mass Observation Archive, University of Sussex, the trustees and staff of the Imperial War Museum archives, the British Library (especially the newsroom), the BBC Archive (especially Kate O'Brien) and the Quakers Library at Friends House. Marigold Atkey at David Higham Associates was a great help in offering advice on permissions.

All quotations from Sir Winston Churchill have been reproduced with permission of Curtis Brown, London on behalf of The Beneficiaries of the Estate of Winston S. Churchill, Copyright © The Beneficiaries of the Estate of Winston S. Churchill. All quotations from Lord Montgomery of Alamein have been reproduced with permission of A. P. Watt, London. All quotations from 1st Viscount Alanbrooke have been reproduced with permission of David Higham Associates, London. All quotations from the Mass Observation Archive, University of Sussex have been reproduced with permission of Curtis Brown, London on behalf of The Trustees of the Mass Observation Archive.

Thank you to Ruth Marsh at the *Daily Telegraph*, Norah Perkins and Richard Pike at Curtis Brown, Georgia Glover and Joe Rogers at David Higham Associates, Helen Wilson at the *Guardian* and Simon Offord at the Imperial War Museum for helping to arrange permissions. Permissions to quote copyrighted material have been sought, but if there have been any errors or omissions, the author and publisher will be happy to rectify them at the earliest opportunity.

For me, the single most important interview I did for the book was with Bernd Koschland, who provided me with a significant emotional link to some of the events that I have described. The value of this cannot be underestimated and I would like to thank him for sharing his story with me. I would also like to thank Mary and Sue Tisdall, Fred Aiken, Ron and Eileen Owen and Ella Glen who all gave up their time to speak to me.

Thanks to Ant, Sue and Edwin Green for their good suggestions and great soup in Finchley. Thanks to Mischa Hewitt, Catherine and Mia for sloe gin and putting me up in Brighton during my visits to the Mass Observation Archive.

Thanks to Wolfgang Ritter for giving me the time to get this book finished, and to Helen and Chris Davis and Jimmy and Tomo Robertson for letting me stay with them in London during my library and archive visits.

Last, but certainly not least, thanks to Bridget, Gilbert and Rafe, who may have collectively hindered my productivity but have helped in many other ways in the past few months.

Although all these people have helped in different ways, if there are any errors or omissions, the responsibility for them is mine alone.

PRICE